scott jason smith

Marble Cake

D1350726

AVERY HILL PUBLISHING

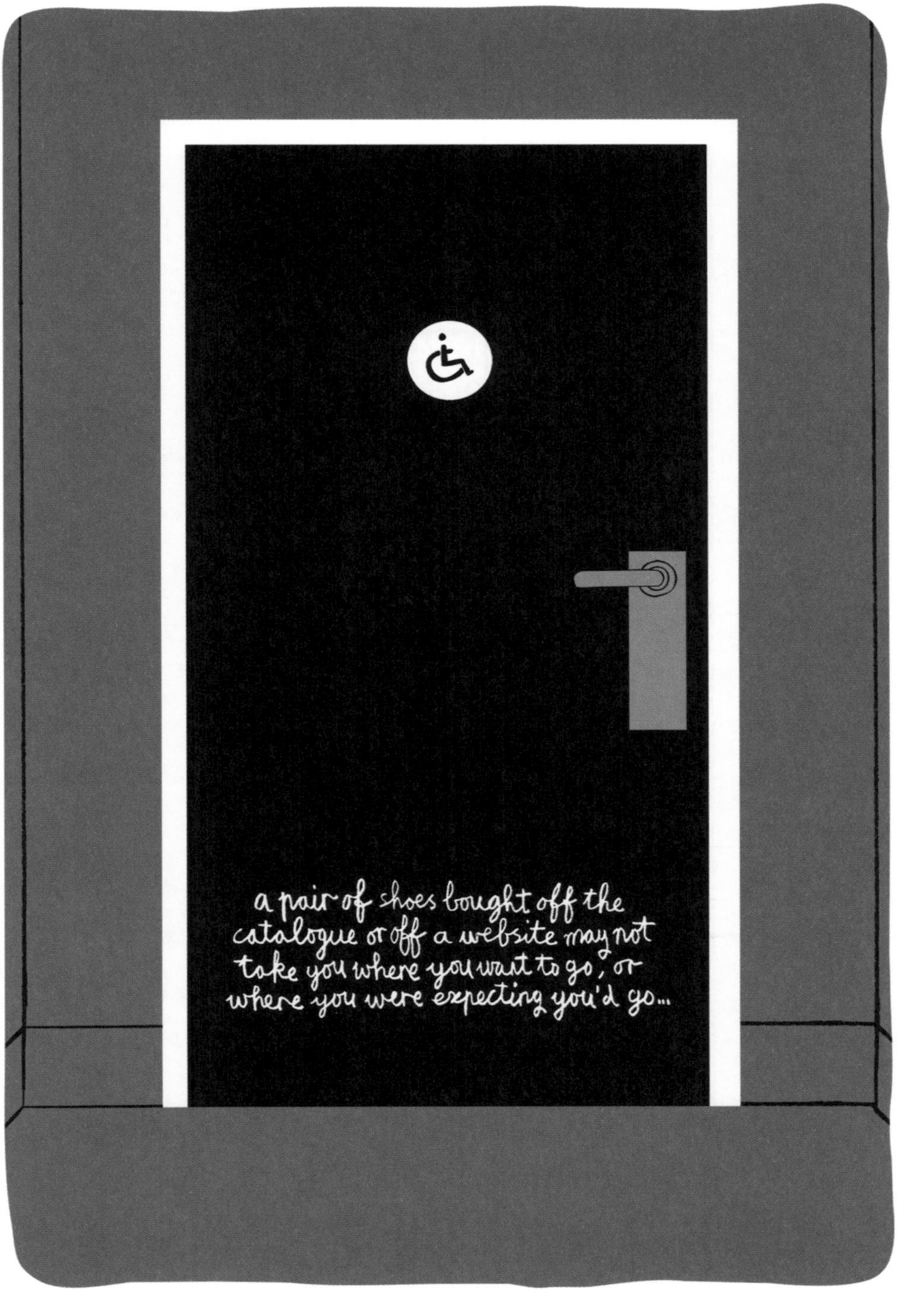
a pair of shoes bought off the
catalogue or off a website may not
take you where you want to go, or
where you were expecting you'd go...

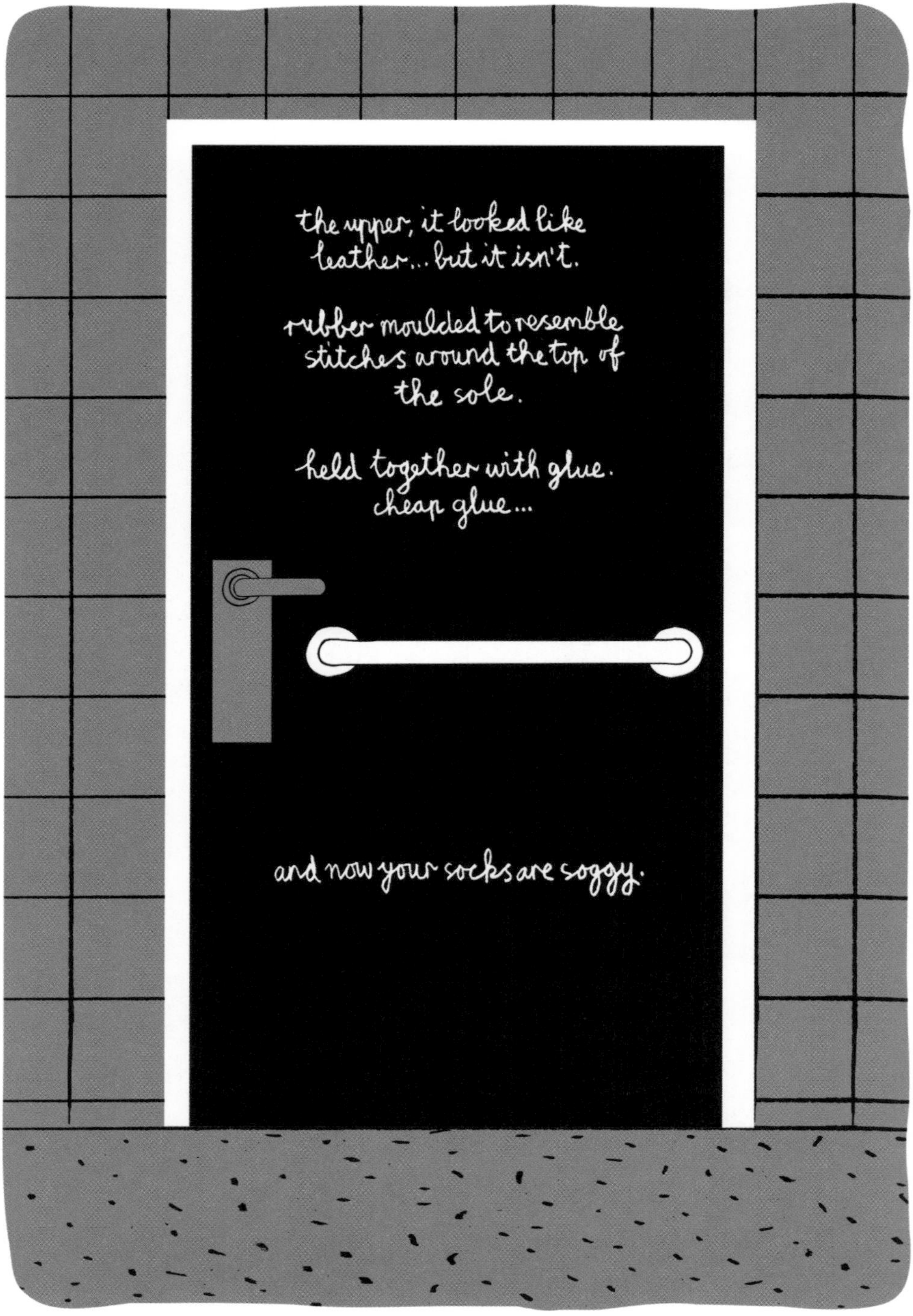
the upper, it looked like leather... but it isn't.
rubber moulded to resemble stitches around the top of the sole.
held together with glue. cheap glue...
and now your socks are soggy.

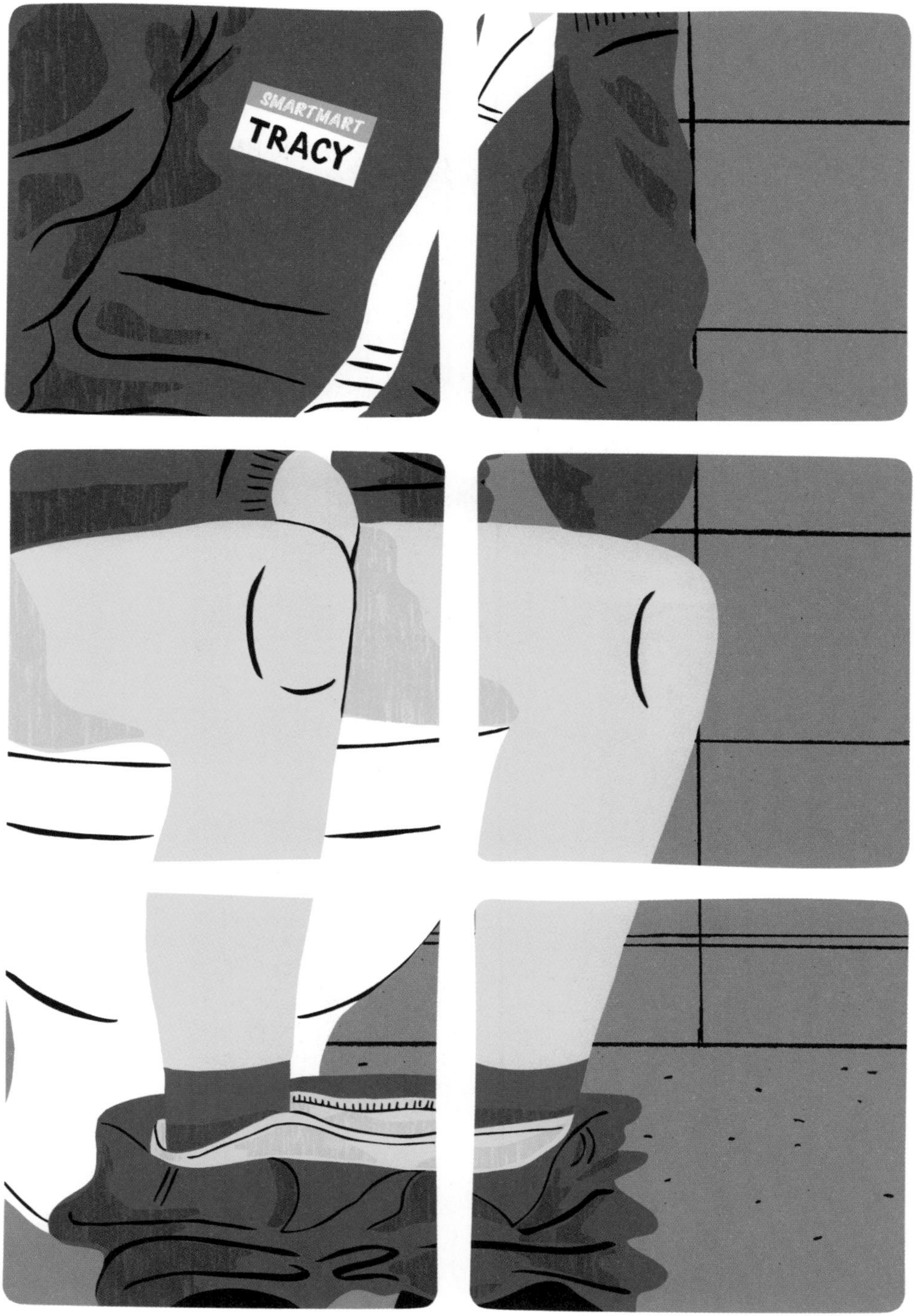
SMARTMART
TRACY

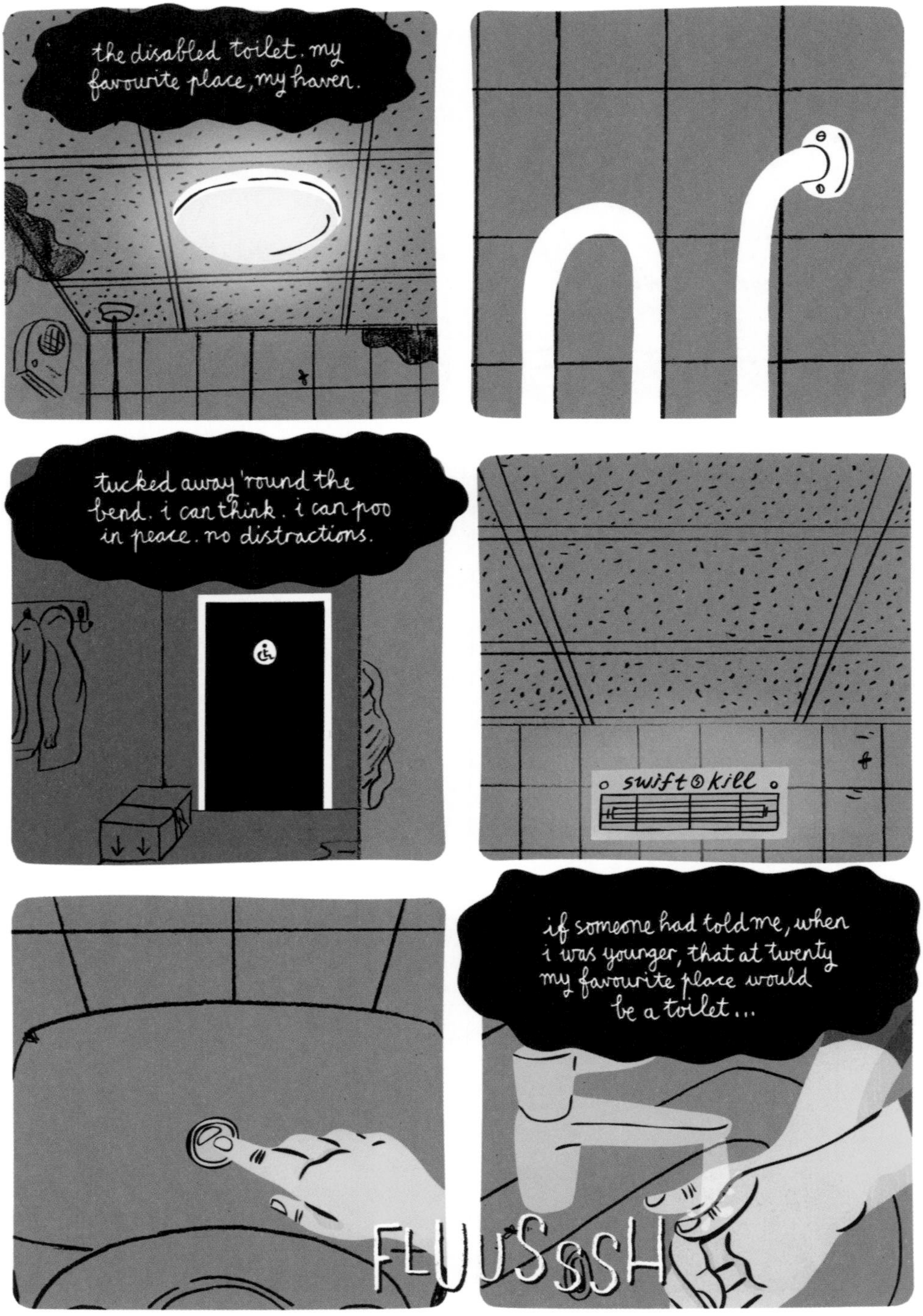
the disabled toilet. my favourite place, my haven.
tucked away 'round the bend. i can think. i can poo in peace. no distractions.
swift kill
if someone had told me, when i was younger, that at twenty my favourite place would be a toilet...
FLUUSSSH

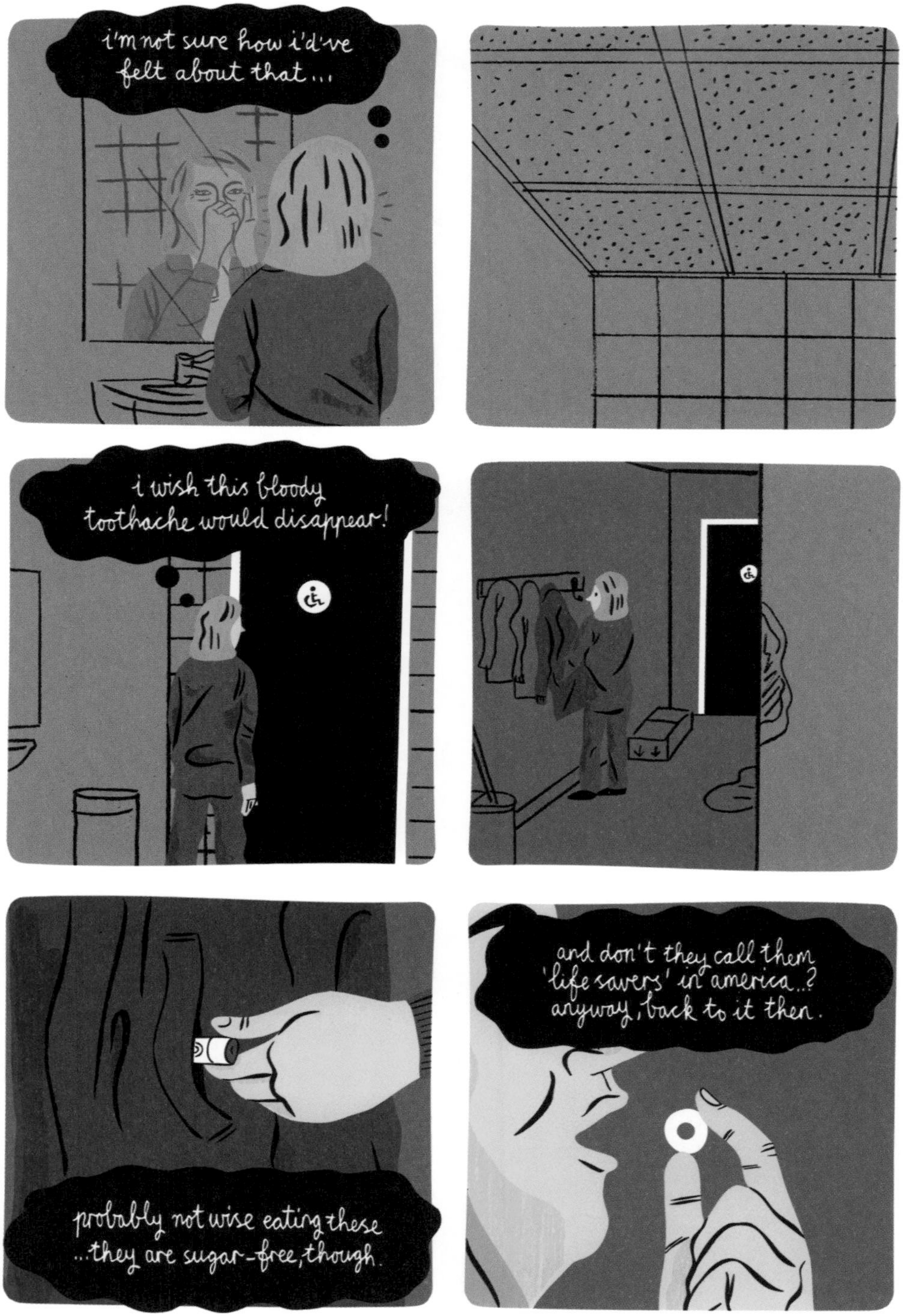
i'm not sure how i'd've felt about that...
i wish this bloody toothache would disappear!
probably not wise eating these ...they are sugar-free, though.
and don't they call them 'life savers' in america..? anyway, back to it then.

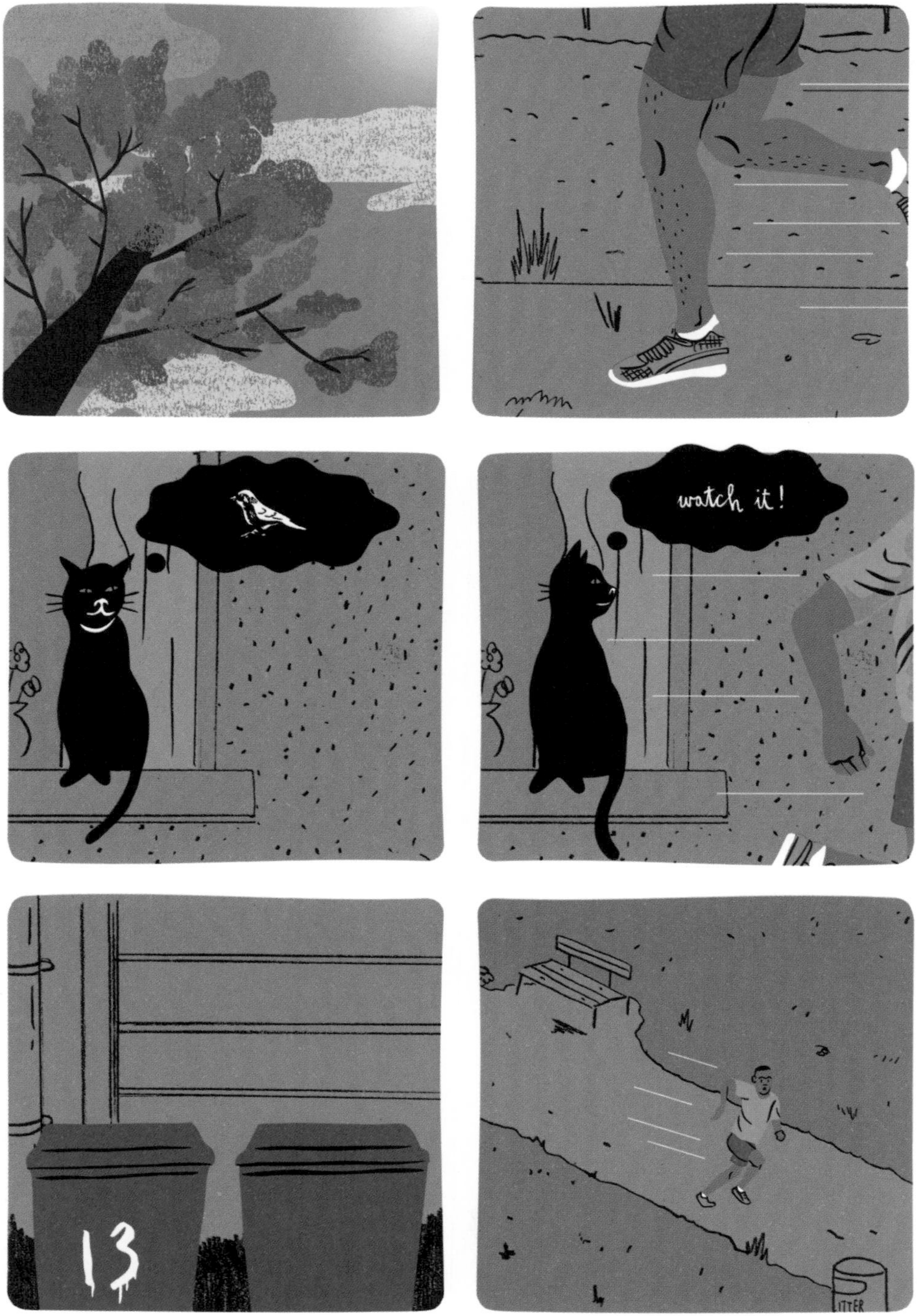
watch it!
13

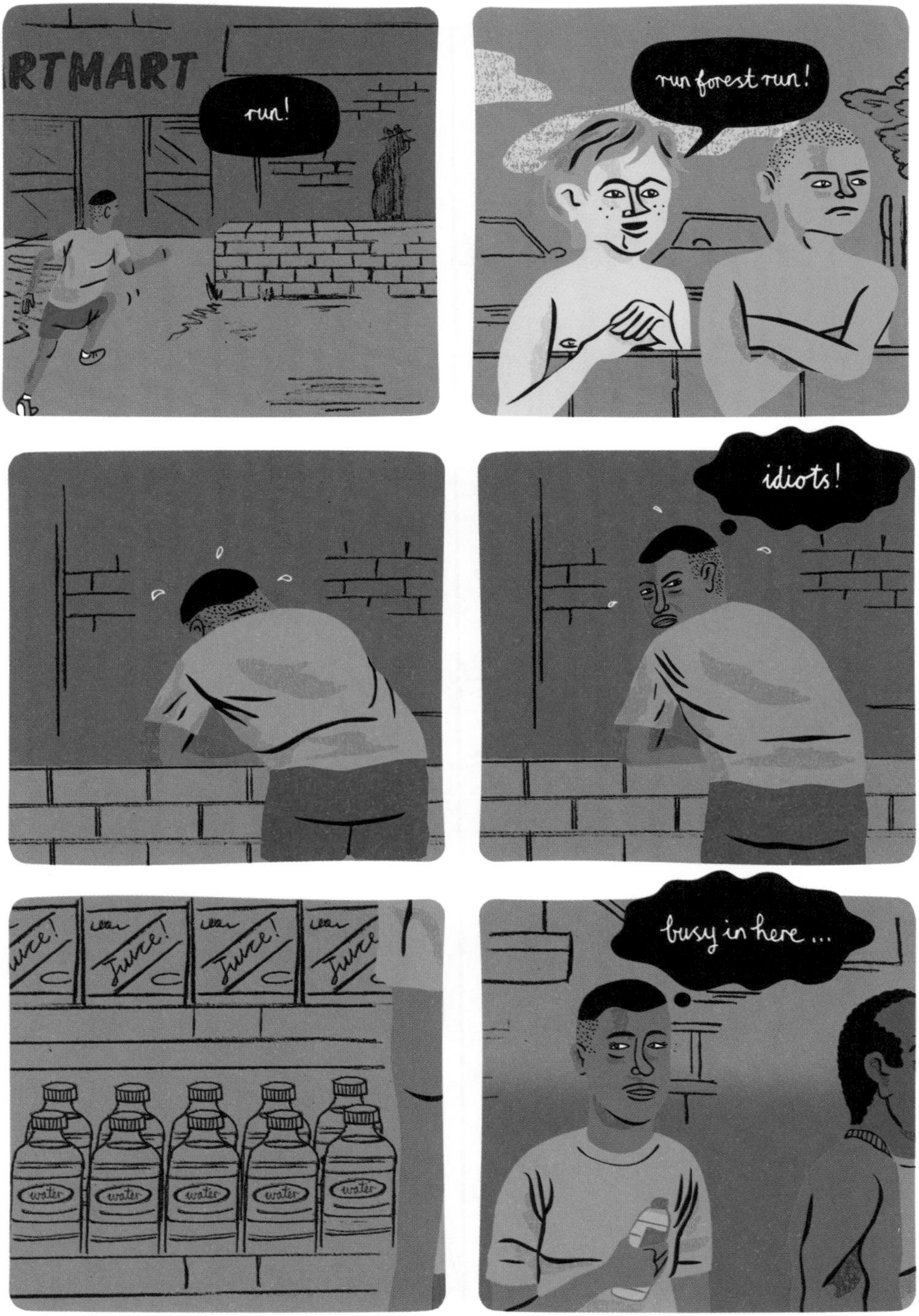
RTMART
run!
run forest run!
idiots!
Juice!
water
busy in here ...

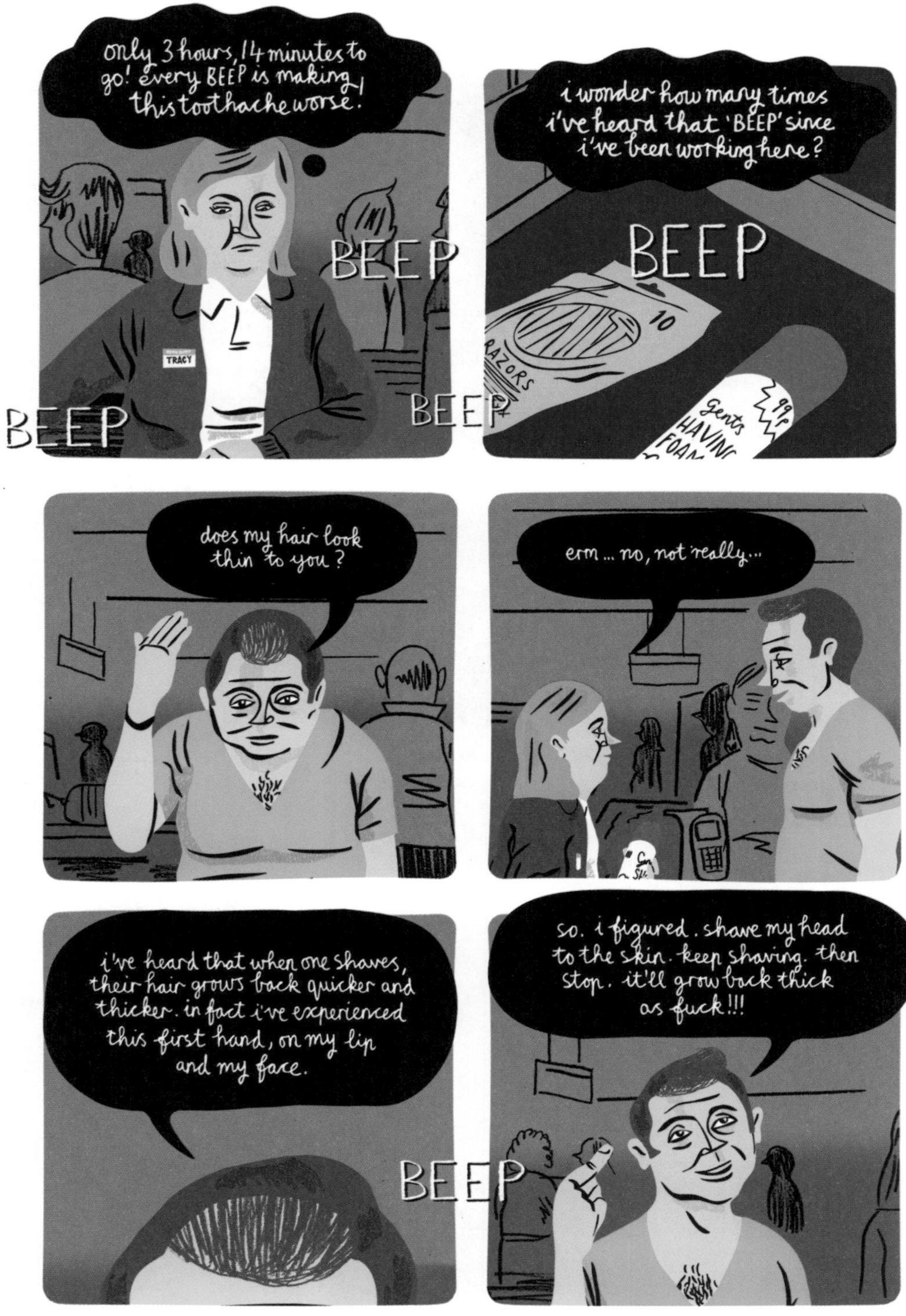
only 3 hours, 14 minutes to go! every BEEP is making this toothache worse!
TRACY
BEEP
BEEP
BEEP
i wonder how many times i've heard that 'BEEP' since i've been working here?
BEEP
10
RAZORS
Gents
99p
does my hair look thin to you?
erm ... no, not really...
i've heard that when one shaves, their hair grows back quicker and thicker. in fact i've experienced this first hand, on my lip and my face.
BEEP
so. i figured. shave my head to the skin. keep shaving. then stop. it'll grow back thick as fuck!!!

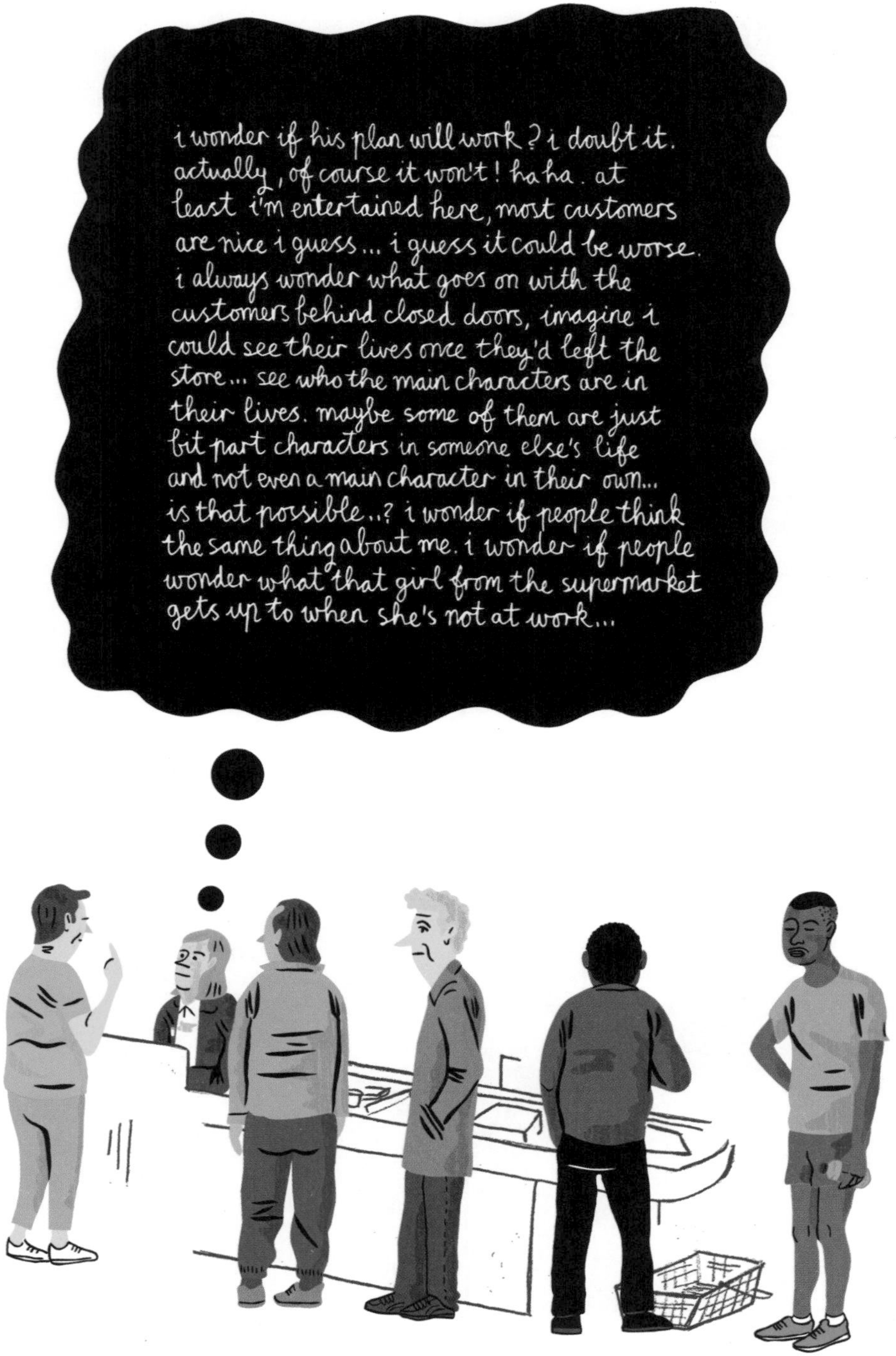
i wonder if his plan will work? i doubt it. actually, of course it won't! ha ha. at least i'm entertained here, most customers are nice i guess... i guess it could be worse. i always wonder what goes on with the customers behind closed doors, imagine i could see their lives once they'd left the store... see who the main characters are in their lives. maybe some of them are just bit part characters in someone else's life and not even a main character in their own... is that possible..? i wonder if people think the same thing about me. i wonder if people wonder what that girl from the supermarket gets up to when she's not at work...

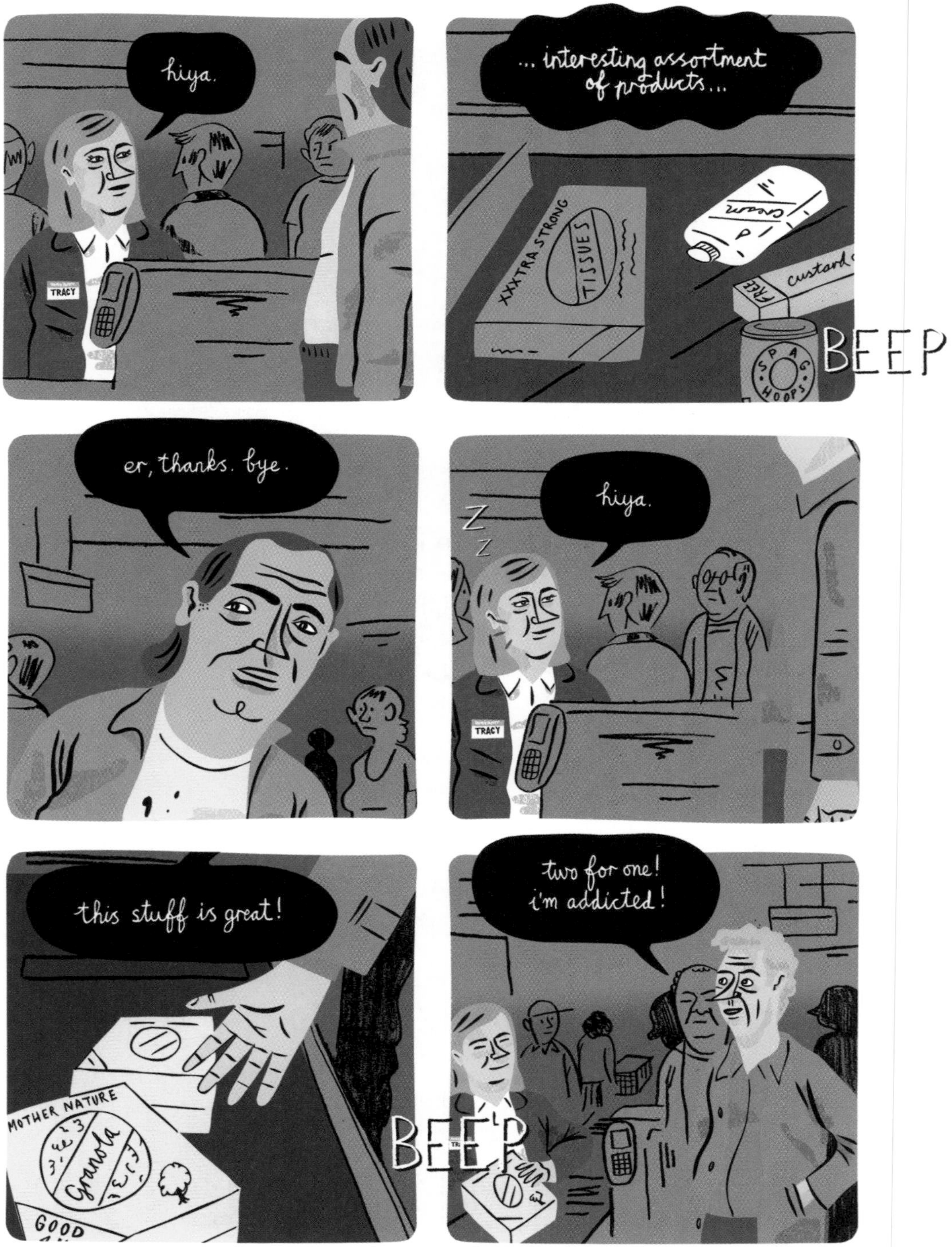
hiya.
TRACY
... interesting assortment of products...
XXXTRA STRONG
TISSUES
cream
custard
FREE
SPAG HOOPS
BEEP
er, thanks. bye.
Z Z
hiya.
TRACY
this stuff is great!
MOTHER NATURE
Granola
GOOD
BEEP
two for one!
i'm addicted!

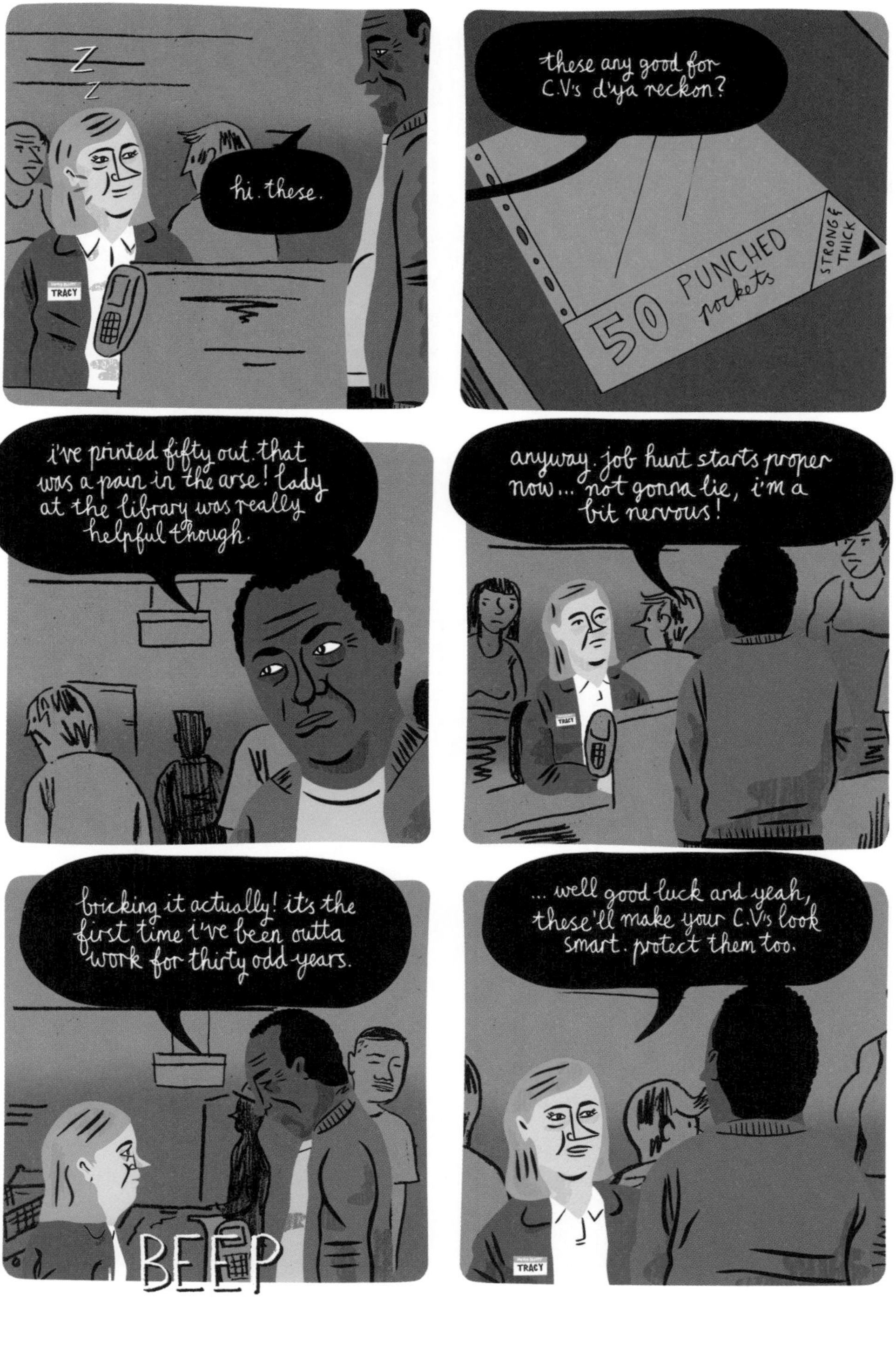
Z
Z
TRACY
hi. these.
these any good for C.V's d'ya reckon?
50 PUNCHED pockets
STRONG & THICK
i've printed fifty out. that was a pain in the arse! lady at the library was really helpful though.
anyway. job hunt starts proper now... not gonna lie, i'm a bit nervous!
bricking it actually! it's the first time i've been outta work for thirty odd years.
BEEP
... well good luck and yeah, these'll make your C.V's look smart. protect them too.
TRACY

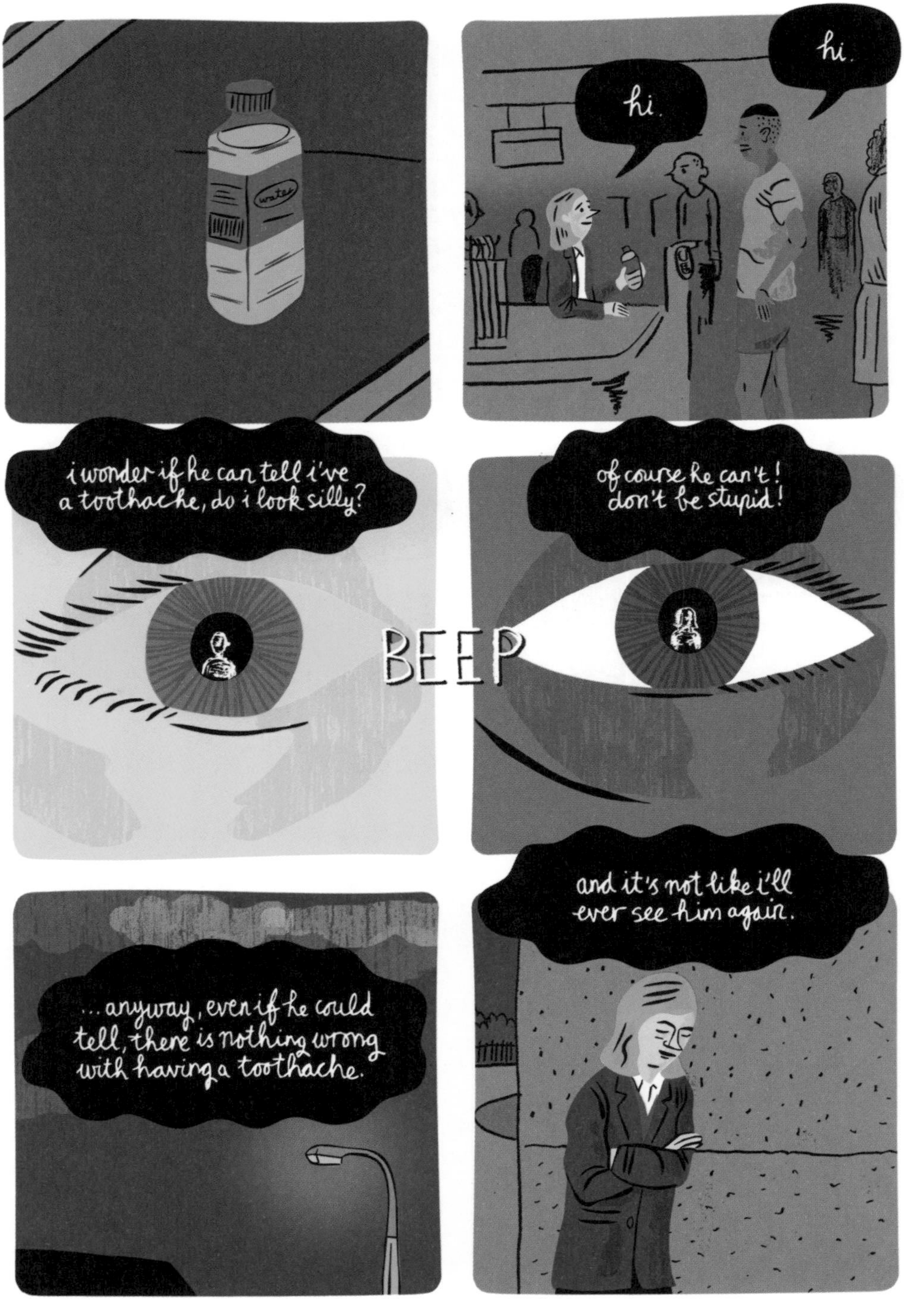
hi.
hi.
i wonder if he can tell i've a toothache, do i look silly?
BEEP
of course he can't! don't be stupid!
...anyway, even if he could tell, there is nothing wrong with having a toothache.
and it's not like i'll ever see him again.

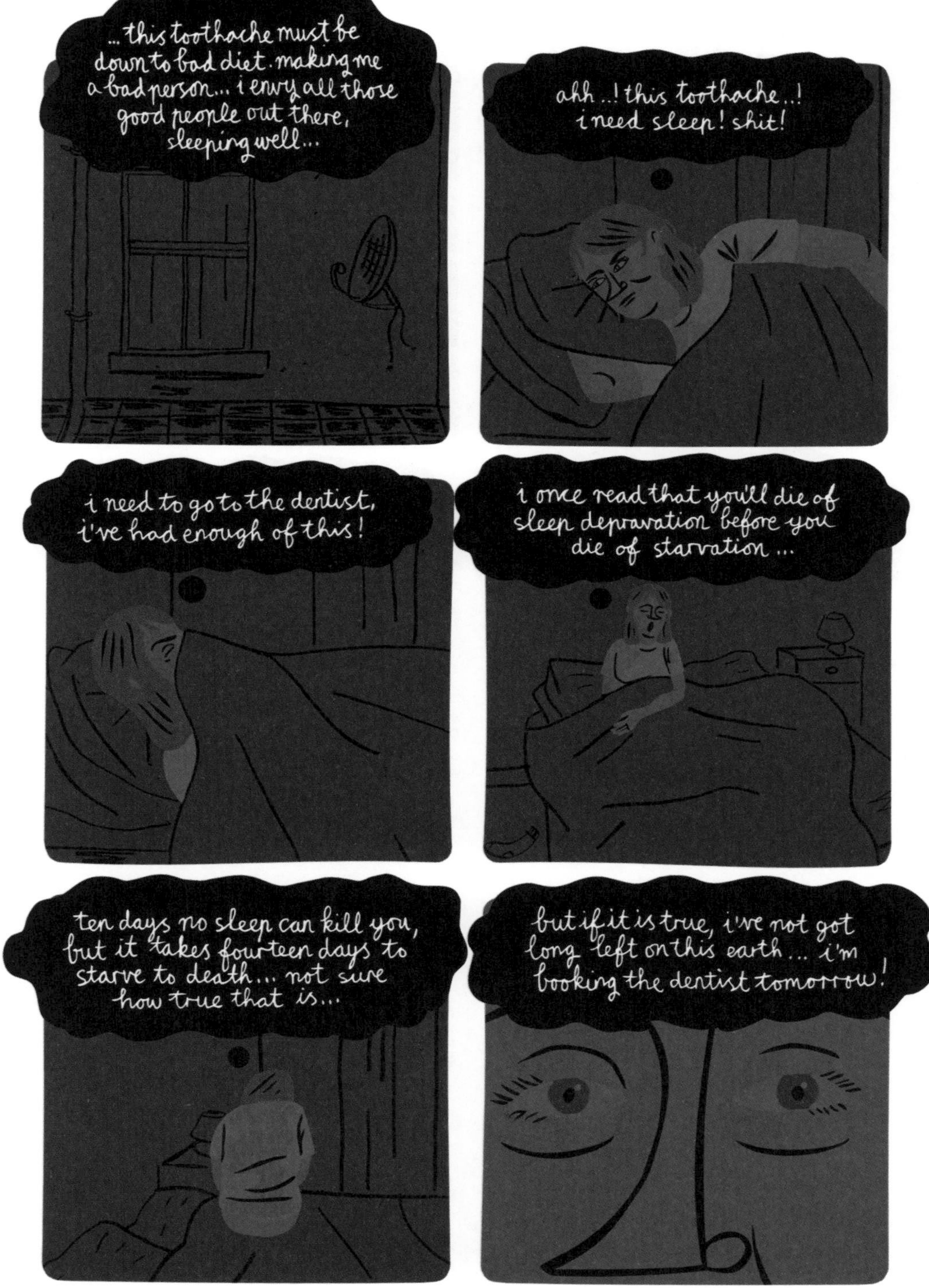
... this toothache must be down to bad diet. making me a bad person... i envy all those good people out there, sleeping well...
ahh..! this toothache..! i need sleep! shit!
i need to go to the dentist, i've had enough of this!
i once read that you'll die of sleep depravation before you die of starvation...
ten days no sleep can kill you, but it takes fourteen days to starve to death... not sure how true that is...
but if it is true, i've not got long left on this earth... i'm booking the dentist tomorrow!

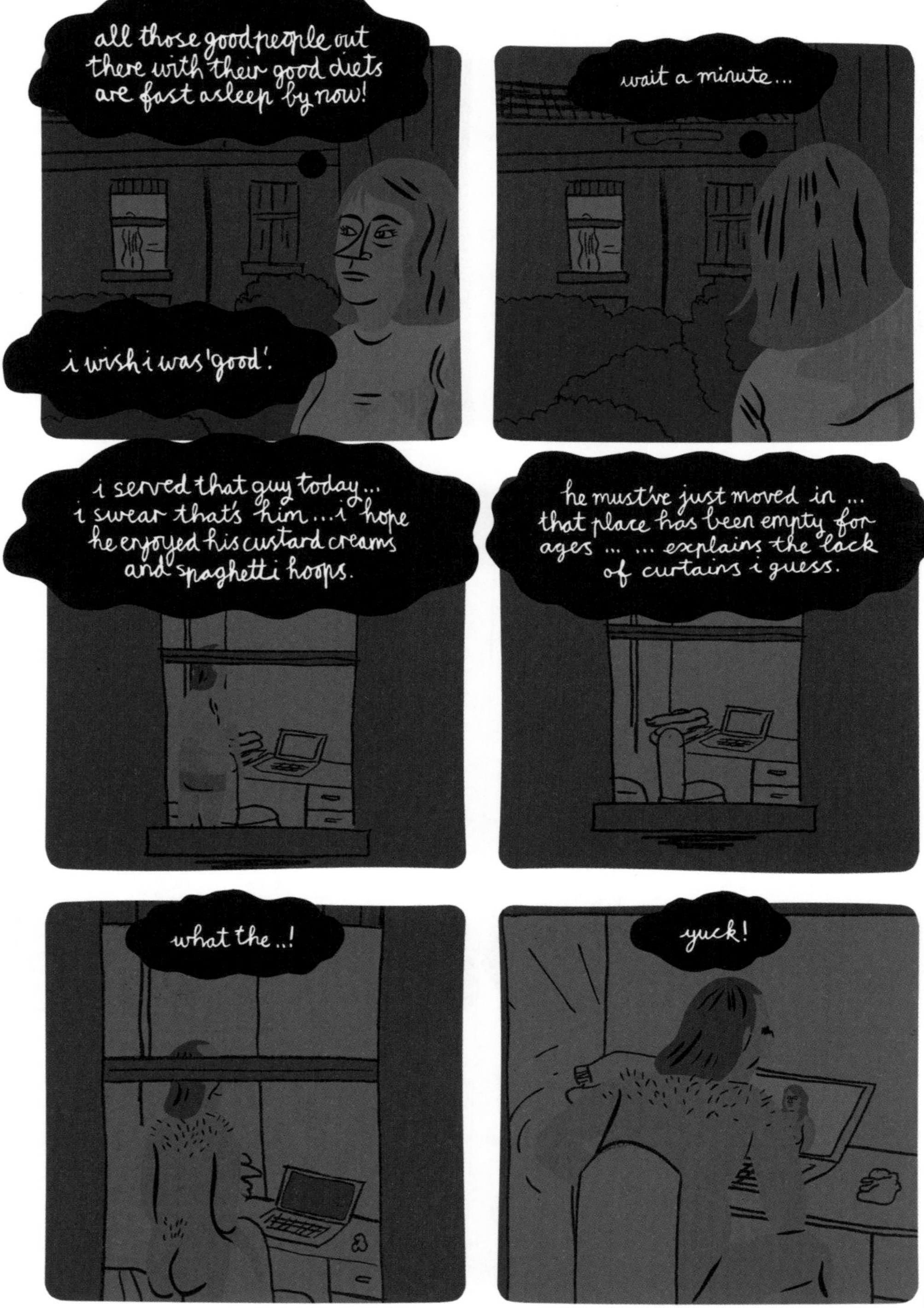
all those good people out there with their good diets are fast asleep by now!
i wish i was 'good'.
wait a minute...
i served that guy today... i swear that's him... i hope he enjoyed his custard creams and spaghetti hoops.
he must've just moved in ... that place has been empty for ages ... ... explains the lack of curtains i guess.
what the..!
yuck!

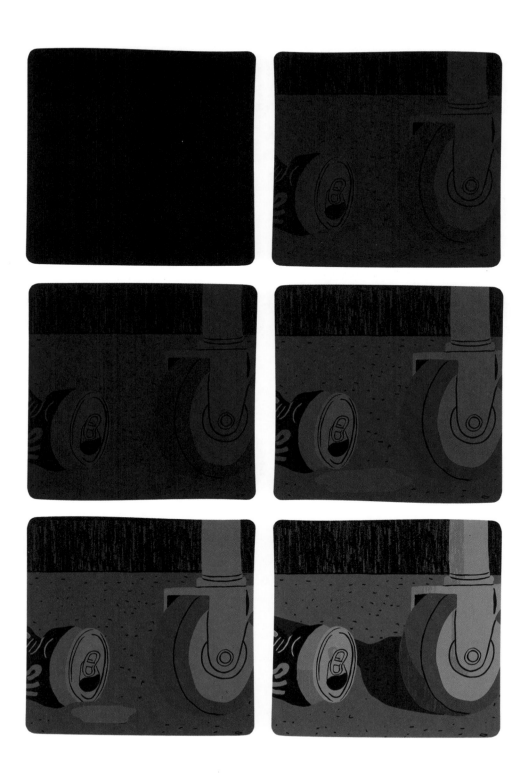

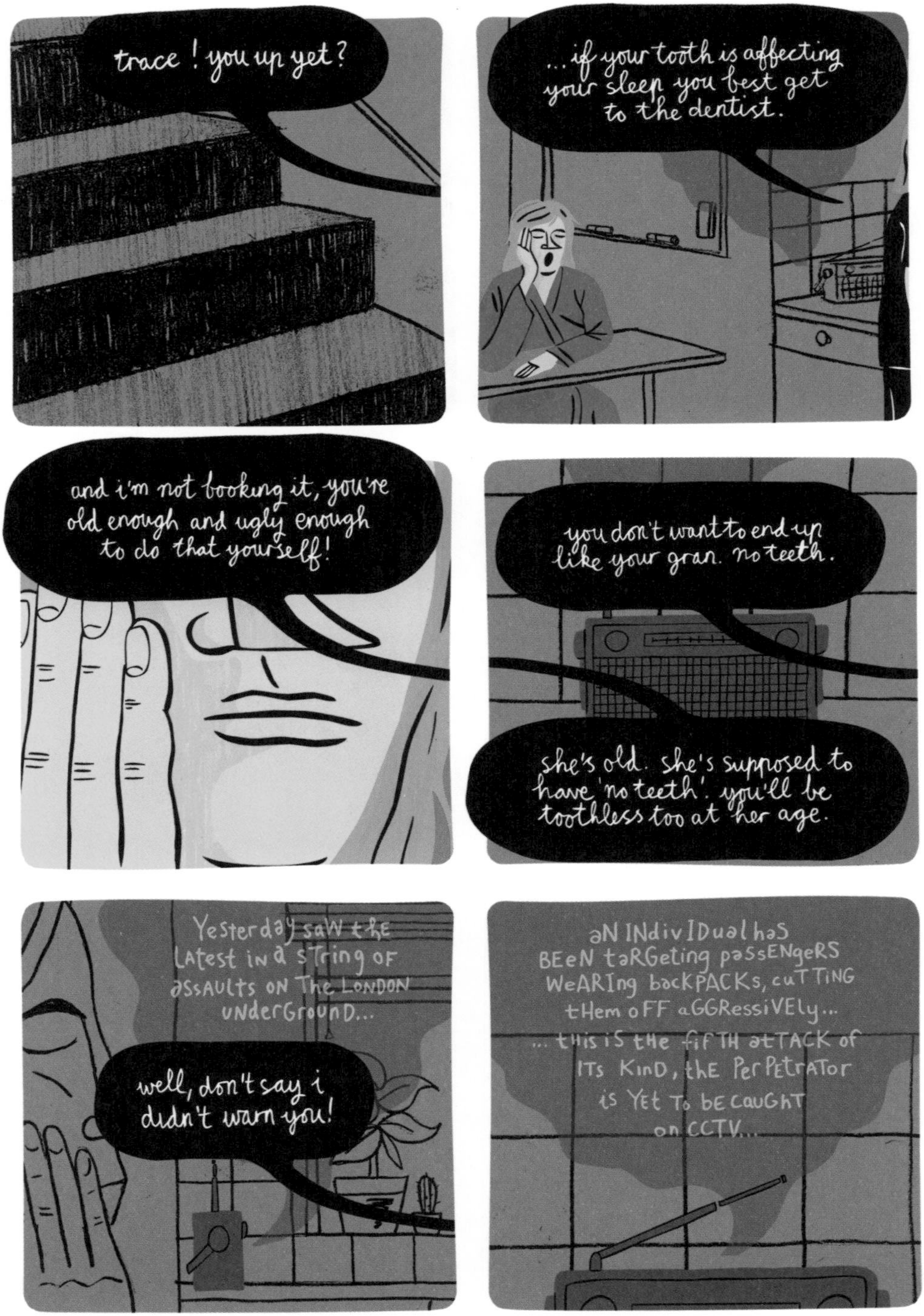
trace! you up yet?
...if your tooth is affecting your sleep you best get to the dentist.
and i'm not booking it, you're old enough and ugly enough to do that yourself!
you don't want to end up like your gran. no teeth.
she's old. she's supposed to have 'no teeth'. you'll be toothless too at her age.
Yesterday saw the latest in a string of assaults on the London underground...
well, don't say i didn't warn you!
an individual has been targeting passengers wearing backpacks, cutting them off aggressively...
...this is the fifth attack of its kind, the perpetrator is yet to be caught on CCTV...

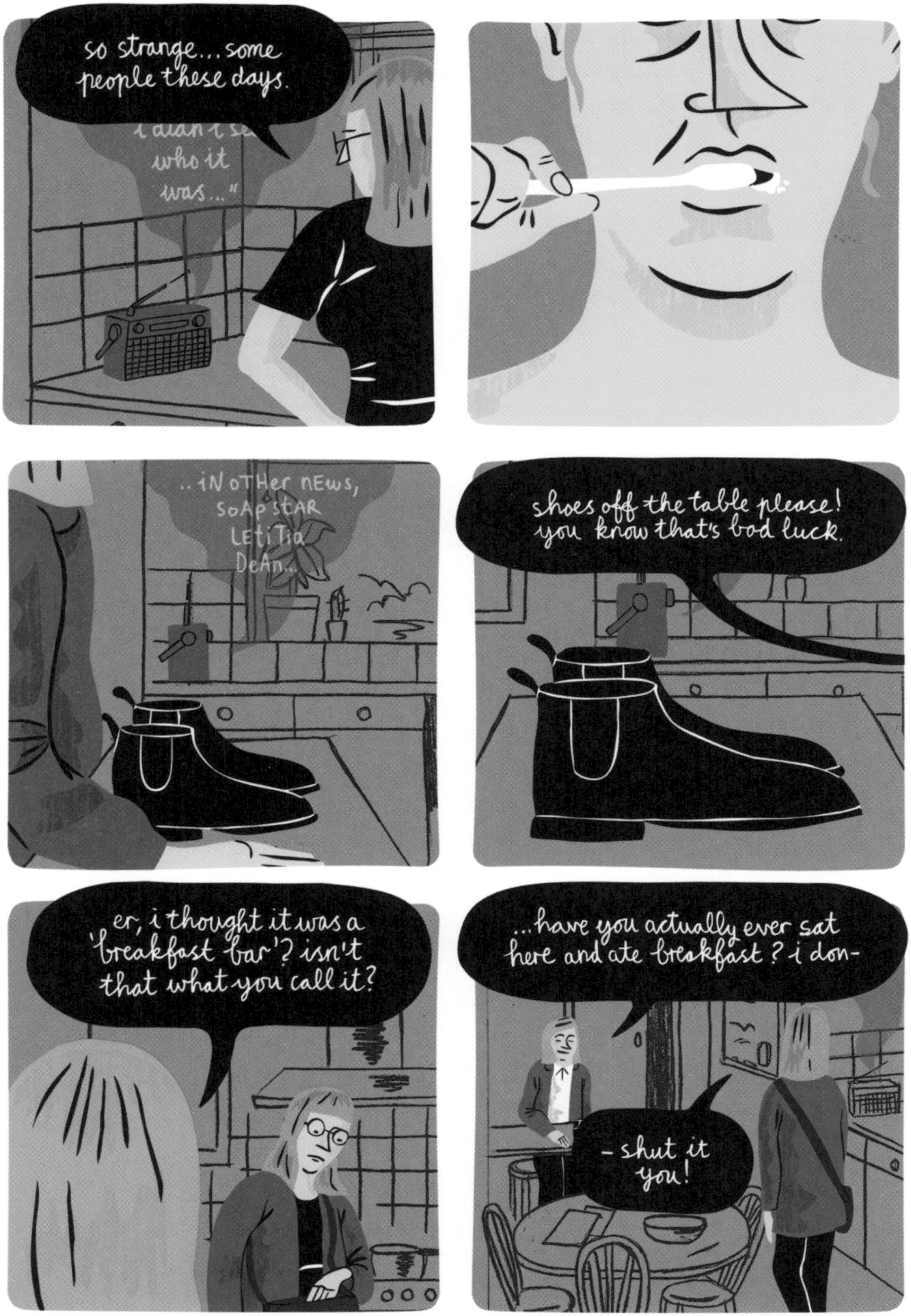
so strange... some people these days.
who it was..."
..iN oTHer nEws, SoAp StAR LEtiTia DeAn...
shoes off the table please! you know that's bad luck.
er, i thought it was a 'breakfast bar'? isn't that what you call it?
...have you actually ever sat here and ate breakfast? i don-
- shut it you!

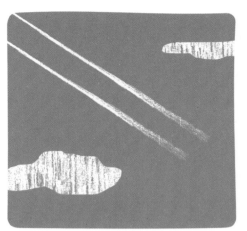

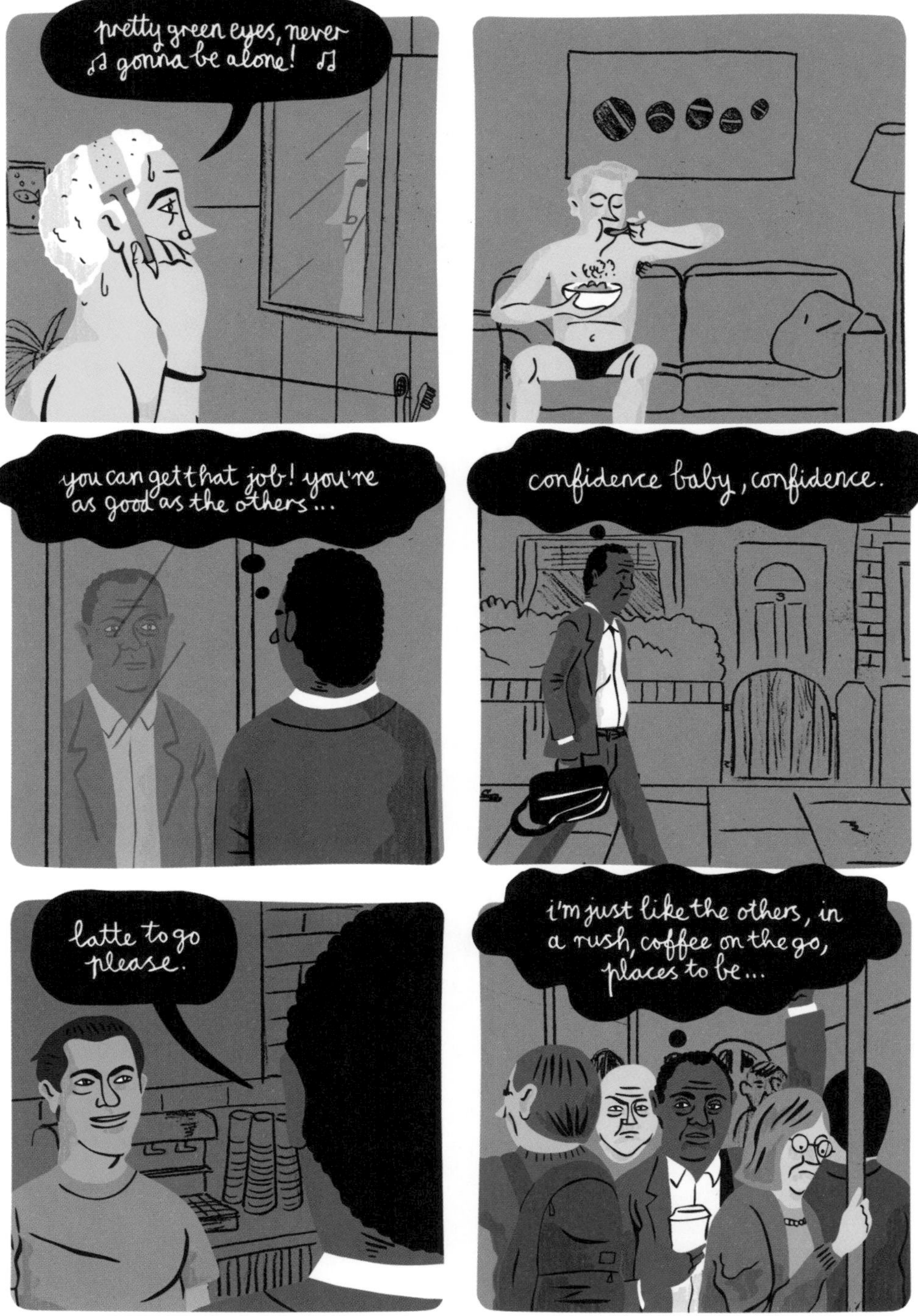
pretty green eyes, never ♫ gonna be alone! ♫
you can get that job! you're as good as the others...
confidence baby, confidence.
latte to go please.
i'm just like the others, in a rush, coffee on the go, places to be...

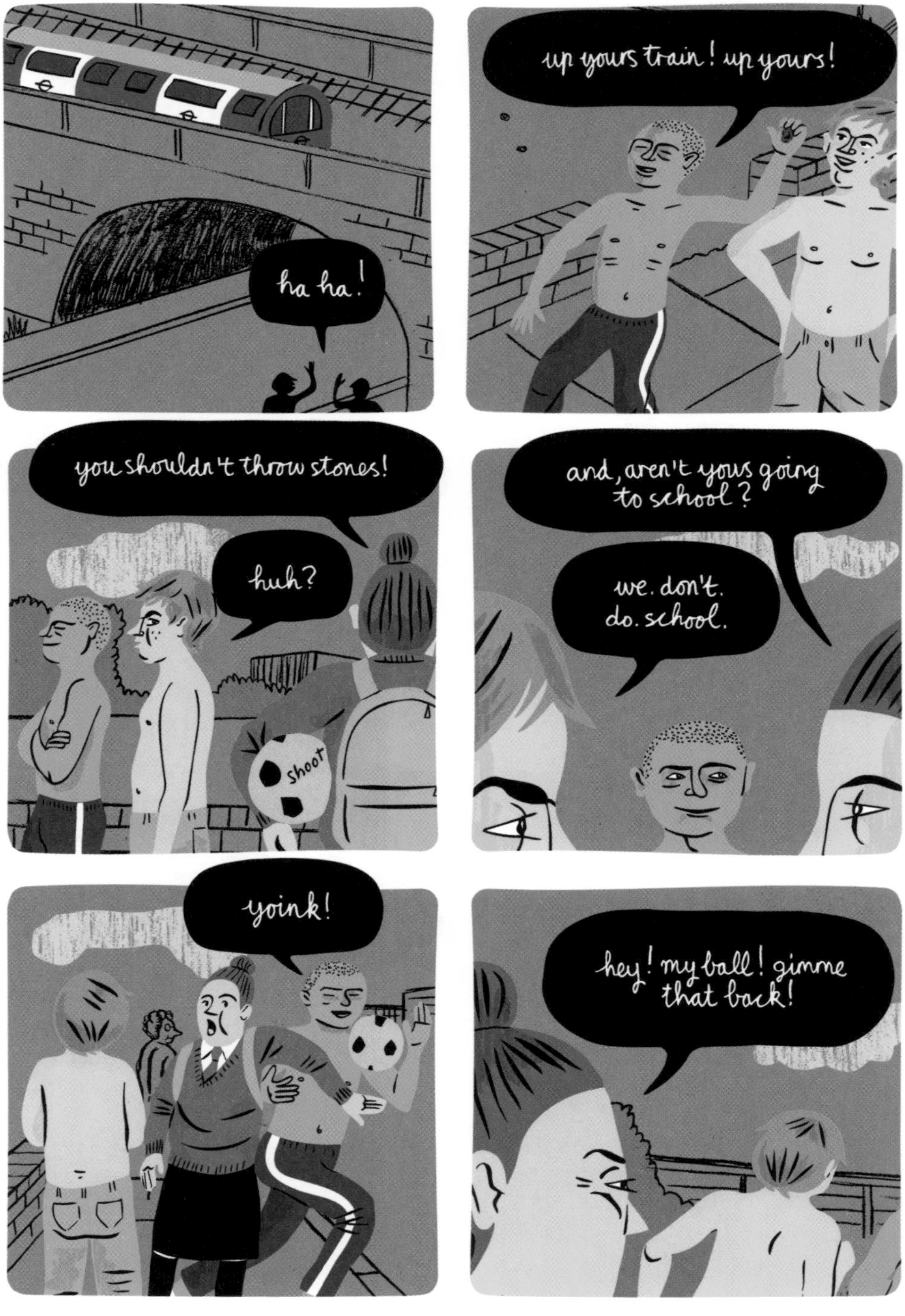
ha ha!
up yours train! up yours!
you shouldn't throw stones!
huh?
shoot
and, aren't yous going to school?
we. don't. do. school.
yoink!
hey! my ball! gimme that back!

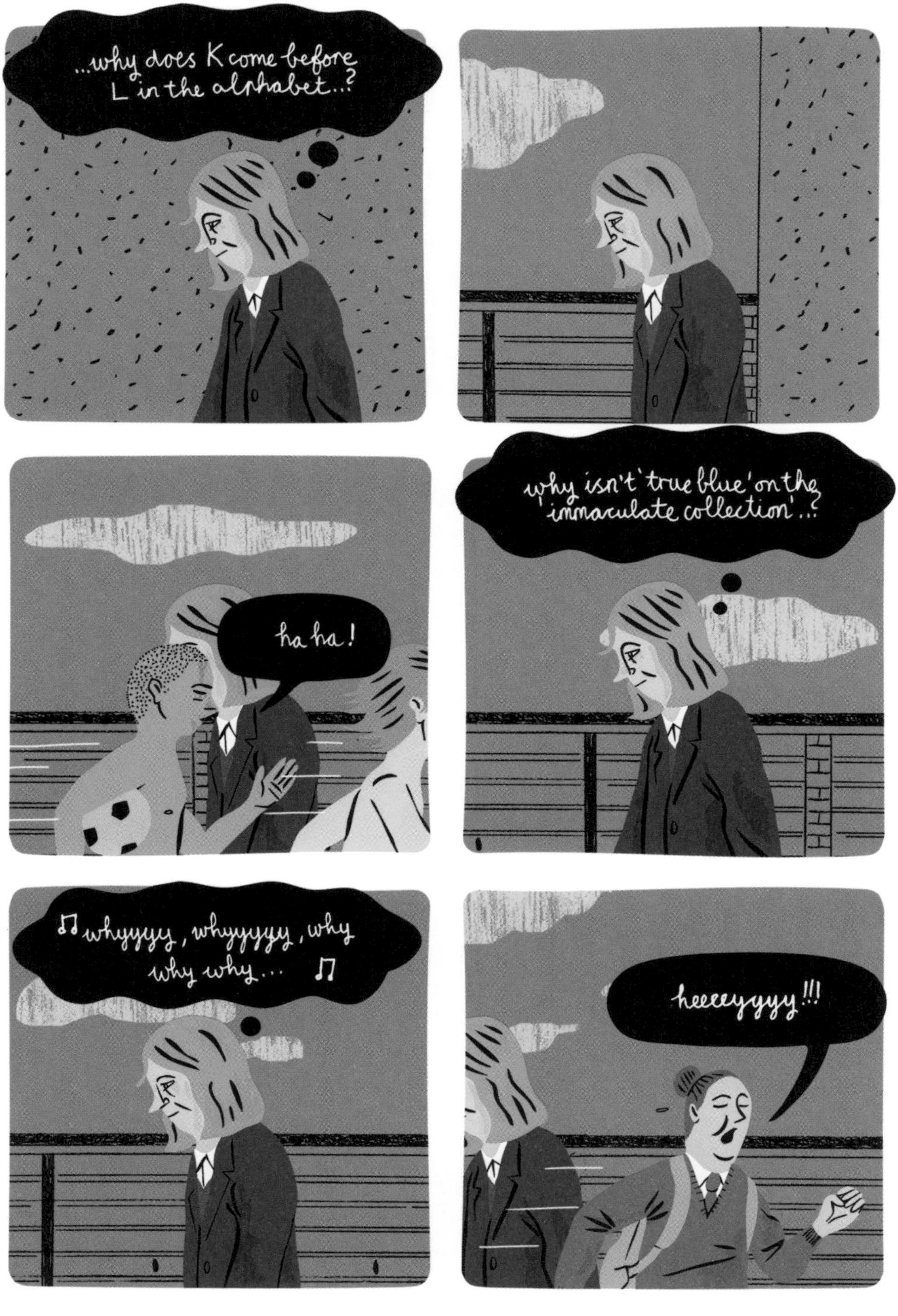
...why does K come before L in the alphabet...?
why isn't 'true blue' on the 'immaculate collection'...?
ha ha!
♫ whyyyy, whyyyyy, why why why... ♫
heeeeyyyy!!!

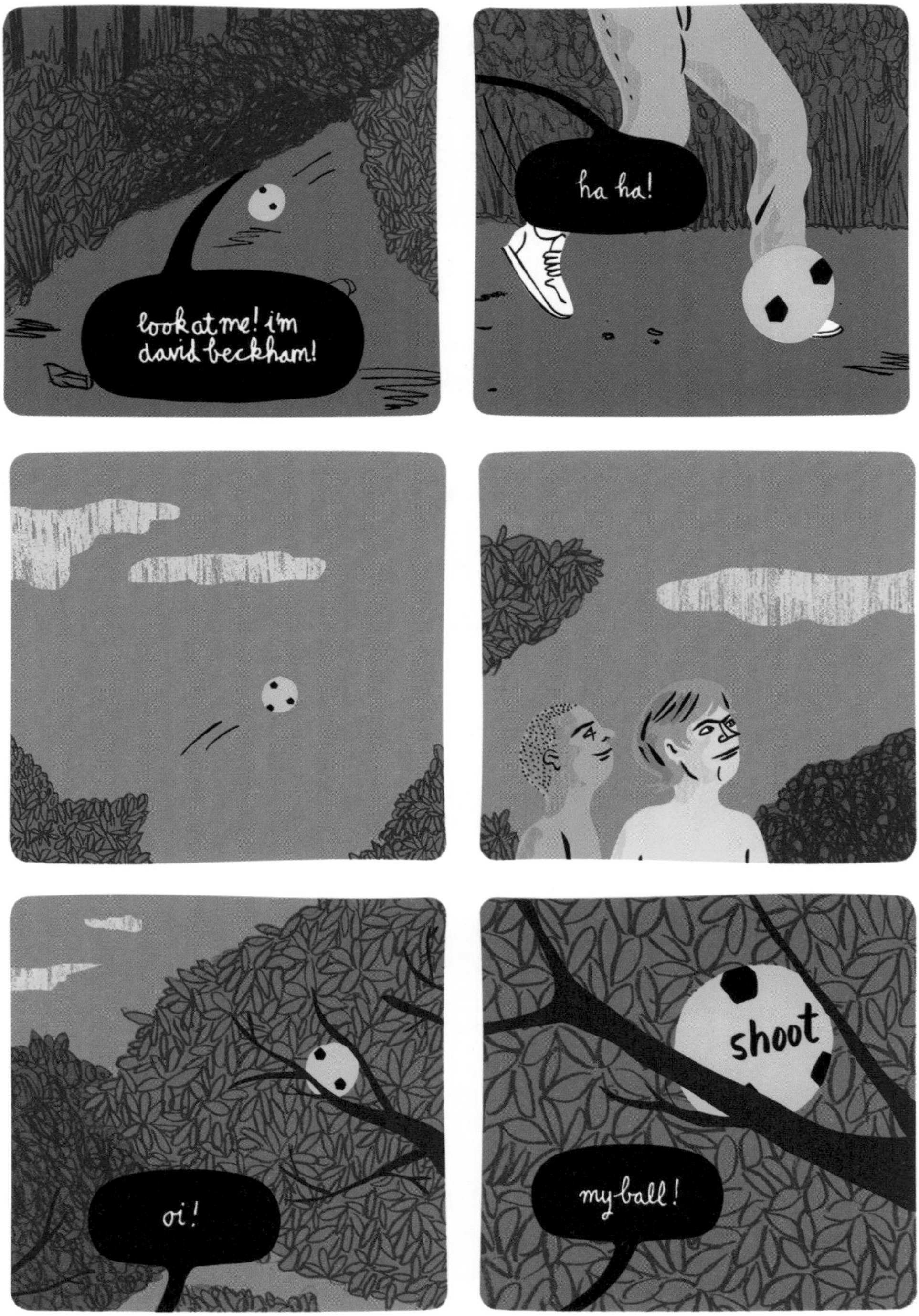
look at me! i'm david beckham!
ha ha!
oi!
shoot
my ball!

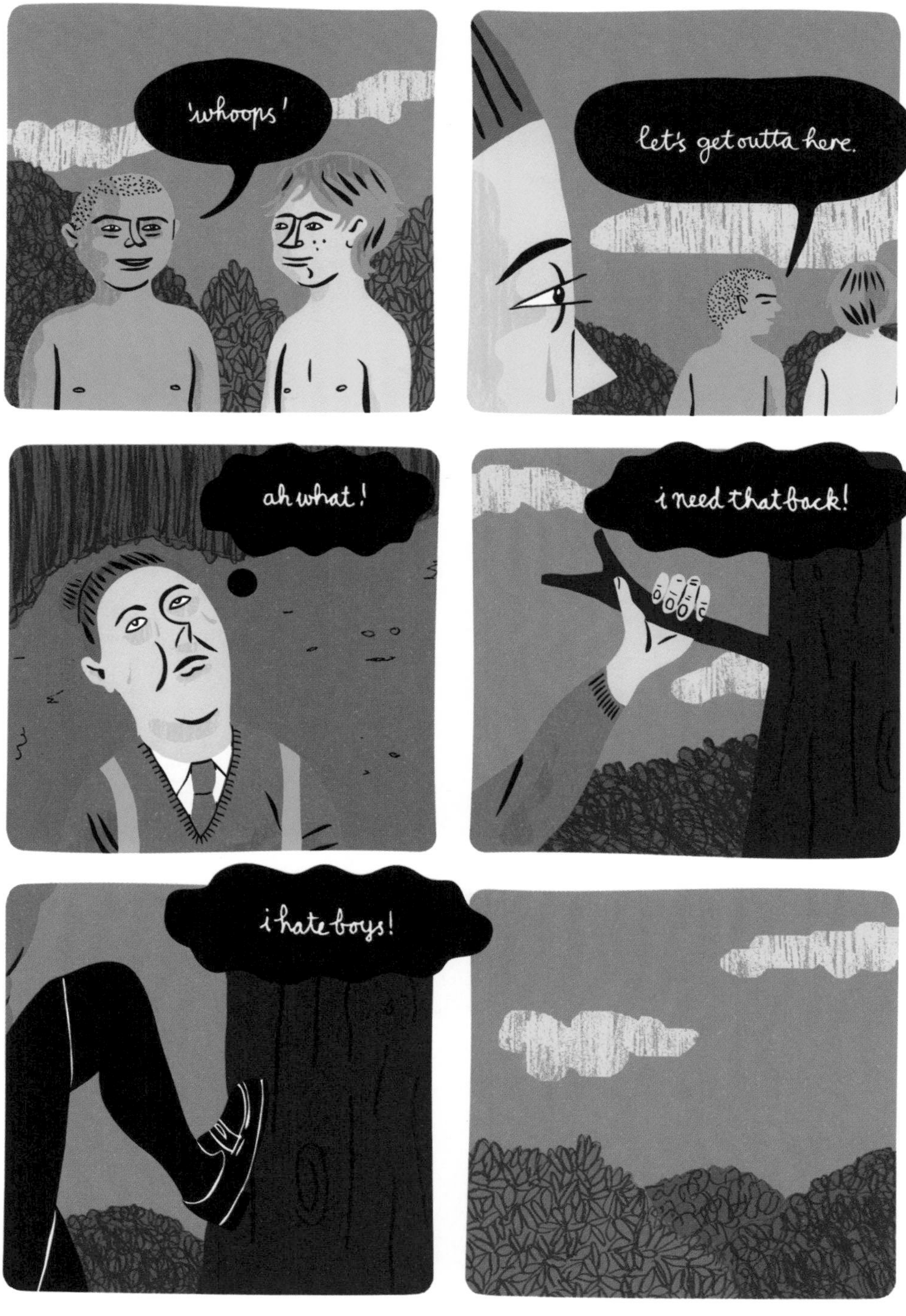
'whoops'
let's get outta here.
ah what!
i need that back!
i hate boys!

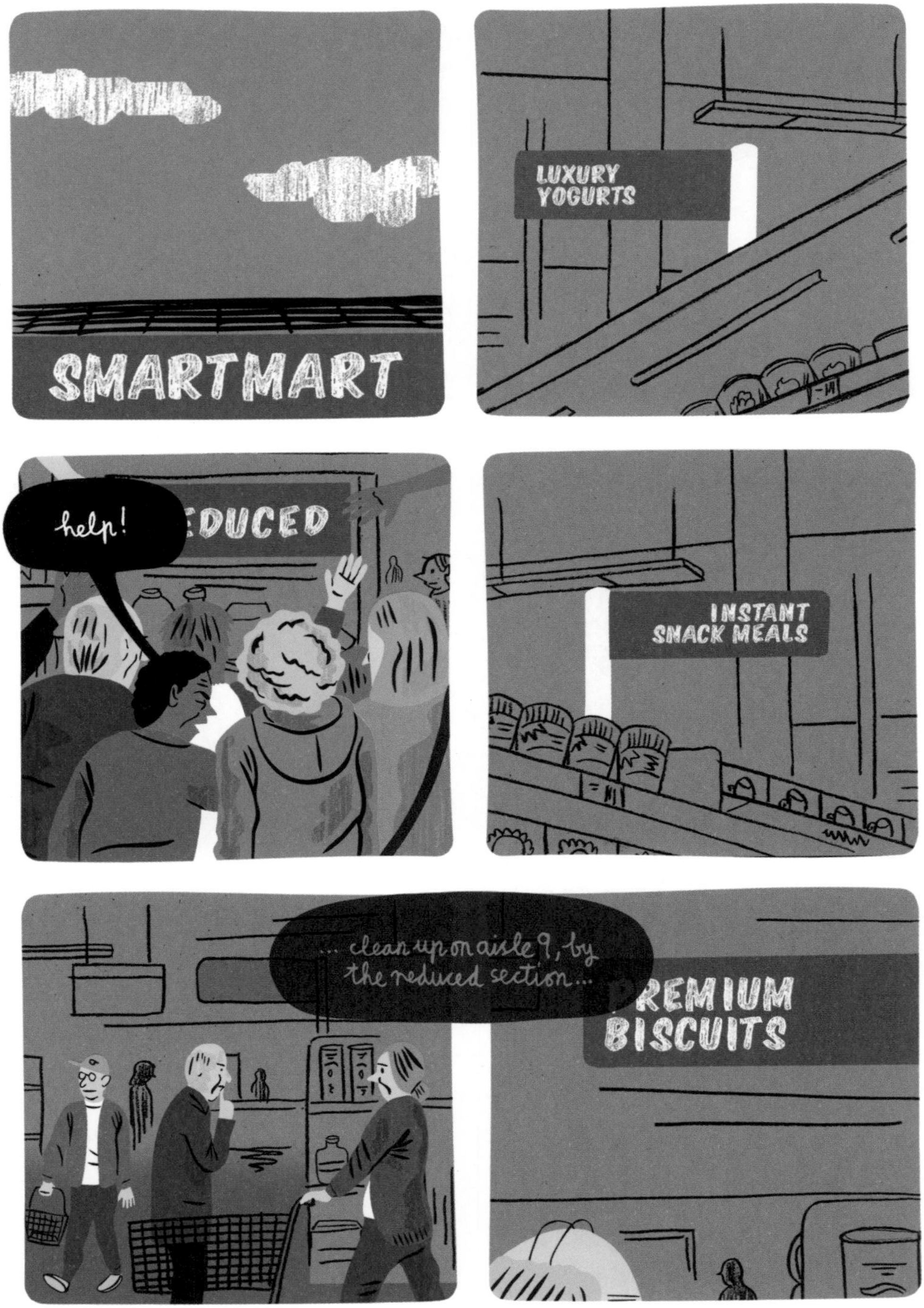

SMARTMART
LUXURY YOGURTS
help!
EDUCED
INSTANT SNACK MEALS
... clean up on aisle 9, by the reduced section...
REMIUM BISCUITS

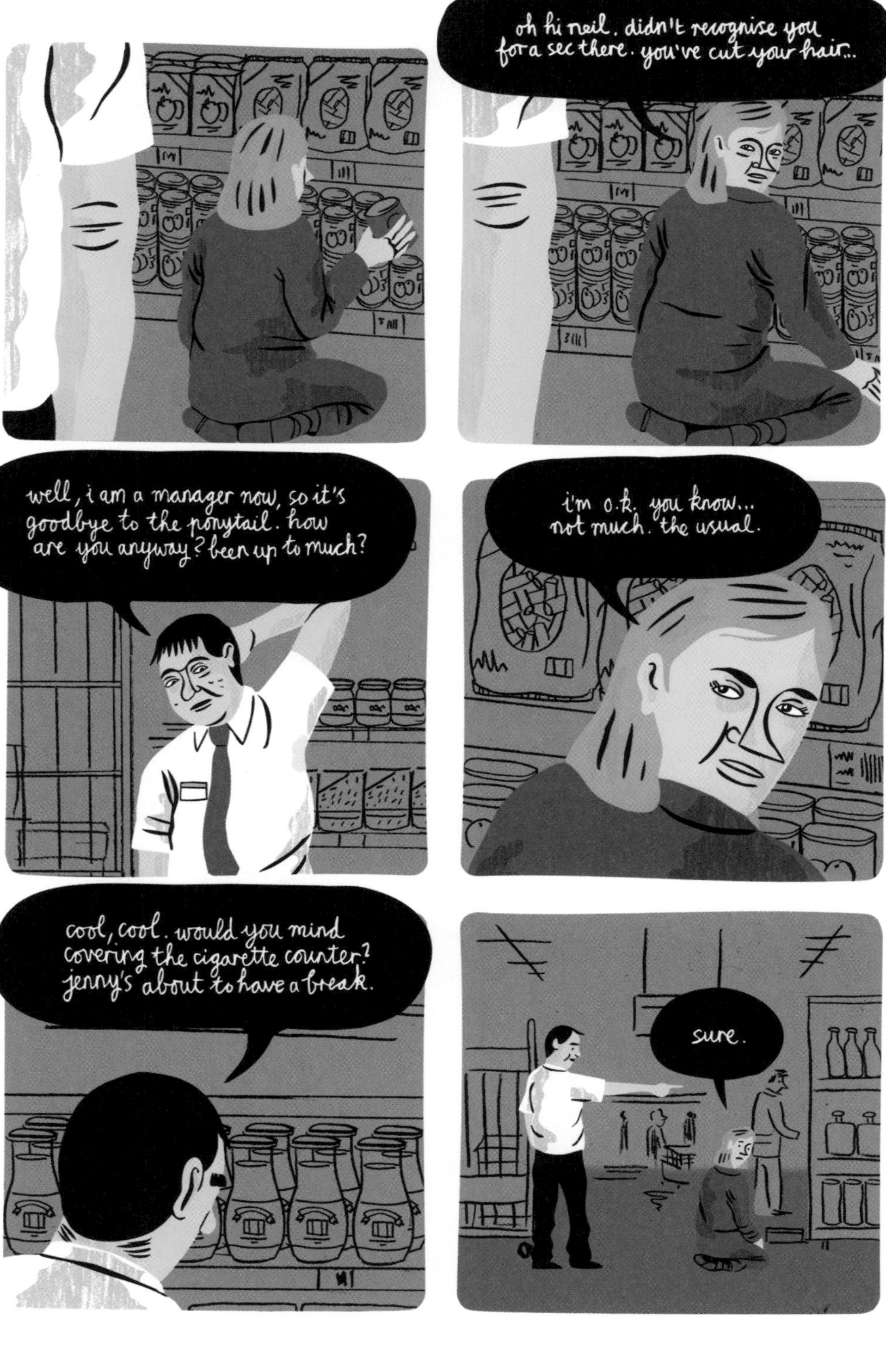
oh hi neil. didn't recognise you for a sec there. you've cut your hair...
well, i am a manager now, so it's goodbye to the ponytail. how are you anyway? been up to much?
i'm o.k. you know... not much. the usual.
cool, cool. would you mind covering the cigarette counter? jenny's about to have a break.
sure.

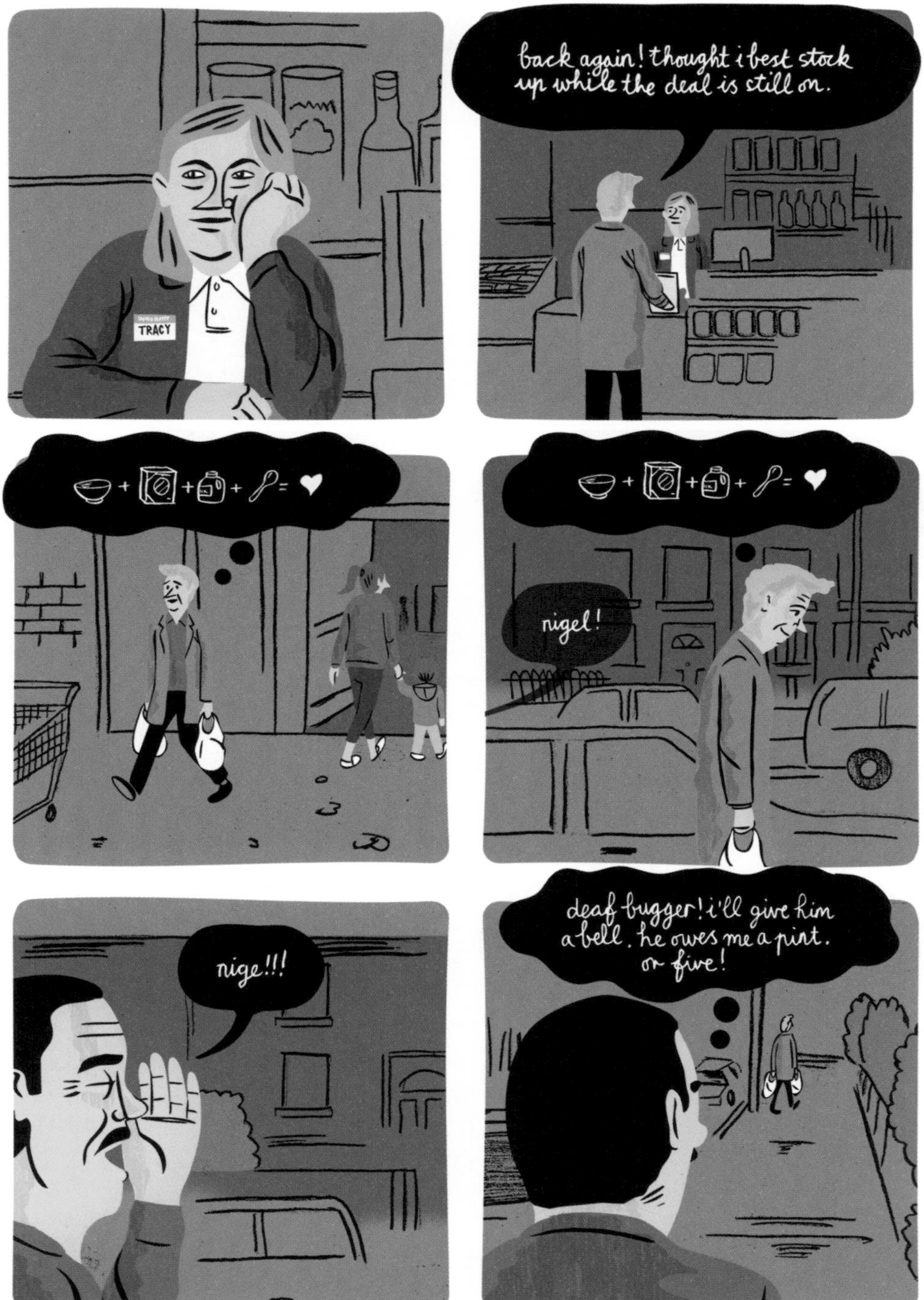
TRACY
back again! thought i best stock up while the deal is still on.
nigel!
nige!!!
deaf bugger! i'll give him a bell. he owes me a pint. or five!

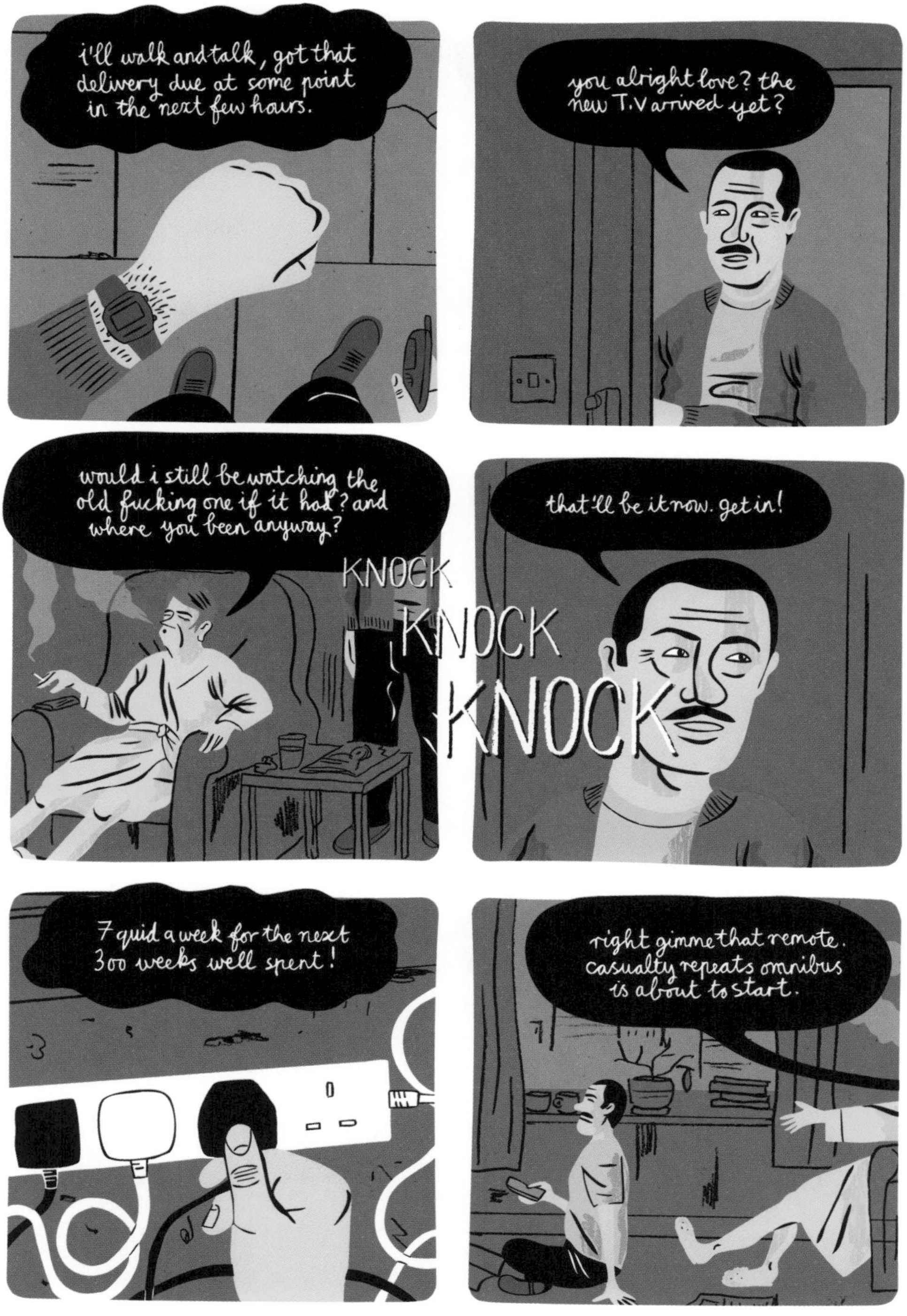

i'll walk and talk, got that delivery due at some point in the next few hours.
you alright love? the new T.V arrived yet?
would i still be watching the old fucking one if it had? and where you been anyway?
that'll be it now. get in!
KNOCK
KNOCK
KNOCK
7 quid a week for the next 300 weeks well spent!
right gimme that remote. casualty repeats omnibus is about to start.

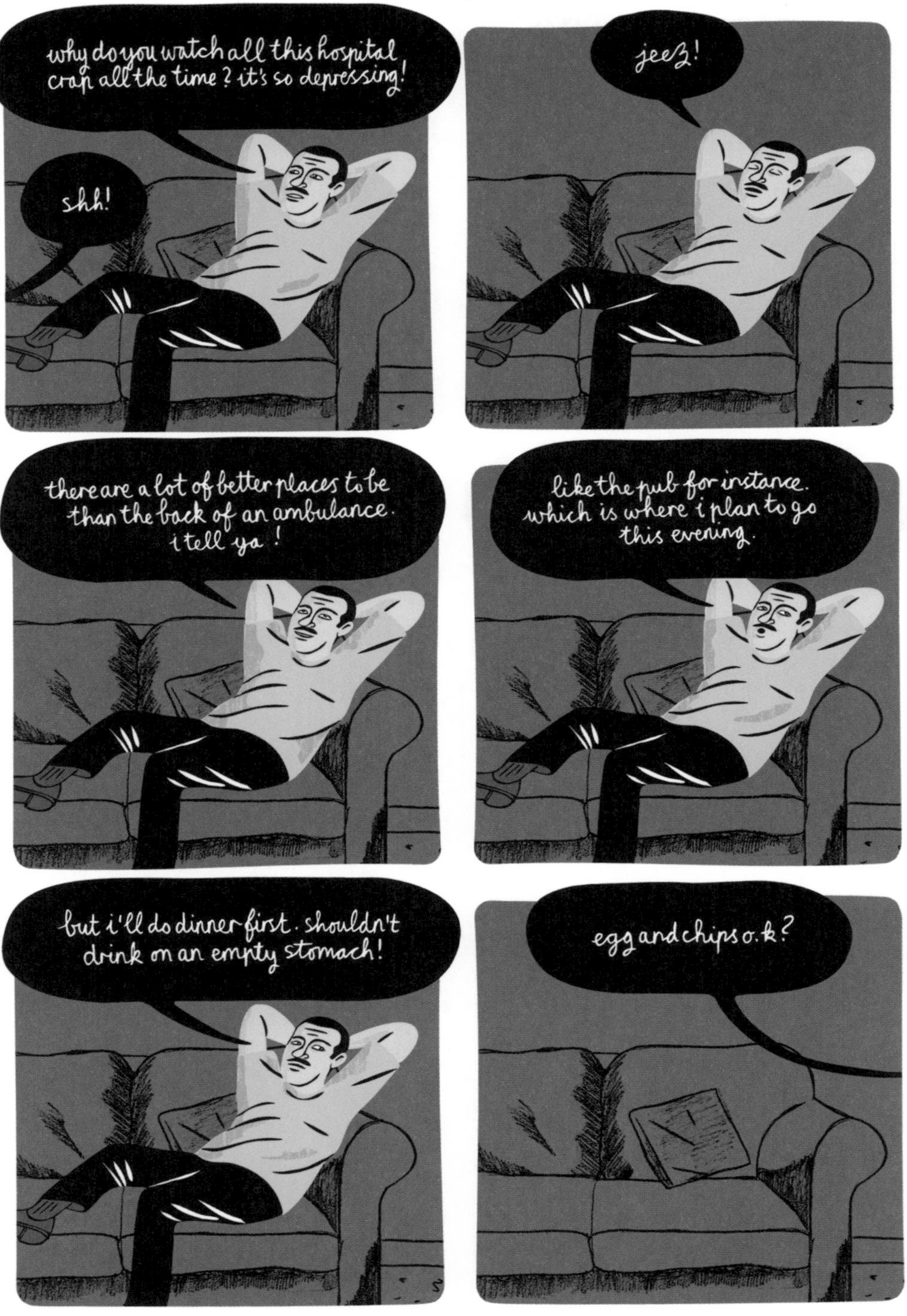
why do you watch all this hospital crap all the time? it's so depressing!
shh!
jeez!
there are a lot of better places to be than the back of an ambulance. i tell ya!
like the pub for instance. which is where i plan to go this evening.
but i'll do dinner first. shouldn't drink on an empty stomach!
egg and chips o.k?

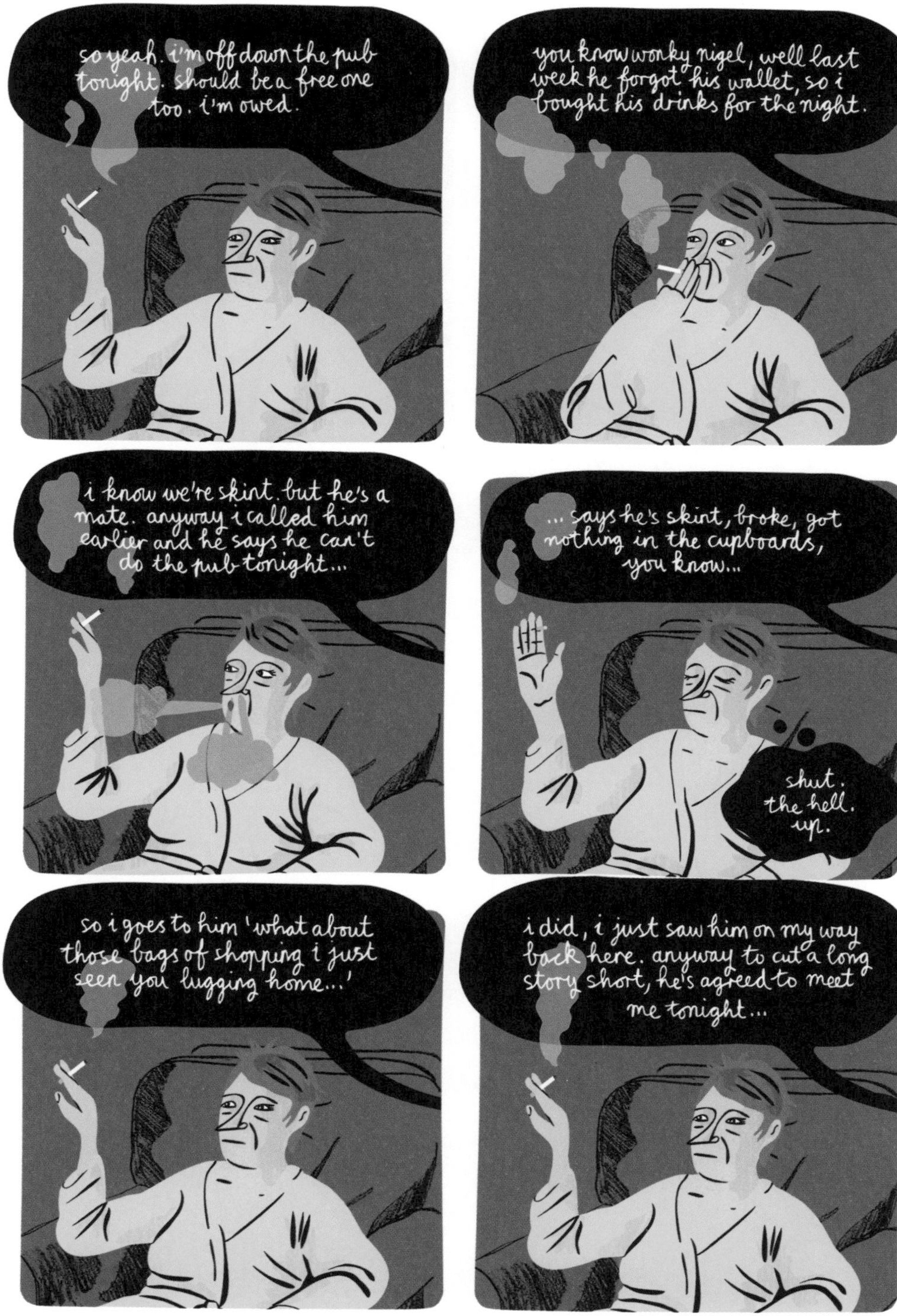
so yeah. i'm off down the pub tonight. should be a free one too. i'm owed.
you know wonky nigel, well last week he forgot his wallet, so i bought his drinks for the night.
i know we're skint. but he's a mate. anyway i called him earlier and he says he can't do the pub tonight...
... says he's skint, broke, got nothing in the cupboards, you know...
shut. the hell. up.
so i goes to him 'what about those bags of shopping i just seen you lugging home...'
i did, i just saw him on my way back here. anyway to cut a long story short, he's agreed to meet me tonight...

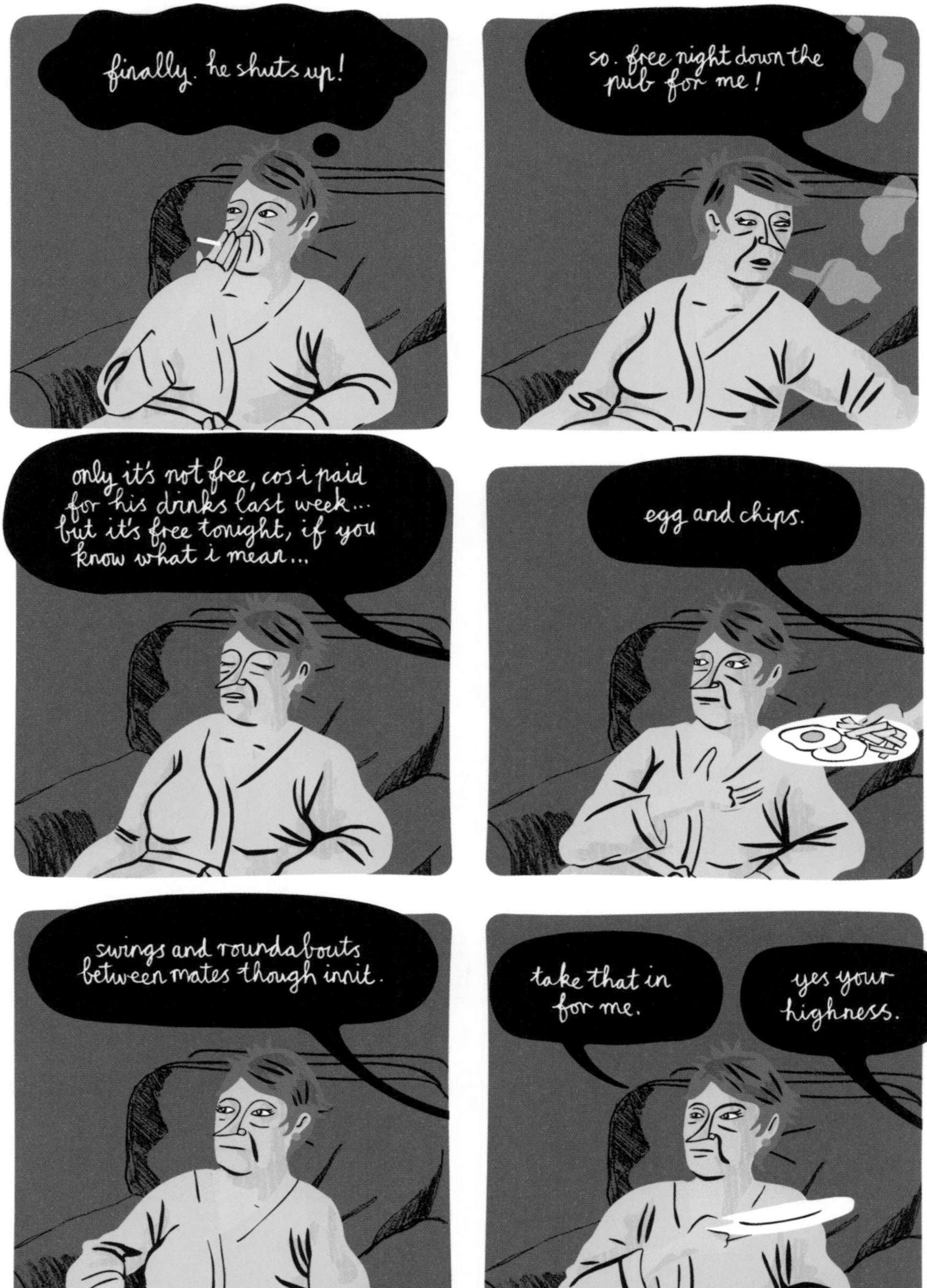
finally. he shuts up!
so. free night down the pub for me!
only it's not free, cos i paid for his drinks last week... but it's free tonight, if you know what i mean...
egg and chips.
swings and roundabouts between mates though innit.
take that in for me.
yes your highness.

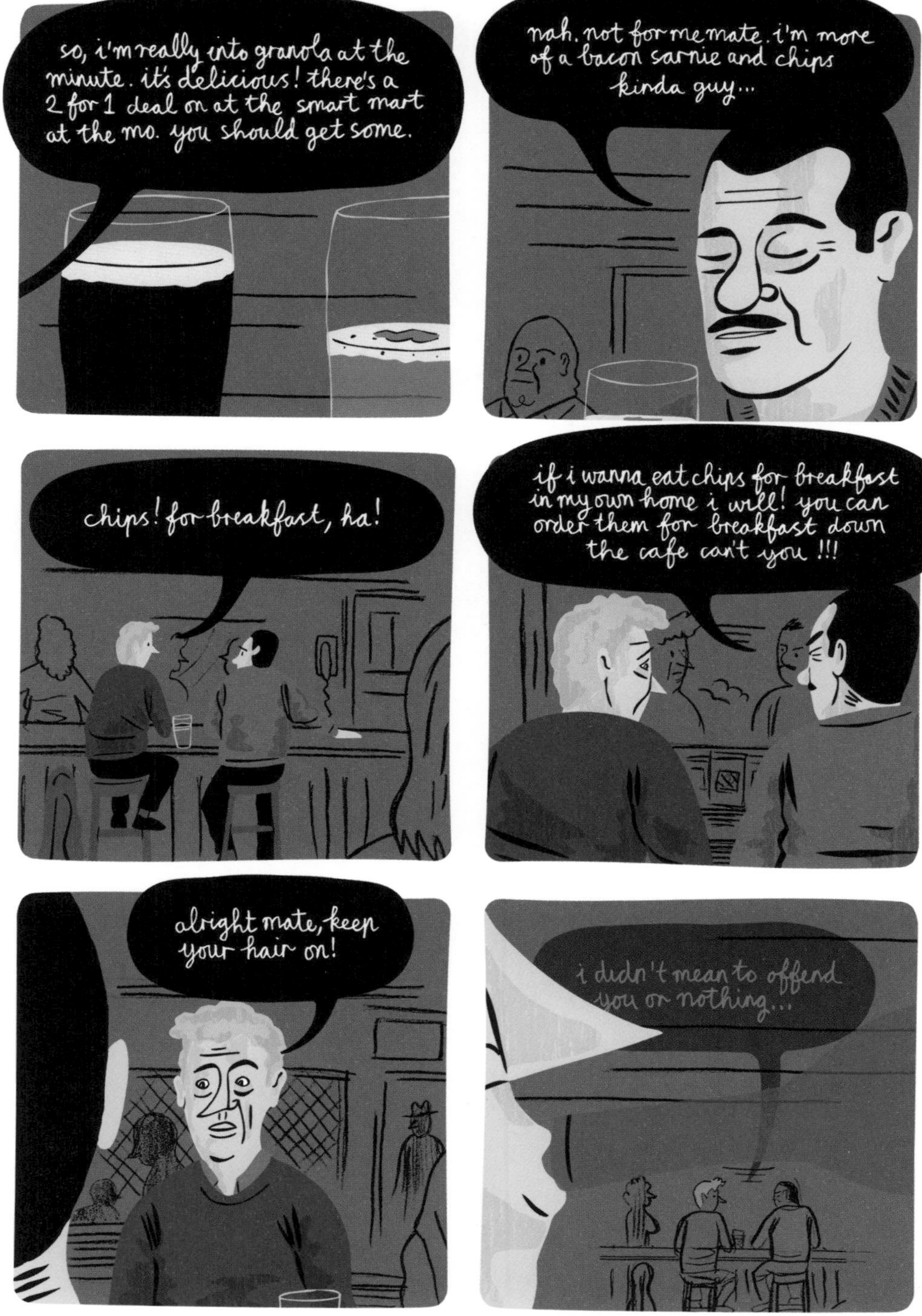
so, i'm really into granola at the minute. it's delicious! there's a 2 for 1 deal on at the smart mart at the mo. you should get some.
nah. not for me mate. i'm more of a bacon sarnie and chips kinda guy...
chips! for breakfast, ha!
if i wanna eat chips for breakfast in my own home i will! you can order them for breakfast down the cafe can't you!!!
alright mate, keep your hair on!
i didn't mean to offend you or nothing...

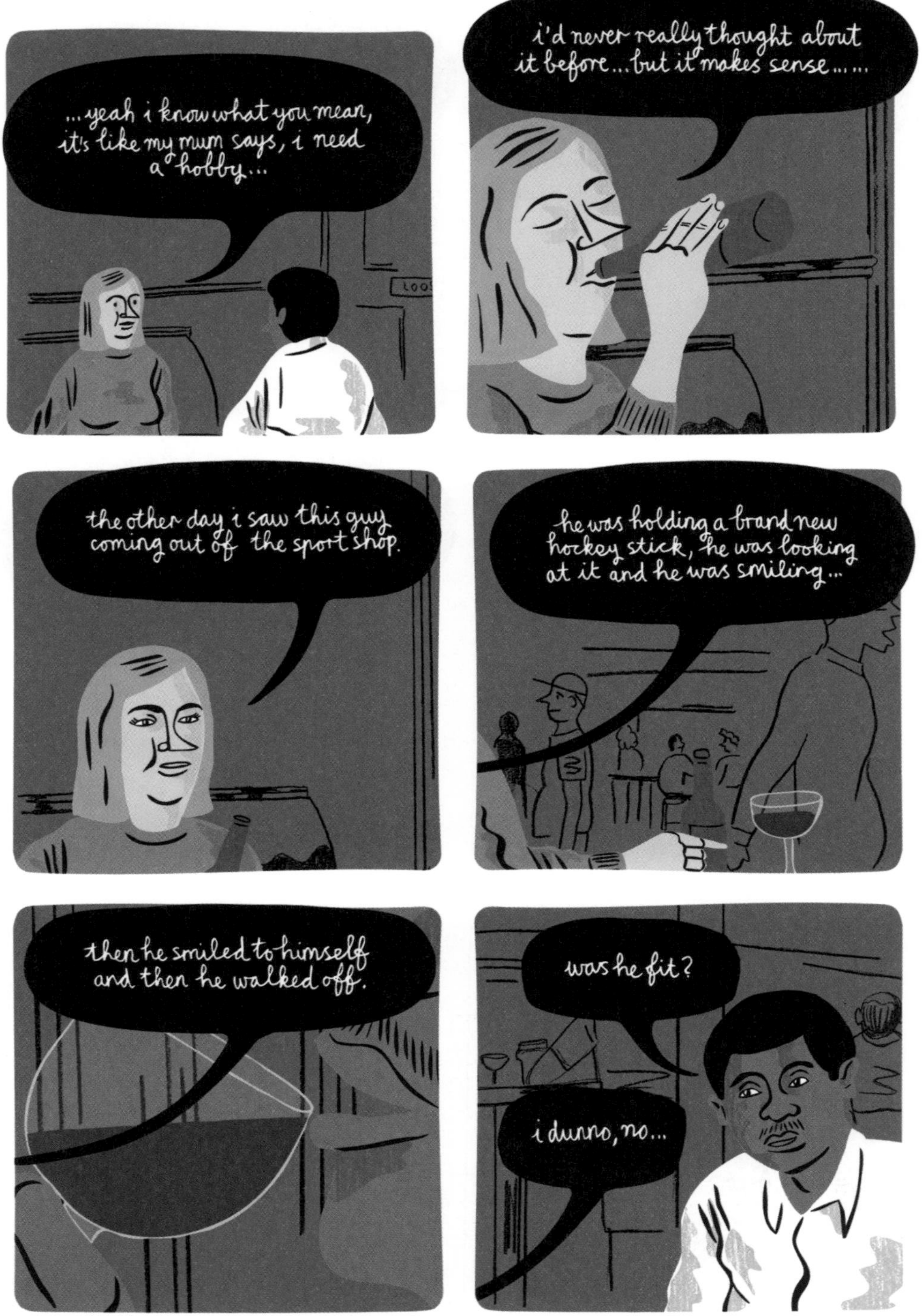
...yeah i know what you mean, it's like my mum says, i need a hobby...
i'd never really thought about it before...but it makes sense......
the other day i saw this guy coming out of the sport shop.
he was holding a brand new hockey stick, he was looking at it and he was smiling...
then he smiled to himself and then he walked off.
was he fit?
i dunno, no...

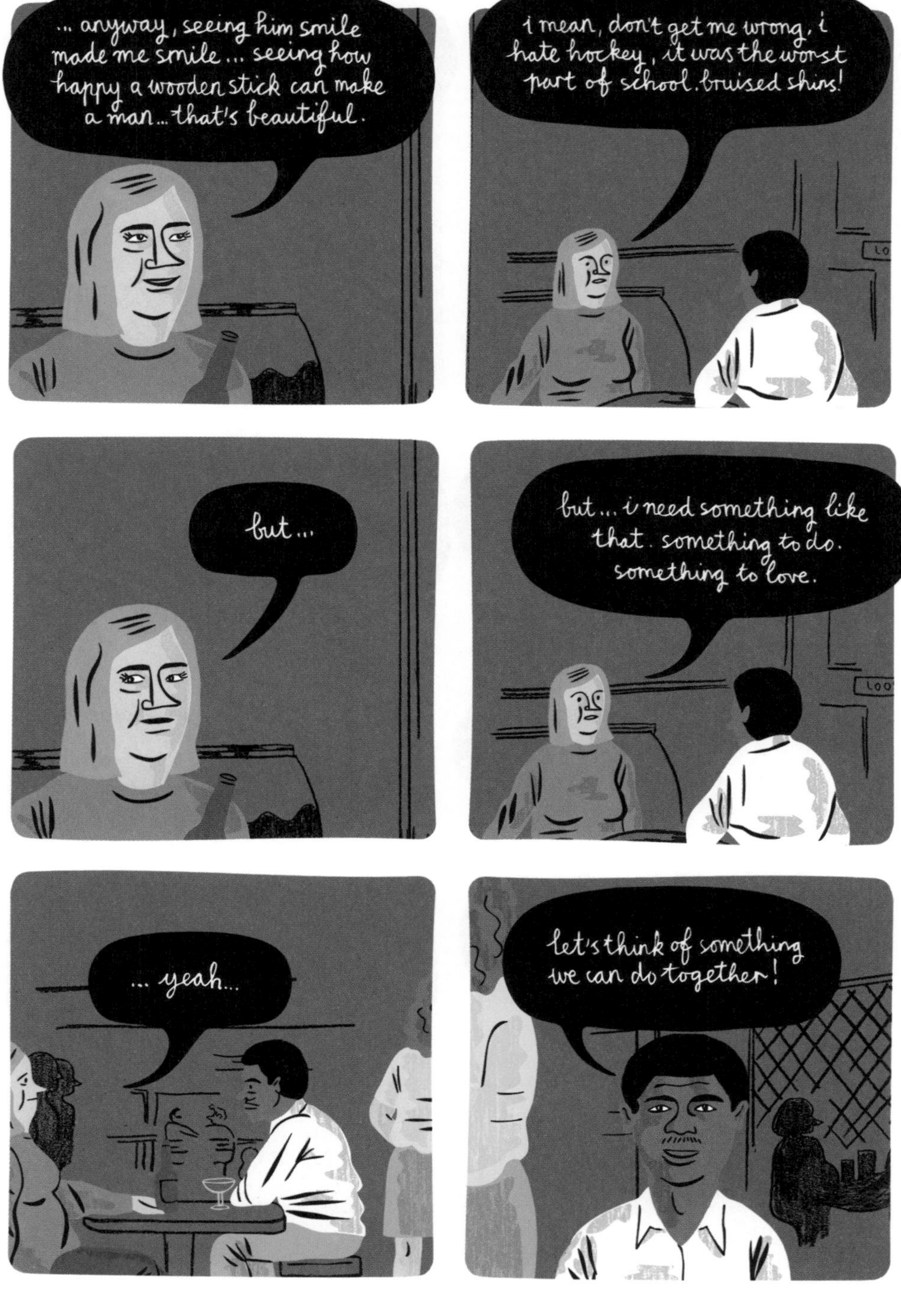
... anyway, seeing him smile made me smile ... seeing how happy a wooden stick can make a man... that's beautiful.
i mean, don't get me wrong, i hate hockey, it was the worst part of school. bruised shins!
but...
but... i need something like that. something to do. something to love.
... yeah...
let's think of something we can do together!

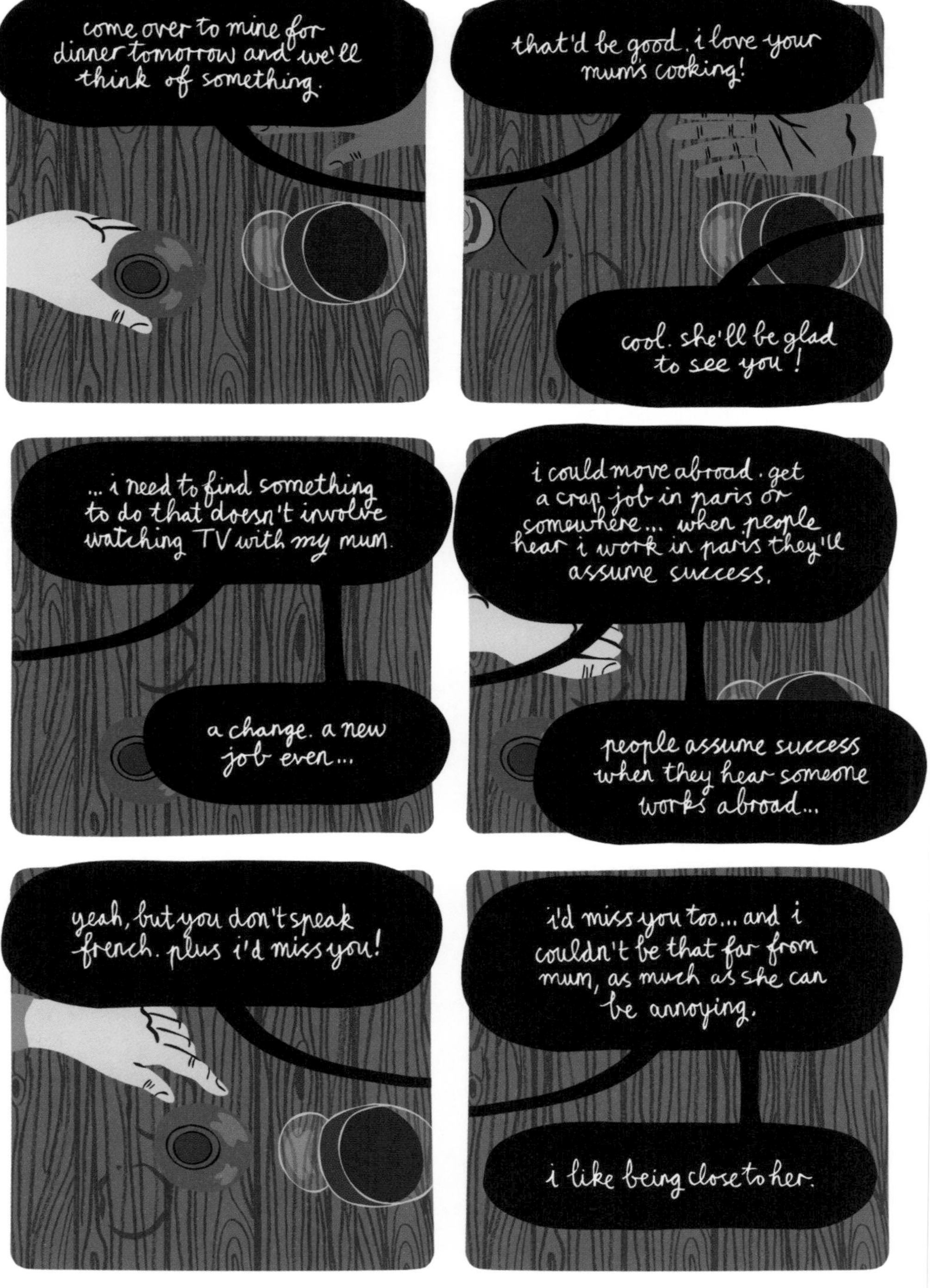
come over to mine for dinner tomorrow and we'll think of something.
that'd be good. i love your mum's cooking!
cool. she'll be glad to see you!
... i need to find something to do that doesn't involve watching TV with my mum.
a change. a new job even...
i could move abroad. get a crap job in paris or somewhere... when people hear i work in paris they'll assume success.
people assume success when they hear someone works abroad...
yeah, but you don't speak french. plus i'd miss you!
i'd miss you too... and i couldn't be that far from mum, as much as she can be annoying.
i like being close to her.

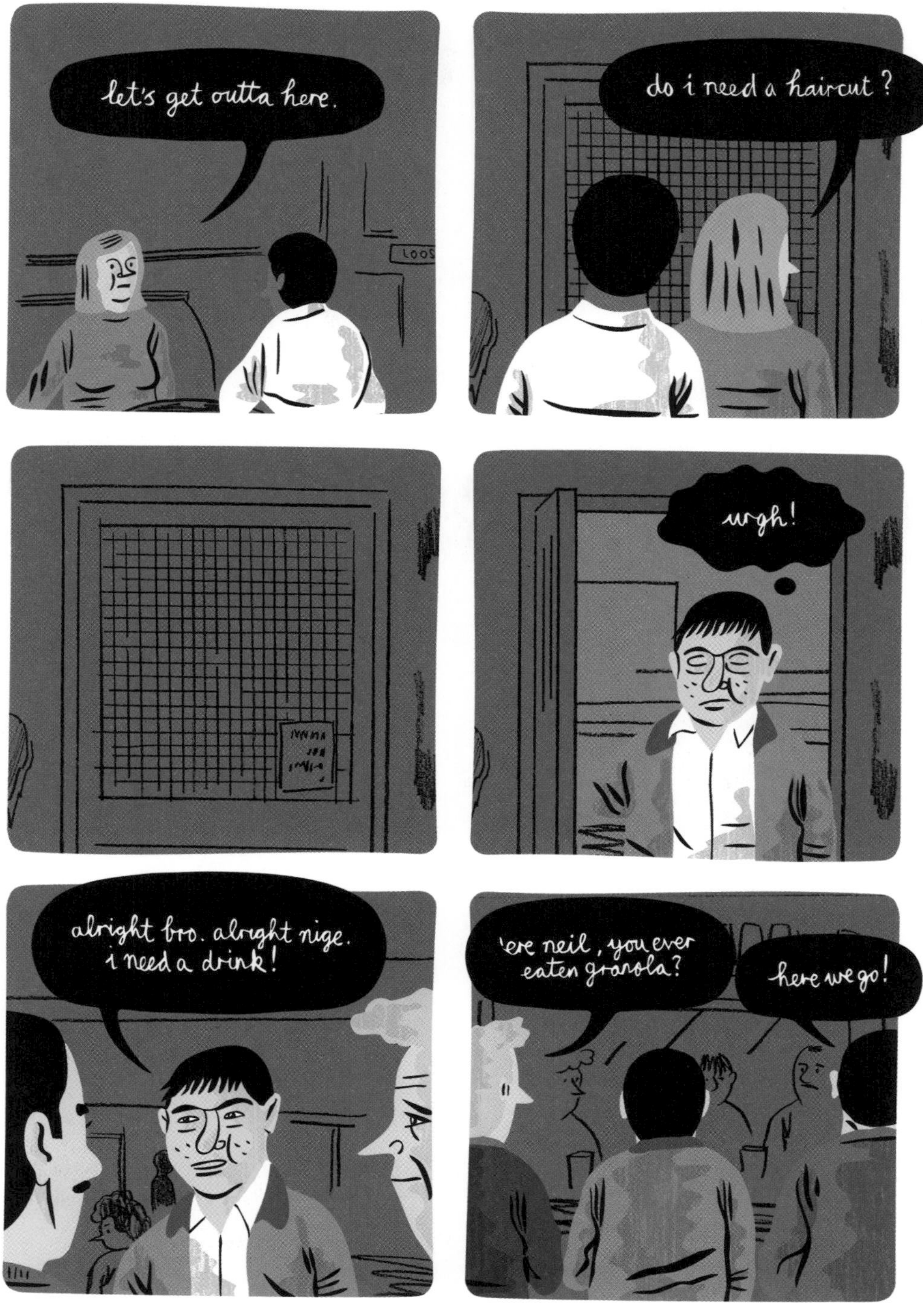
let's get outta here.
do i need a haircut?
urgh!
alright bro. alright nige. i need a drink!
'ere neil, you ever eaten granola?
here we go!

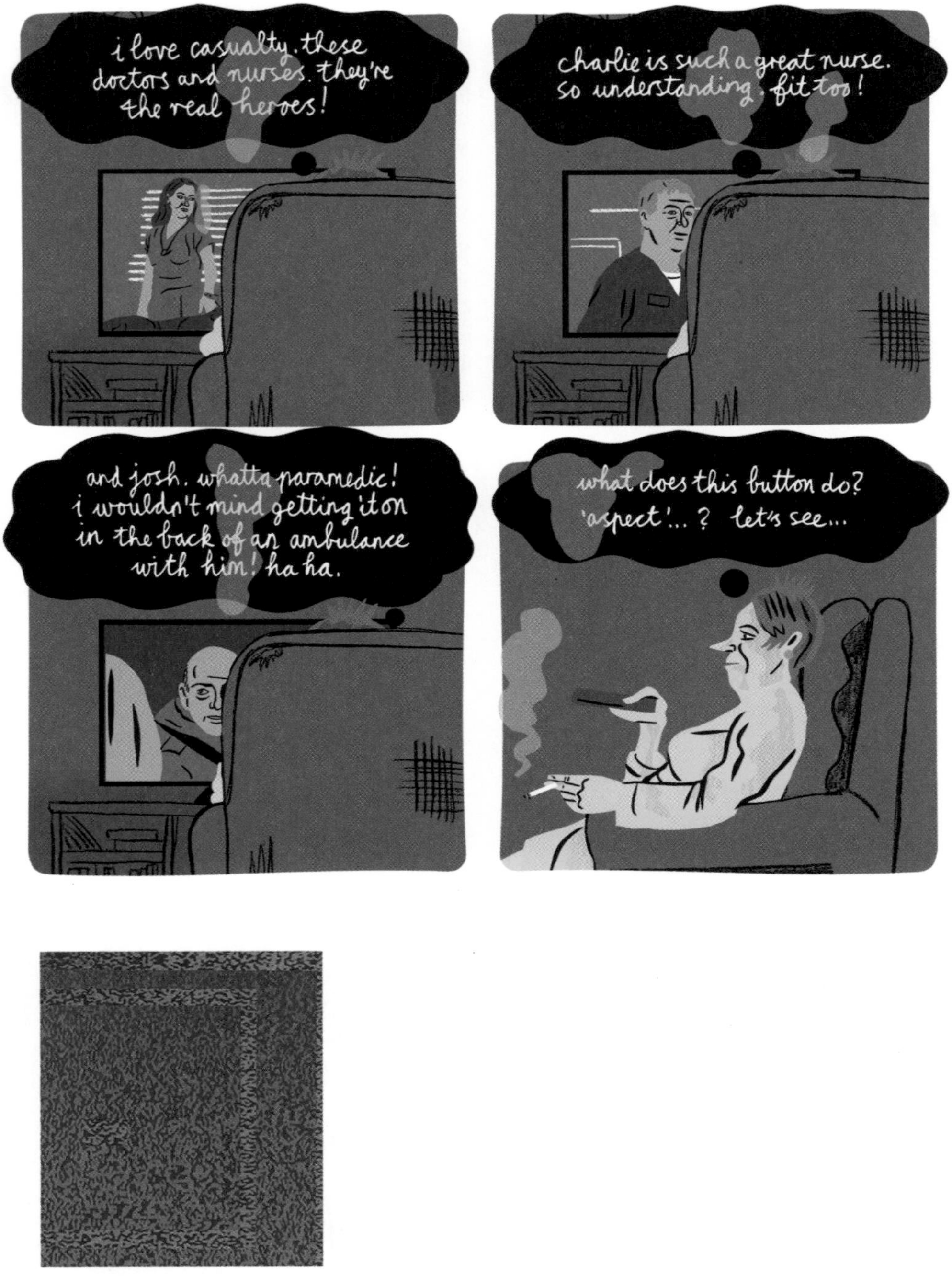
i love casualty. these doctors and nurses. they're the real heroes!
charlie is such a great nurse. so understanding. fit too!
and josh. whatta paramedic! i wouldn't mind getting it on in the back of an ambulance with him! ha ha.
what does this button do? 'aspect'... ? let's see...

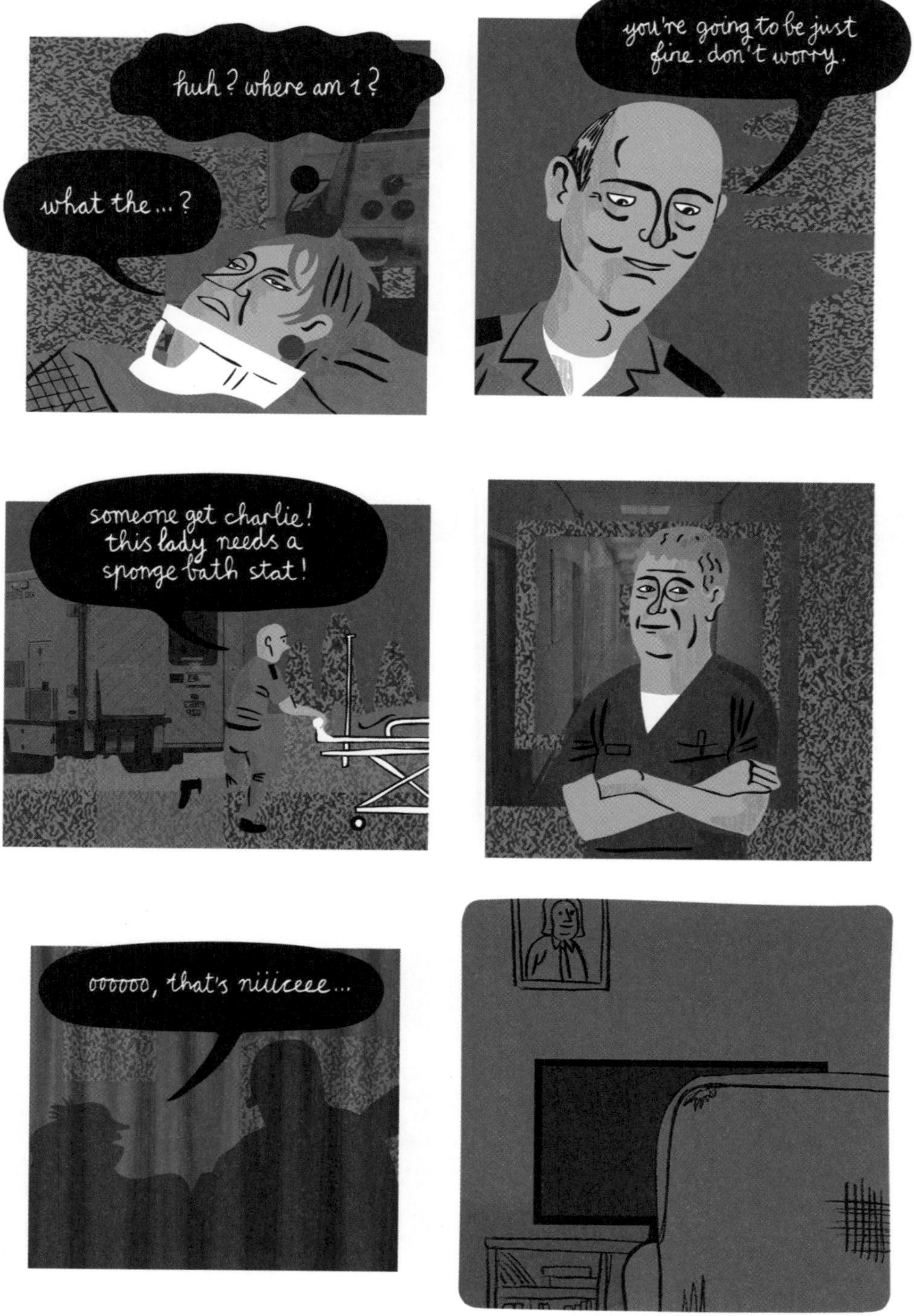
what the...?
huh? where am i?
you're going to be just fine. don't worry.
someone get charlie! this lady needs a sponge bath stat!
oooooo, that's niiiceee...

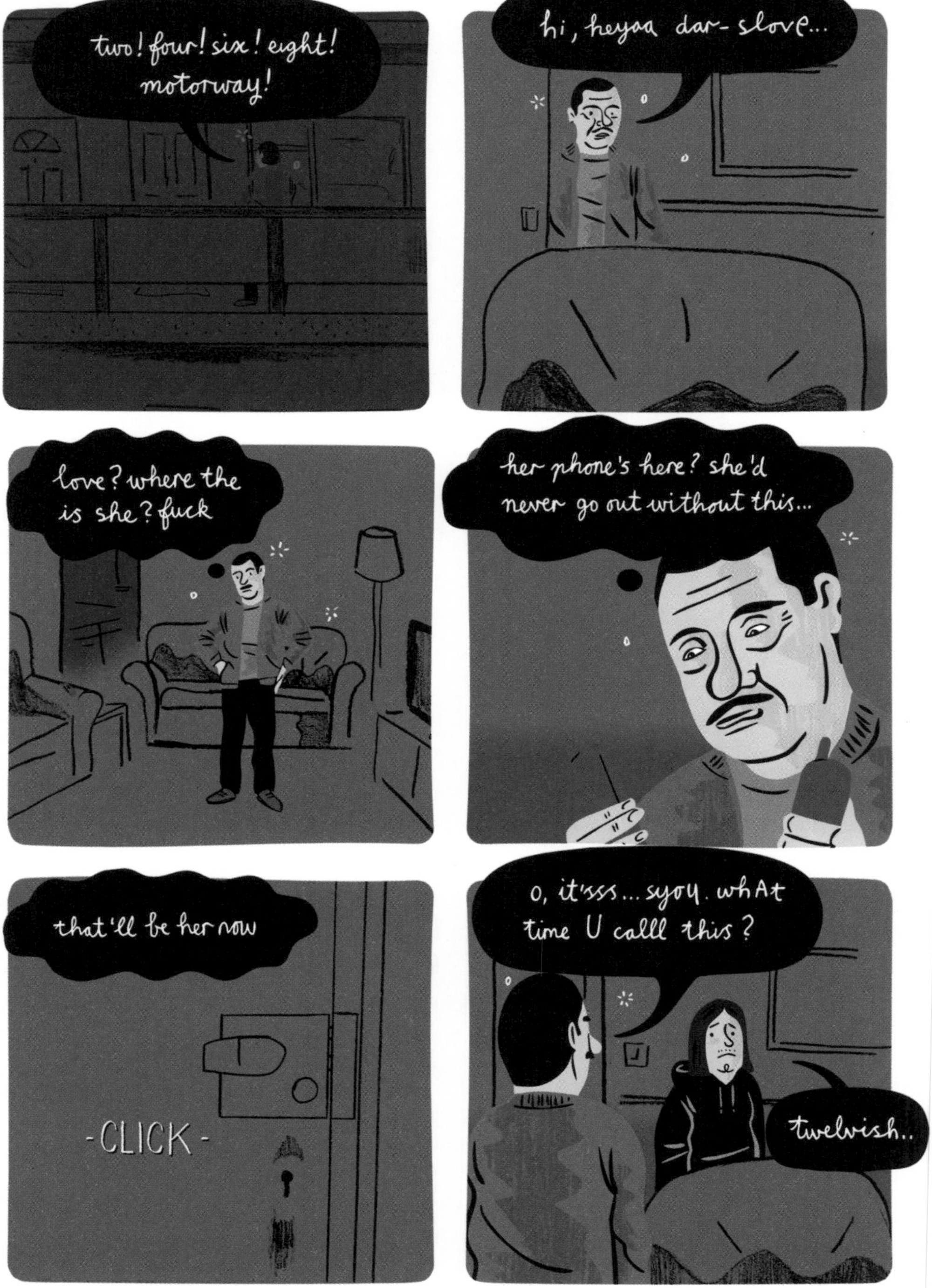
two! four! six! eight! motorway!
hi, heyaa dar- slove...
love? where the is she? fuck
her phone's here? she'd never go out without this...
that'll be her now
-CLICK-
o, it'sss... syou. whAt time U calll this?
twelvish..

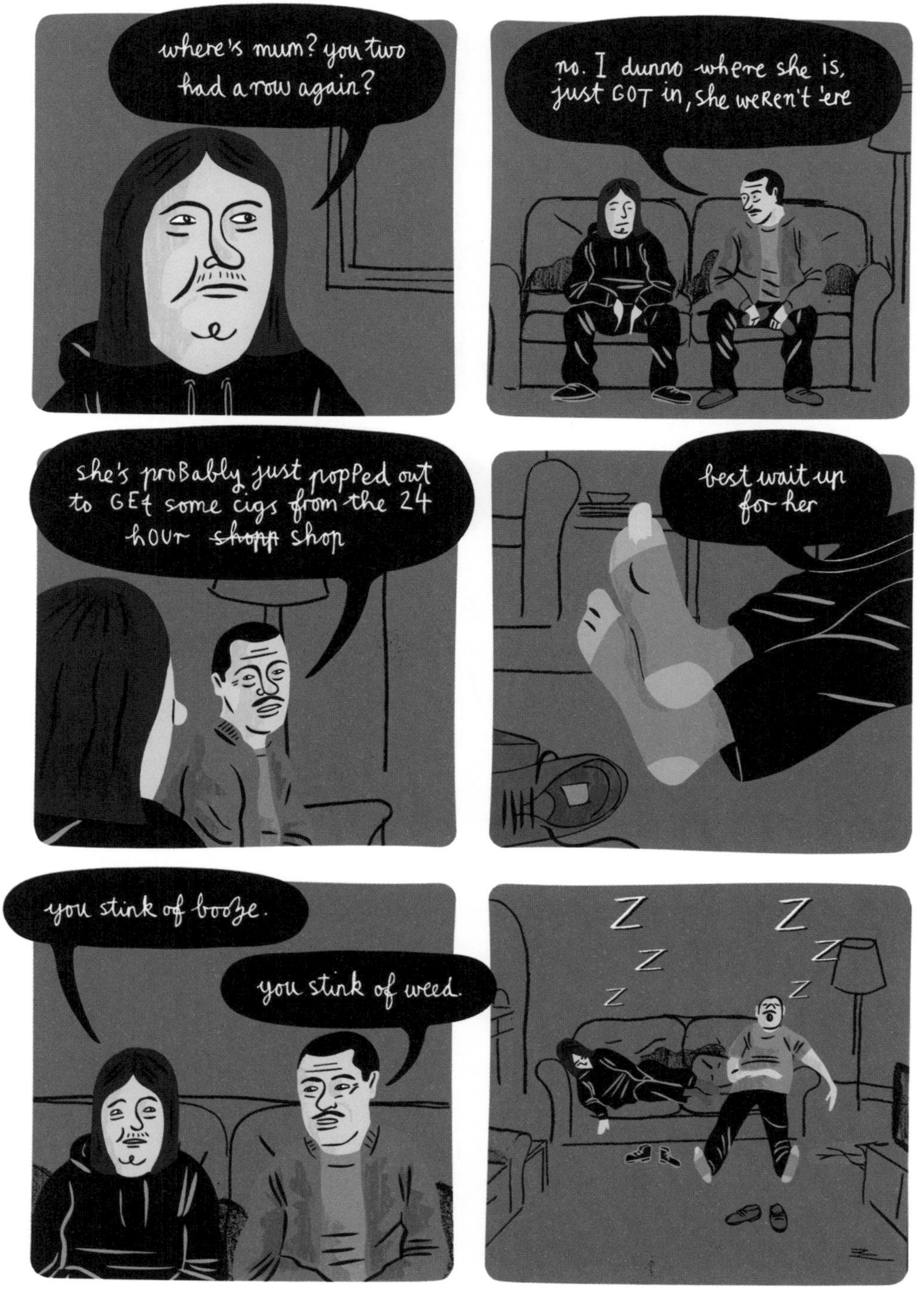
where's mum? you two had a row again?
no. I dunno where she is, just GOT in, she weren't 'ere
she's proBaBly just popped out to GEt some cigs from the 24 hour shopp shop
best wait up for her
you stink of booze.
you stink of weed.
Z Z Z Z Z Z

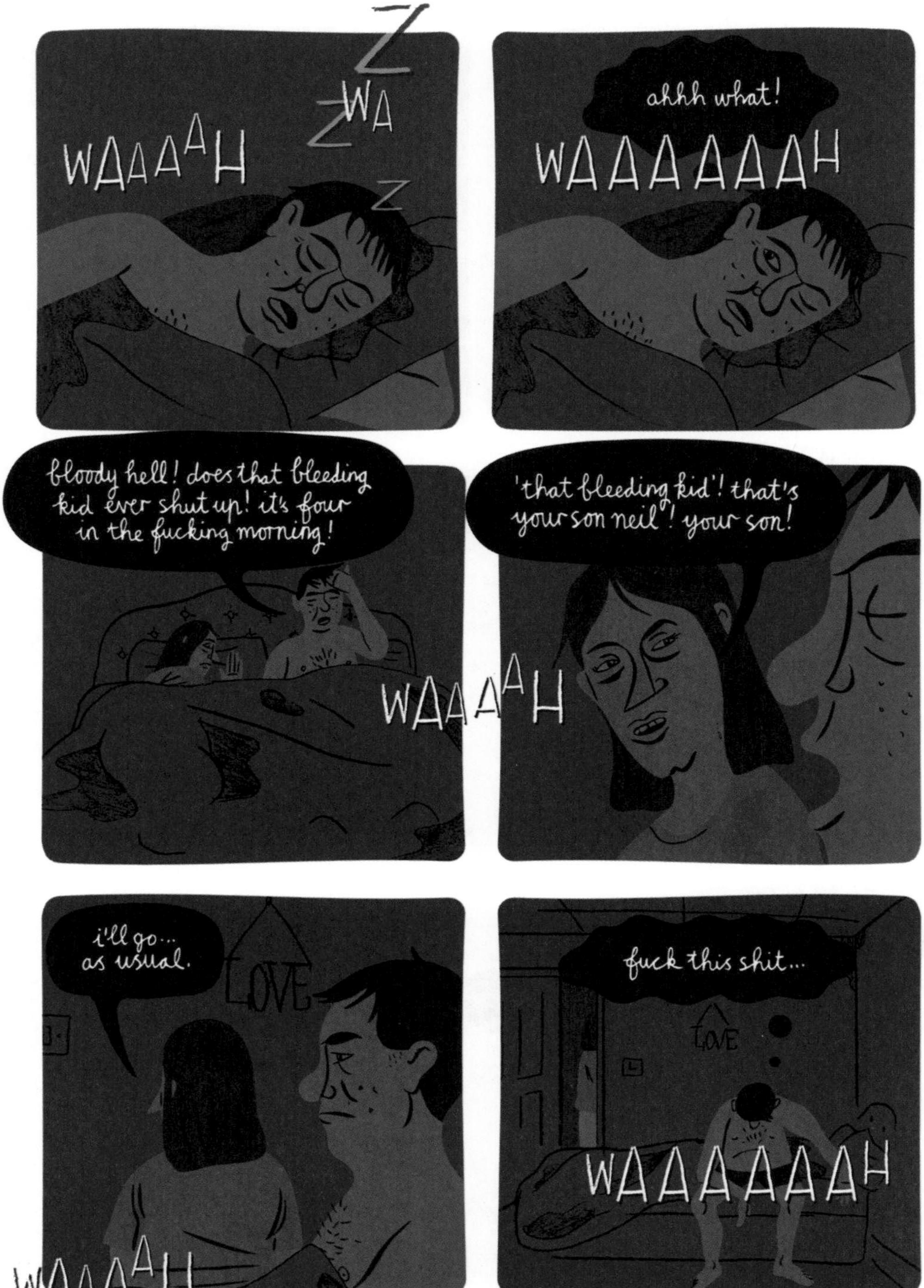
WAAAAH
WA
ahhh what!
WAAAAAAH
bloody hell! does that bleeding kid ever shut up! it's four in the fucking morning!
'that bleeding kid'! that's your son neil! your son!
WAAAAH
i'll go... as usual.
LOVE
WAAAAH
fuck this shit...
LOVE
WAAAAAAH

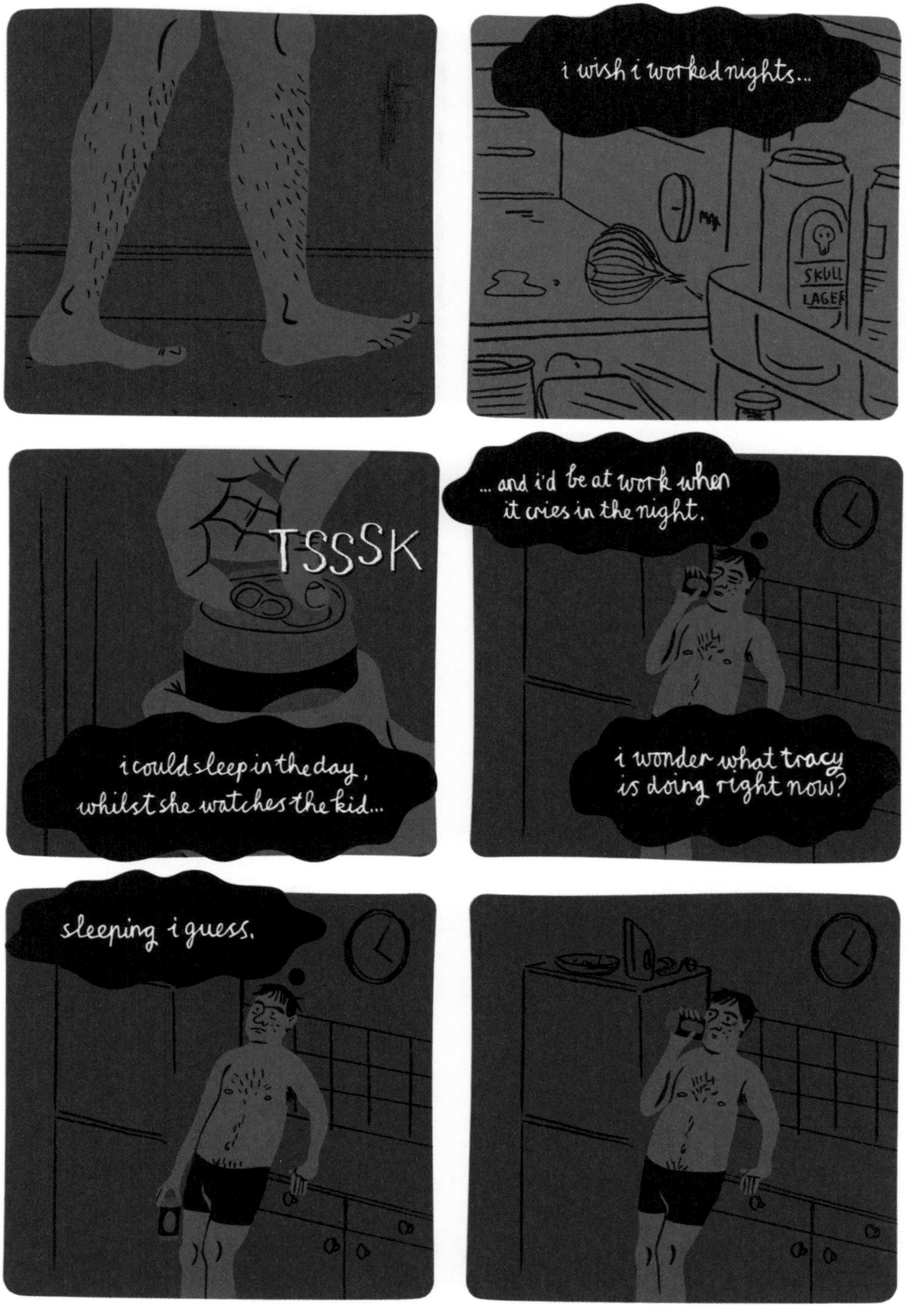
i wish i worked nights...
SKULL LAGER
TSSSK
i could sleep in the day, whilst she watches the kid...
... and i'd be at work when it cries in the night.
i wonder what tracy is doing right now?
sleeping i guess.

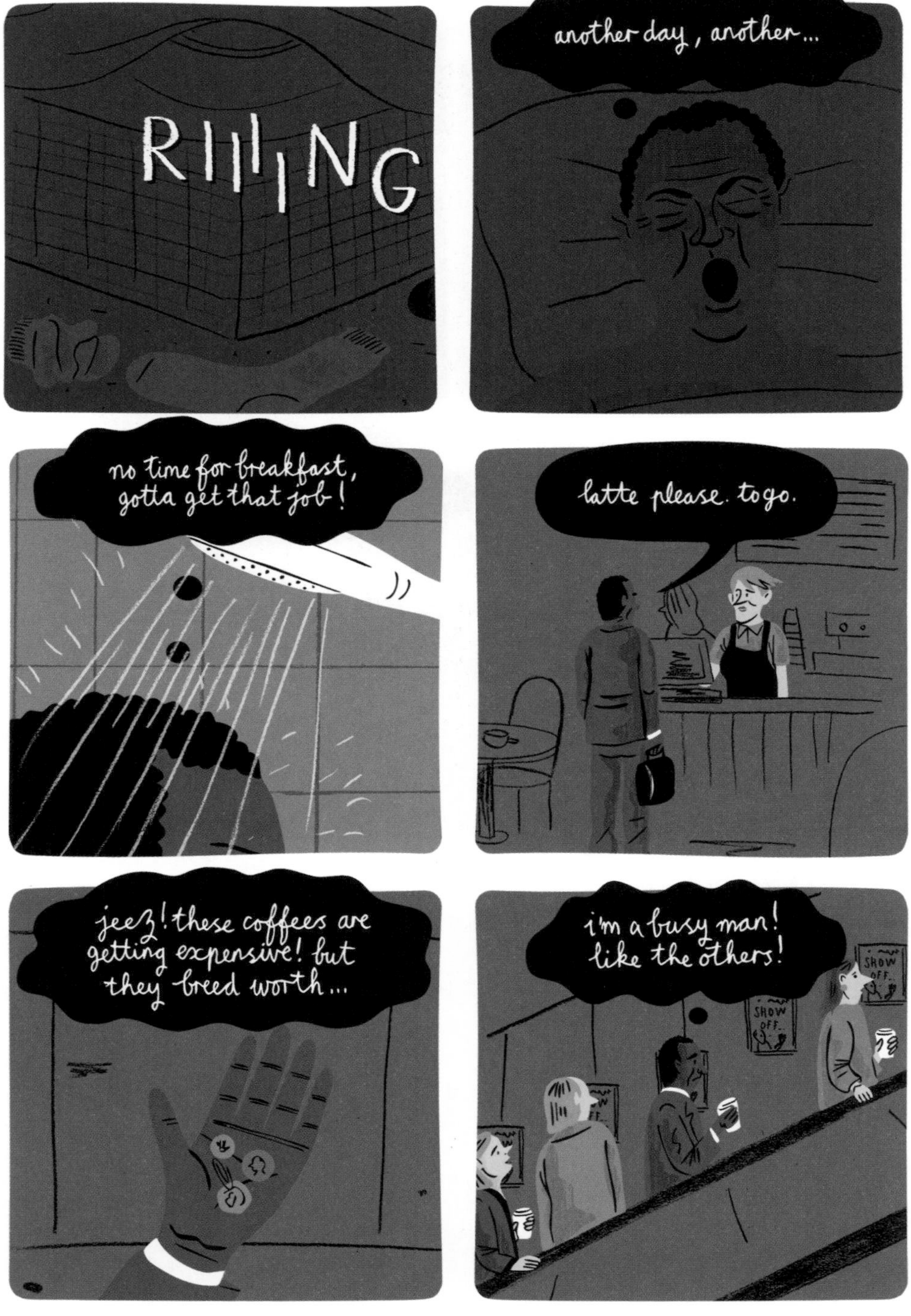
RIIIING
another day, another...
no time for breakfast, gotta get that job!
latte please. to go.
jeez! these coffees are getting expensive! but they breed worth...
i'm a busy man! like the others!
SHOW OFF..
SHOW OFF..

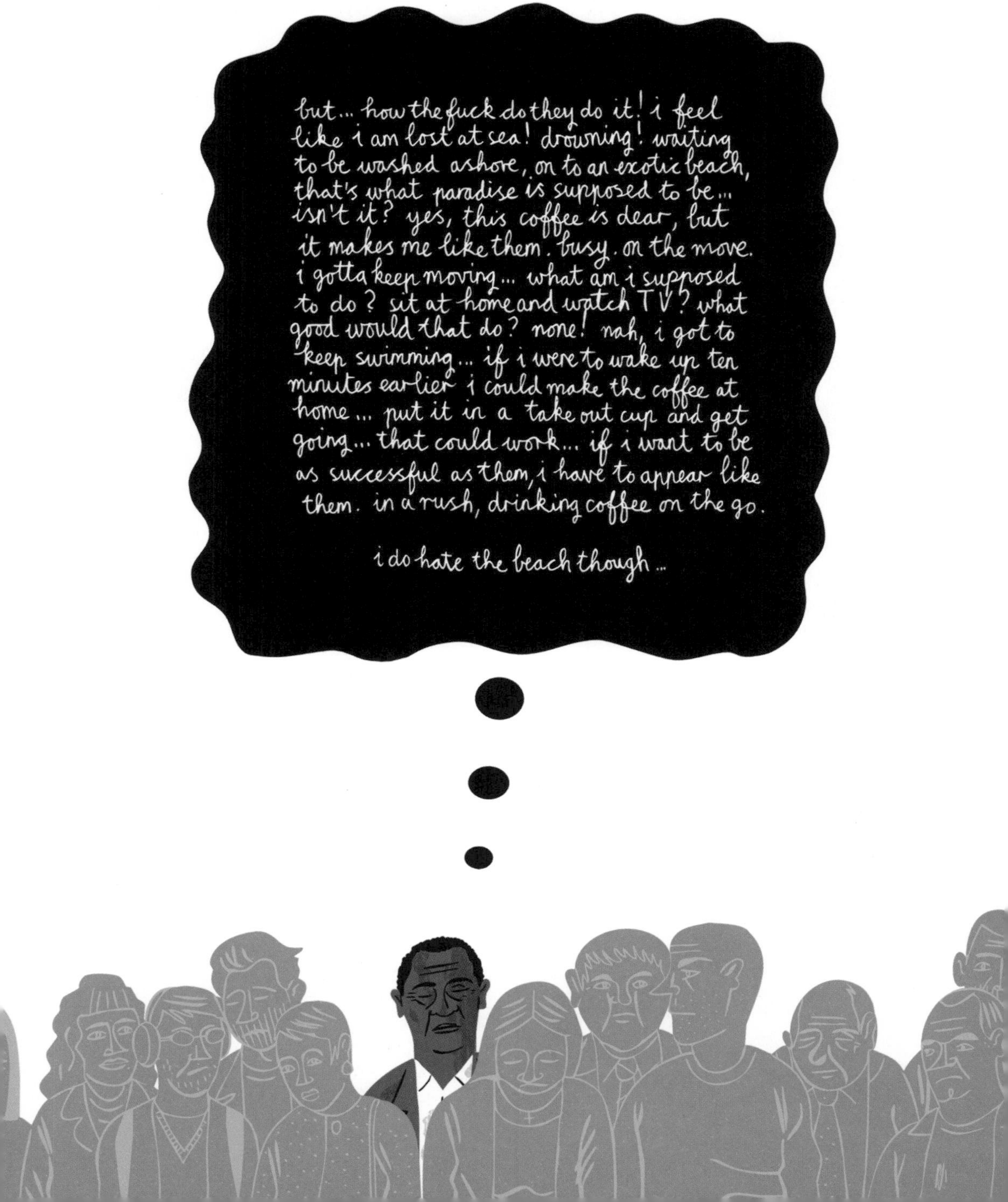
but... how the fuck do they do it! i feel like i am lost at sea! drowning! waiting to be washed ashore, on to an exotic beach, that's what paradise is supposed to be... isn't it? yes, this coffee is dear, but it makes me like them. busy. on the move. i gotta keep moving... what am i supposed to do? sit at home and watch TV? what good would that do? none! nah, i got to keep swimming... if i were to wake up ten minutes earlier i could make the coffee at home... put it in a take out cup and get going... that could work... if i want to be as successful as them, i have to appear like them. in a rush, drinking coffee on the go.
i do hate the beach though...

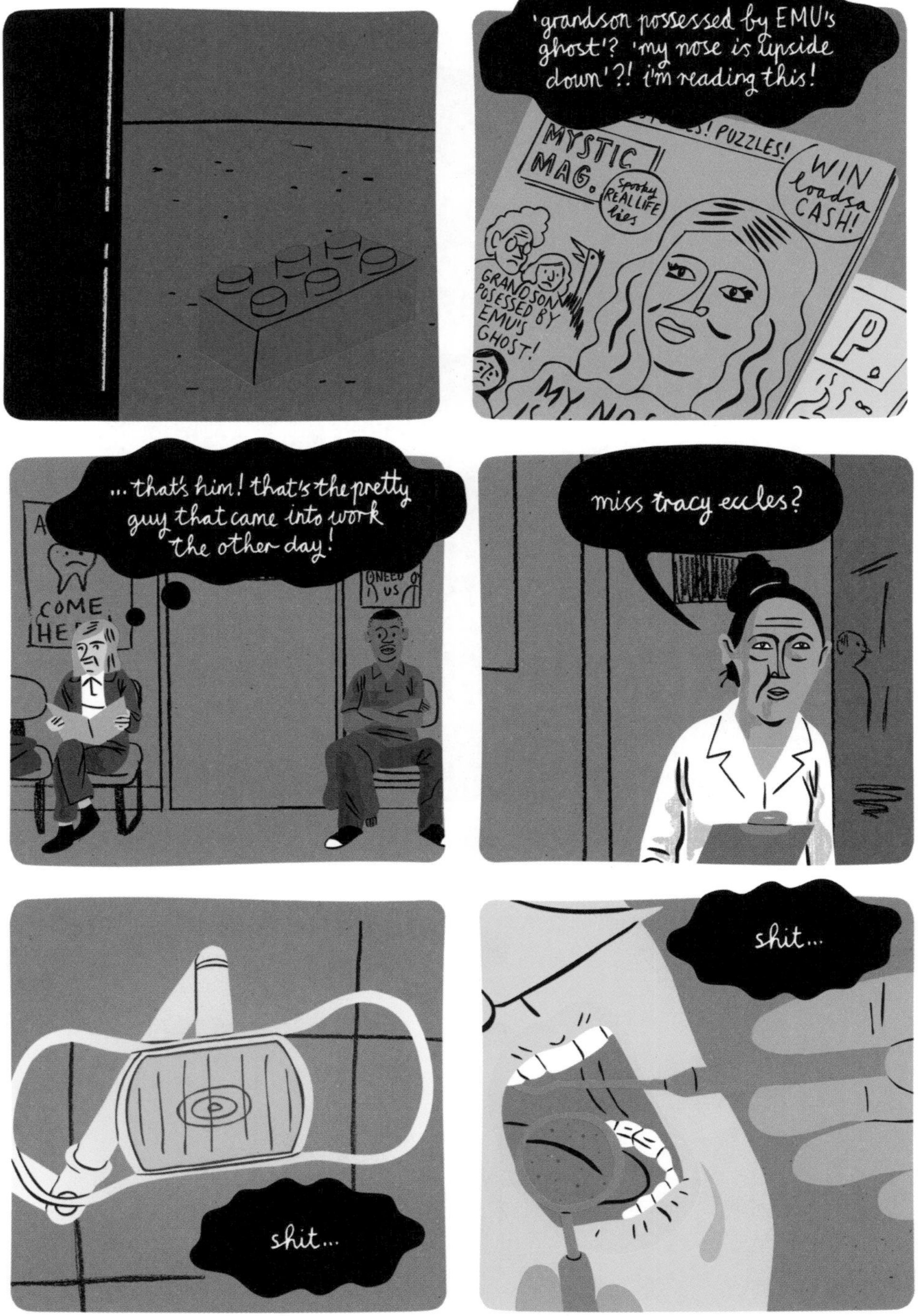
'grandson possessed by EMU's ghost'? 'my nose is upside down'?! i'm reading this!
MYSTIC MAG.
PUZZLES!
WIN loadsa CASH!
Spooky REALLIFE lies
GRANDSON POSESSED BY EMU'S GHOST!
... that's him! that's the pretty guy that came into work the other day!
COME HE
miss tracy eccles?
shit...
shit...

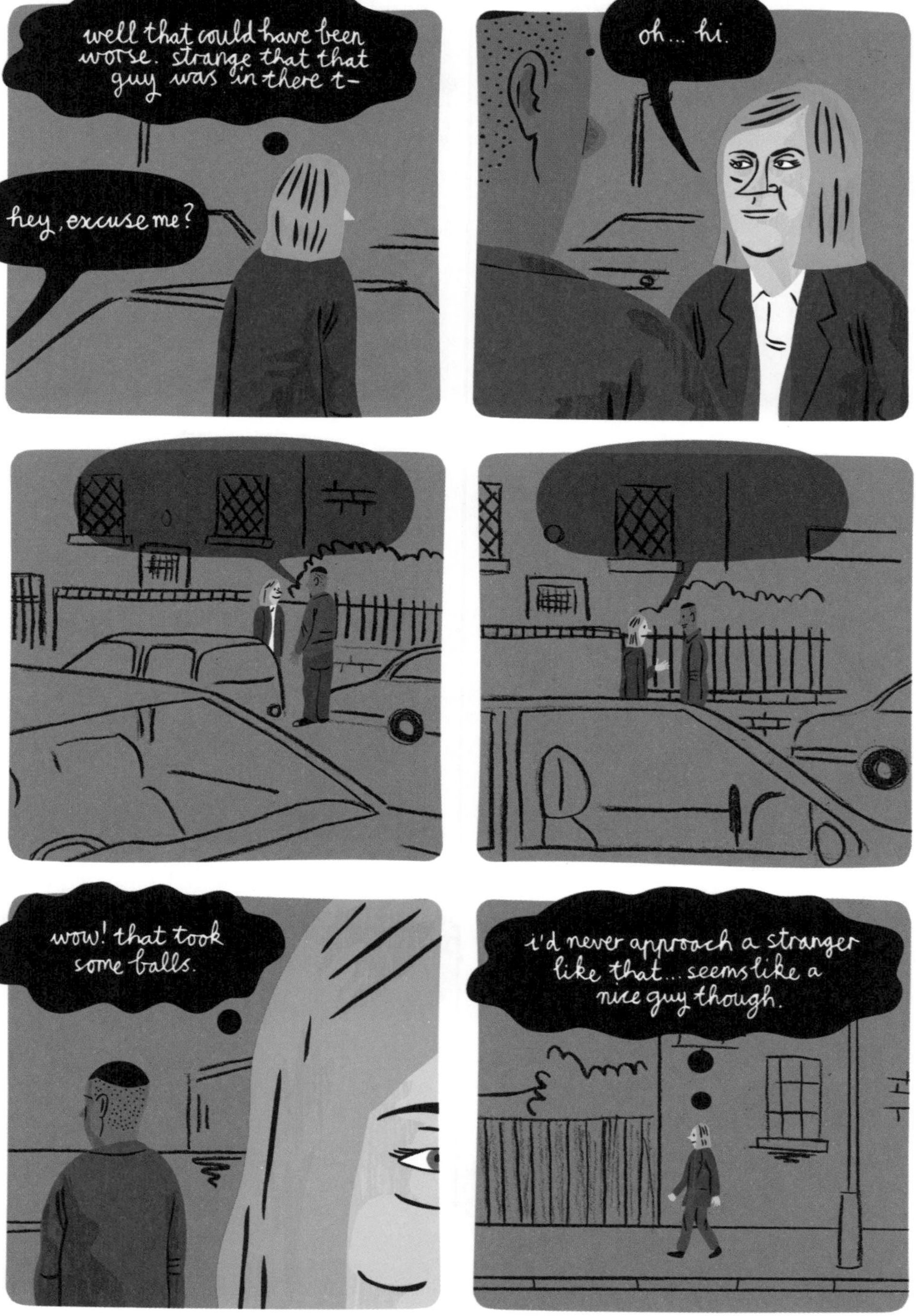

well that could have been worse. strange that that guy was in there t-
hey, excuse me?
oh... hi.
wow! that took some balls.
i'd never approach a stranger like that... seems like a nice guy though.

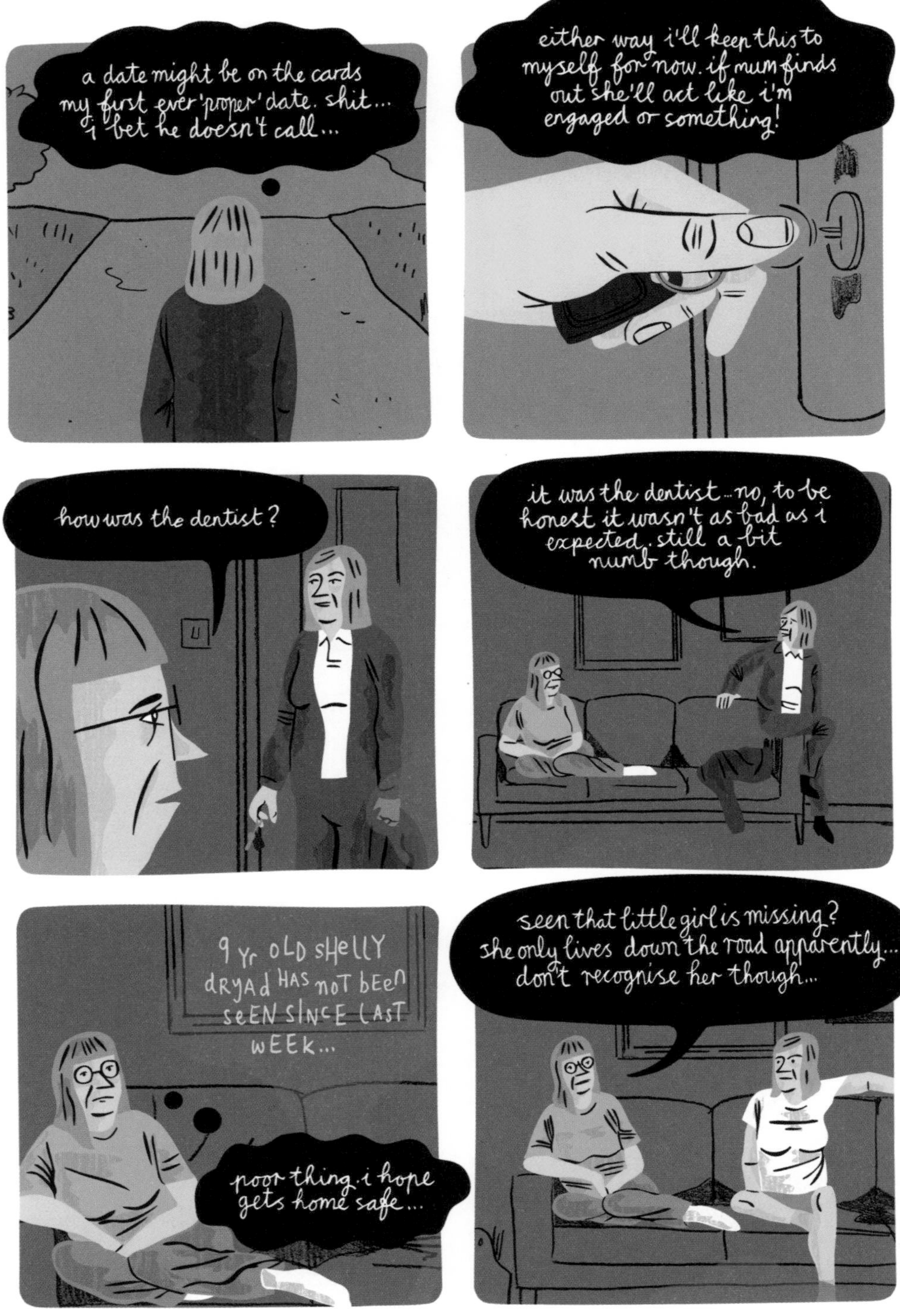
a date might be on the cards my first ever 'proper' date. shit... i bet he doesn't call...
either way i'll keep this to myself for now. if mum finds out she'll act like i'm engaged or something!
how was the dentist?
it was the dentist... no, to be honest it wasn't as bad as i expected. still a bit numb though.
9 Yr OLD SHELLY DRYAD HAS NOT BEEN SEEN SINCE LAST WEEK...
poor thing. i hope gets home safe...
seen that little girl is missing? she only lives down the road apparently... don't recognise her though...

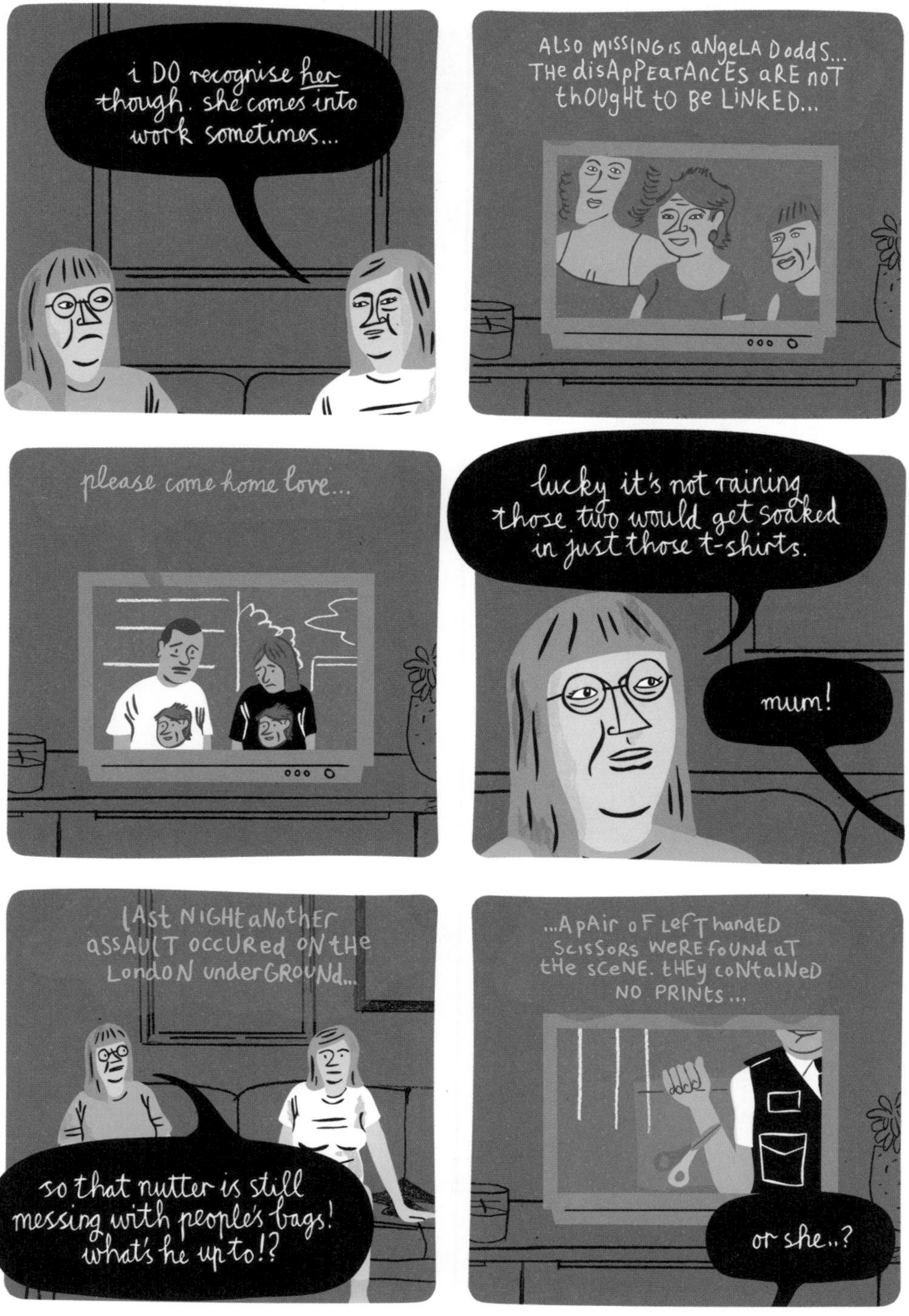
i DO recognise her though. she comes into work sometimes...
ALSO MISSING IS ANGELA DODDS... THE DISAPPEARANCES ARE NOT THOUGHT TO BE LINKED...
please come home love...
lucky it's not raining those two would get soaked in just those t-shirts.
mum!
LAST NIGHT ANOTHER ASSAULT OCCURED ON THE LONDON UNDERGROUND...
so that nutter is still messing with people's bags! what's he up to!?
...A PAIR OF LEFT HANDED SCISSORS WERE FOUND AT THE SCENE. THEY CONTAINED NO PRINTS...
or she..?

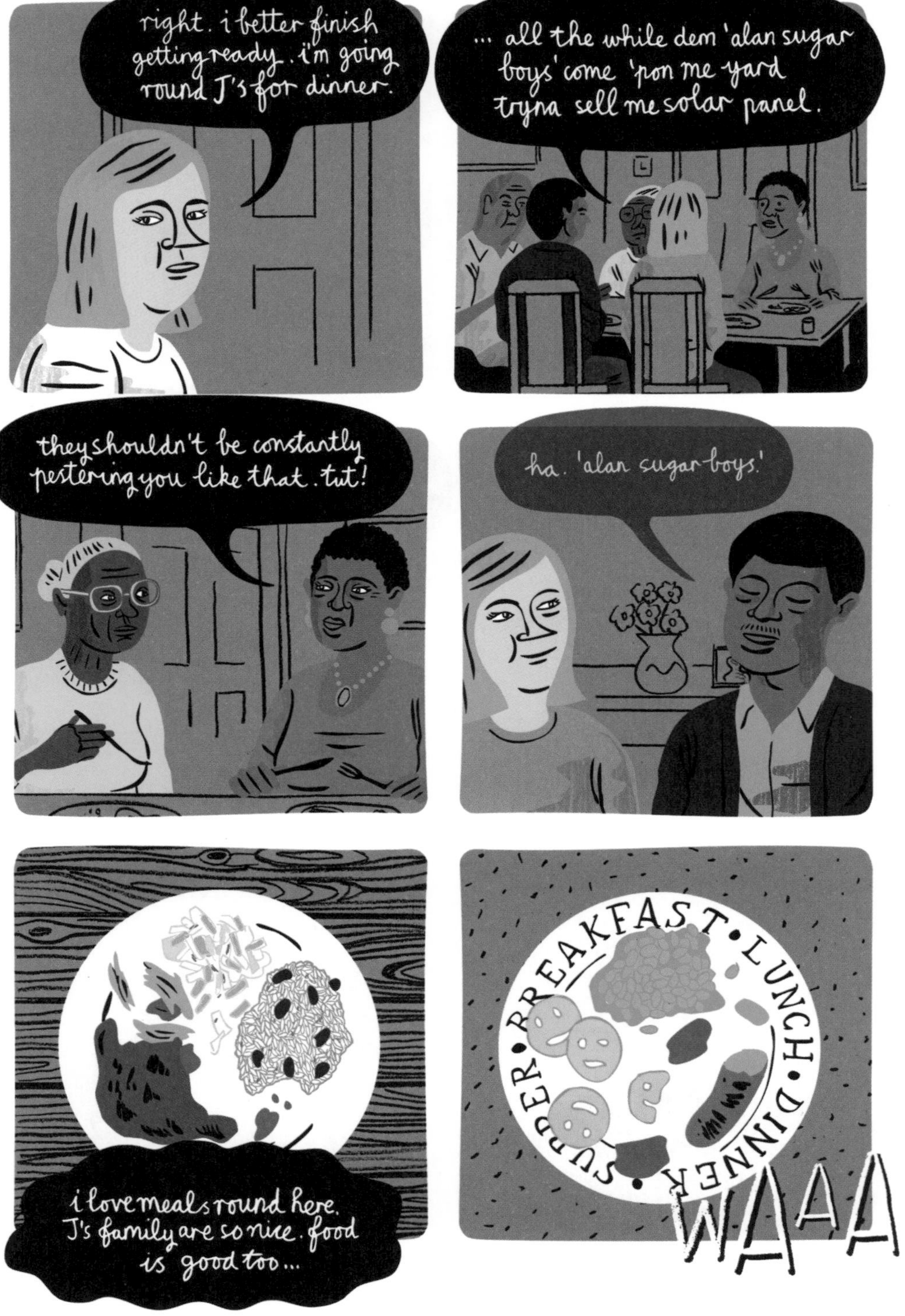
right. i better finish getting ready. i'm going round J's for dinner.
... all the while dem 'alan sugar boys' come 'pon me yard tryna sell me solar panel.
they shouldn't be constantly pestering you like that. tut!
ha. 'alan sugar boys.'
i love meals round here. J's family are so nice. food is good too...
BREAKFAST • LUNCH • DINNER • SUPPER •
WAAA

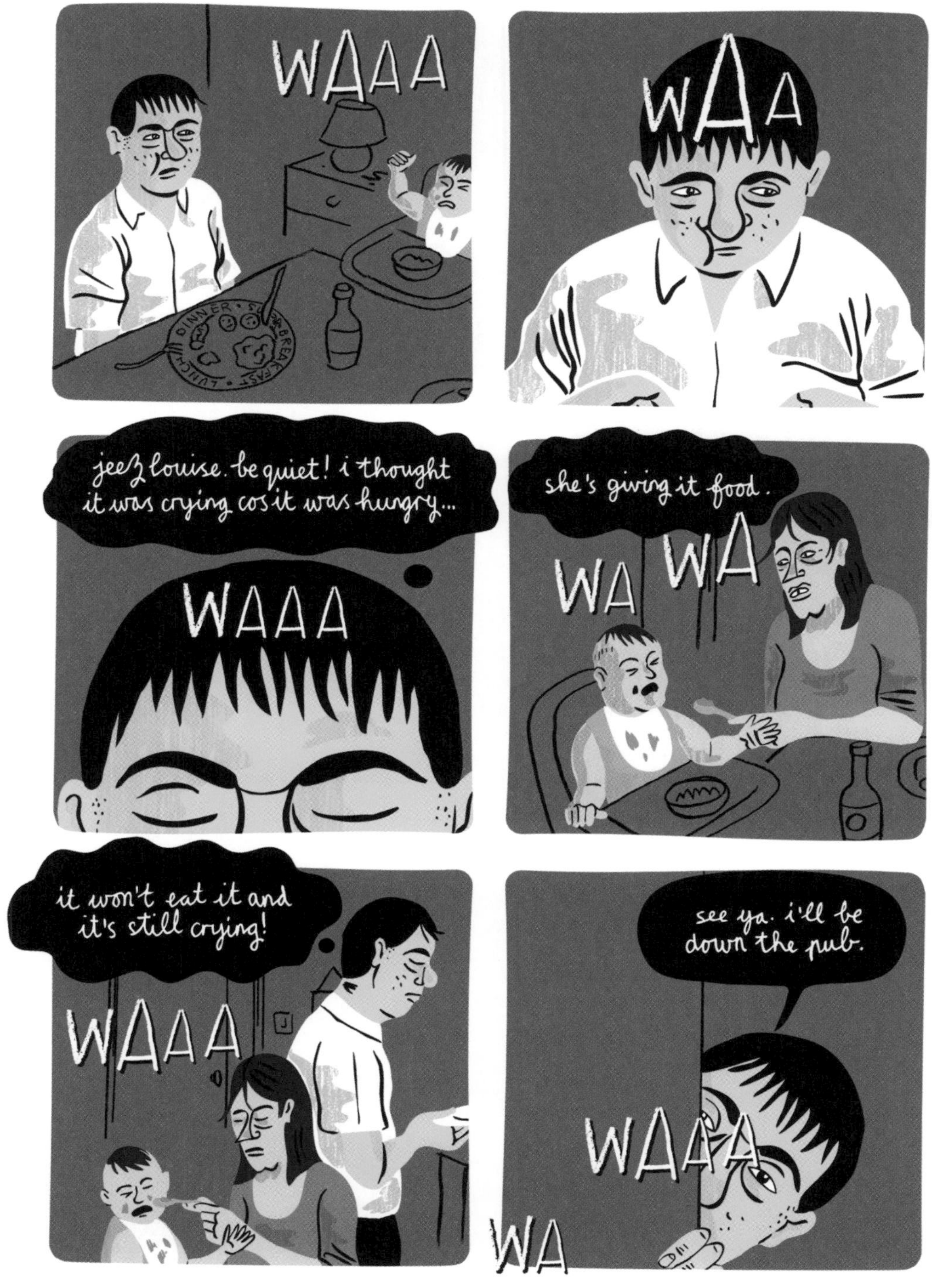

WAAA
WAA
jeez louise. be quiet! i thought it was crying cos it was hungry...
WAAA
she's giving it food.
WA
WA
it won't eat it and it's still crying!
WAAA
see ya. i'll be down the pub.
WAAA
WA

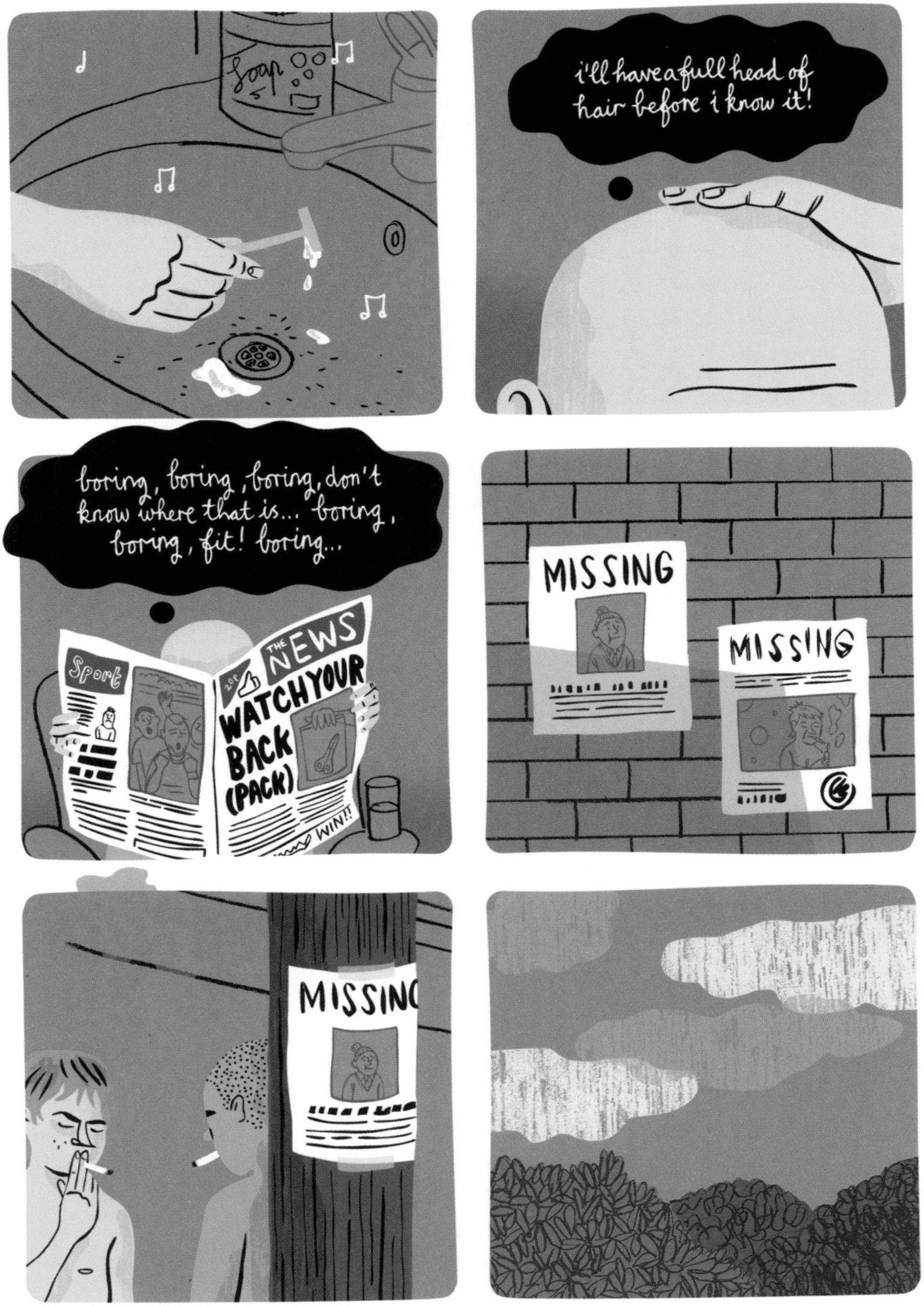
Soap
i'll have a full head of hair before i know it!
boring, boring, boring, don't know where that is... boring, boring, fit! boring...
Sport
THE NEWS
WATCH YOUR BACK (PACK)
WIN!!
MISSING
MISSING
MISSIN

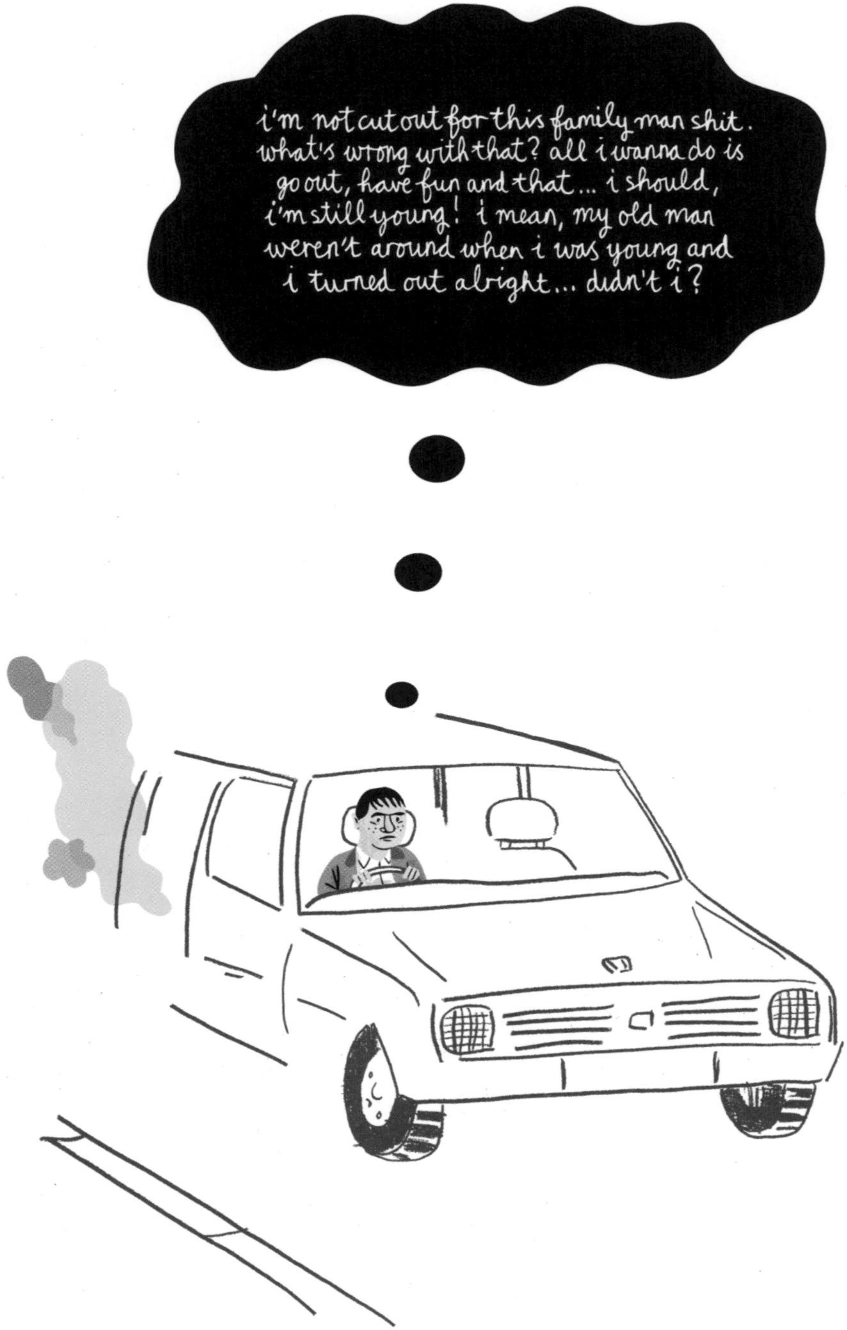
i'm not cut out for this family man shit. what's wrong with that? all i wanna do is go out, have fun and that... i should, i'm still young! i mean, my old man weren't around when i was young and i turned out alright... didn't i?

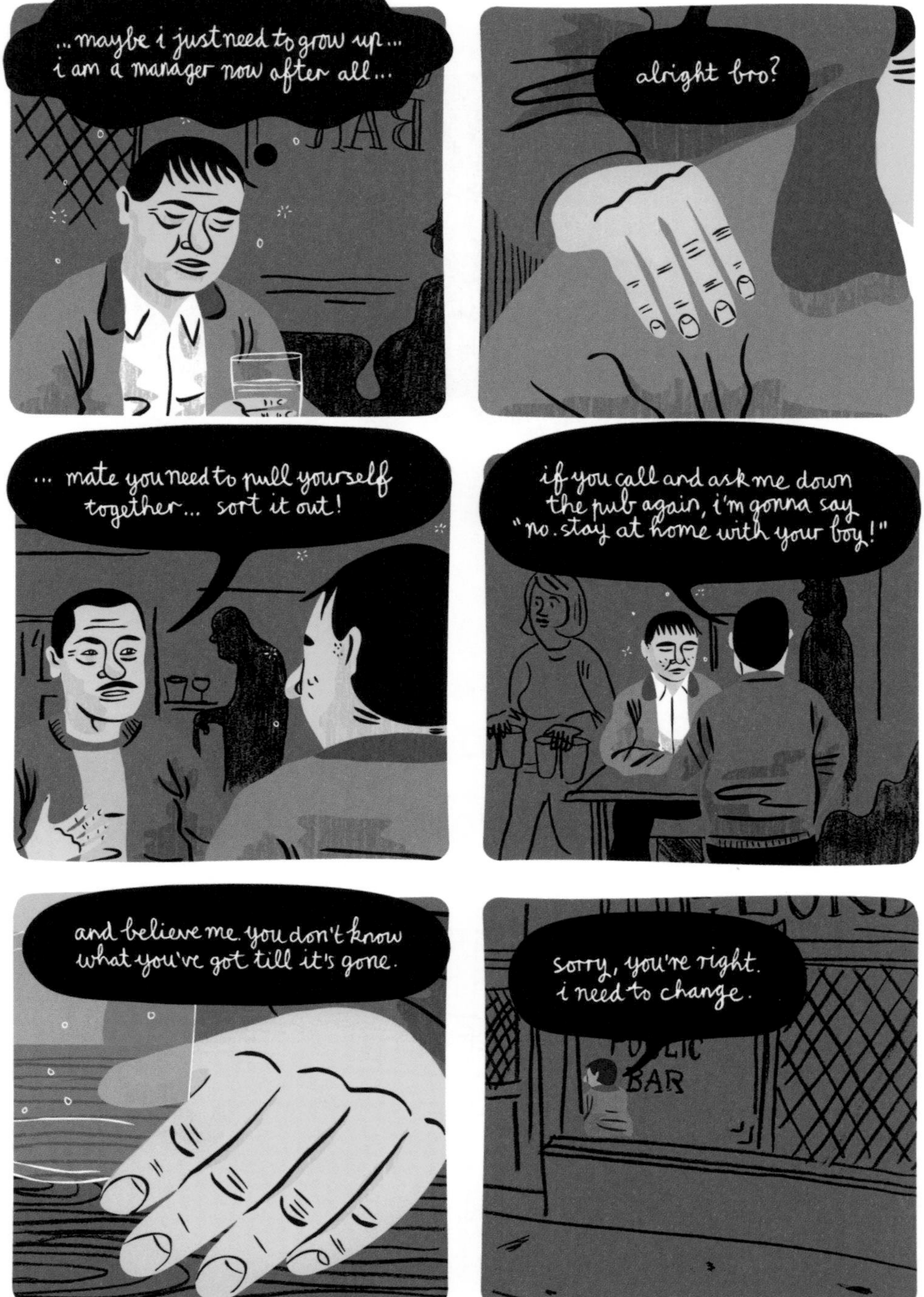
... maybe i just need to grow up...
i am a manager now after all...
alright bro?
... mate you need to pull yourself together... sort it out!
if you call and ask me down the pub again, i'm gonna say "no. stay at home with your boy!"
and believe me. you don't know what you've got till it's gone.
sorry, you're right. i need to change.
PUBLIC
BAR

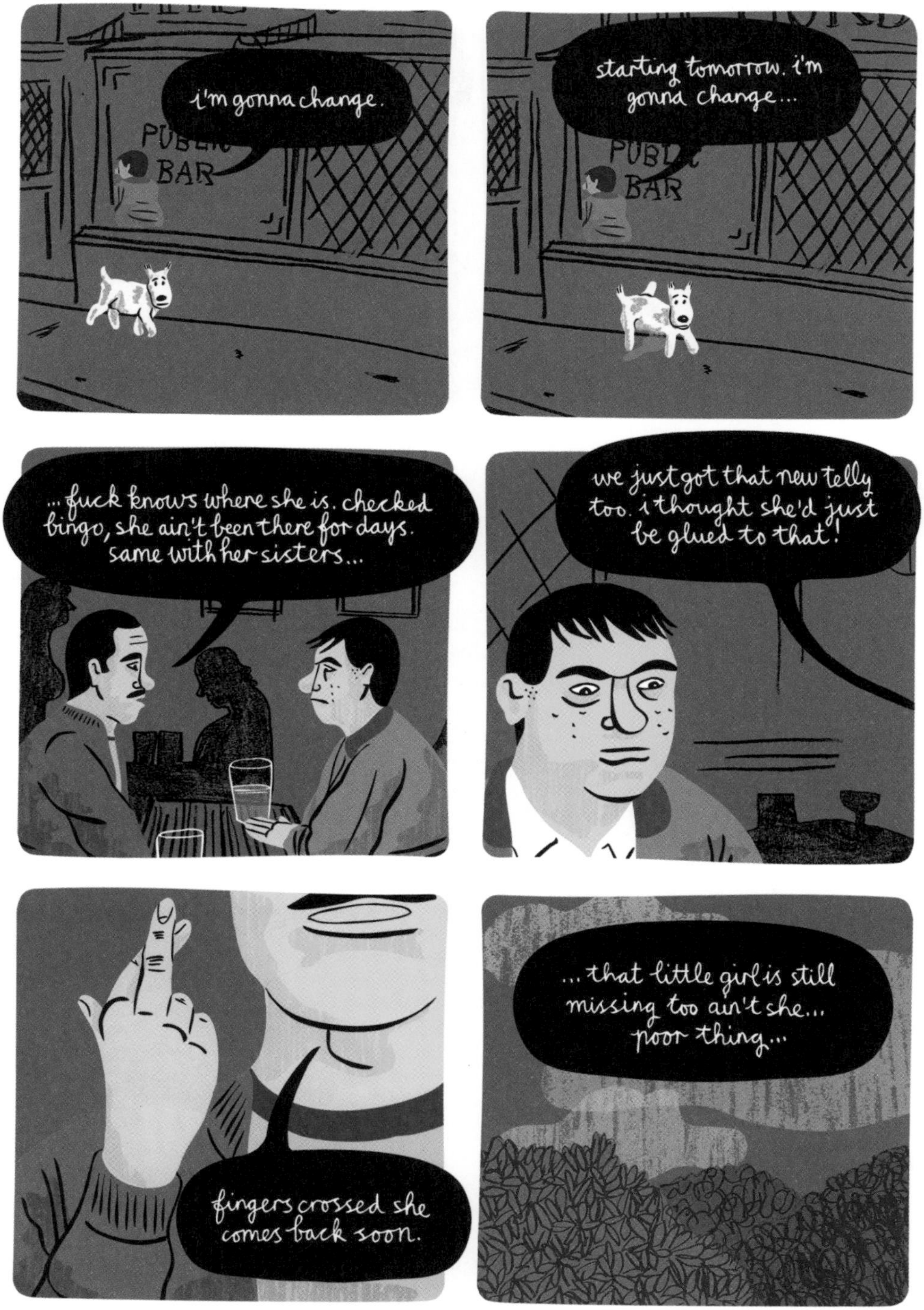
i'm gonna change.
PUBLIC BAR
starting tomorrow. i'm gonna change...
...fuck knows where she is. checked bingo, she ain't been there for days. same with her sisters...
we just got that new telly too. i thought she'd just be glued to that!
fingers crossed she comes back soon.
...that little girl is still missing too ain't she... poor thing...

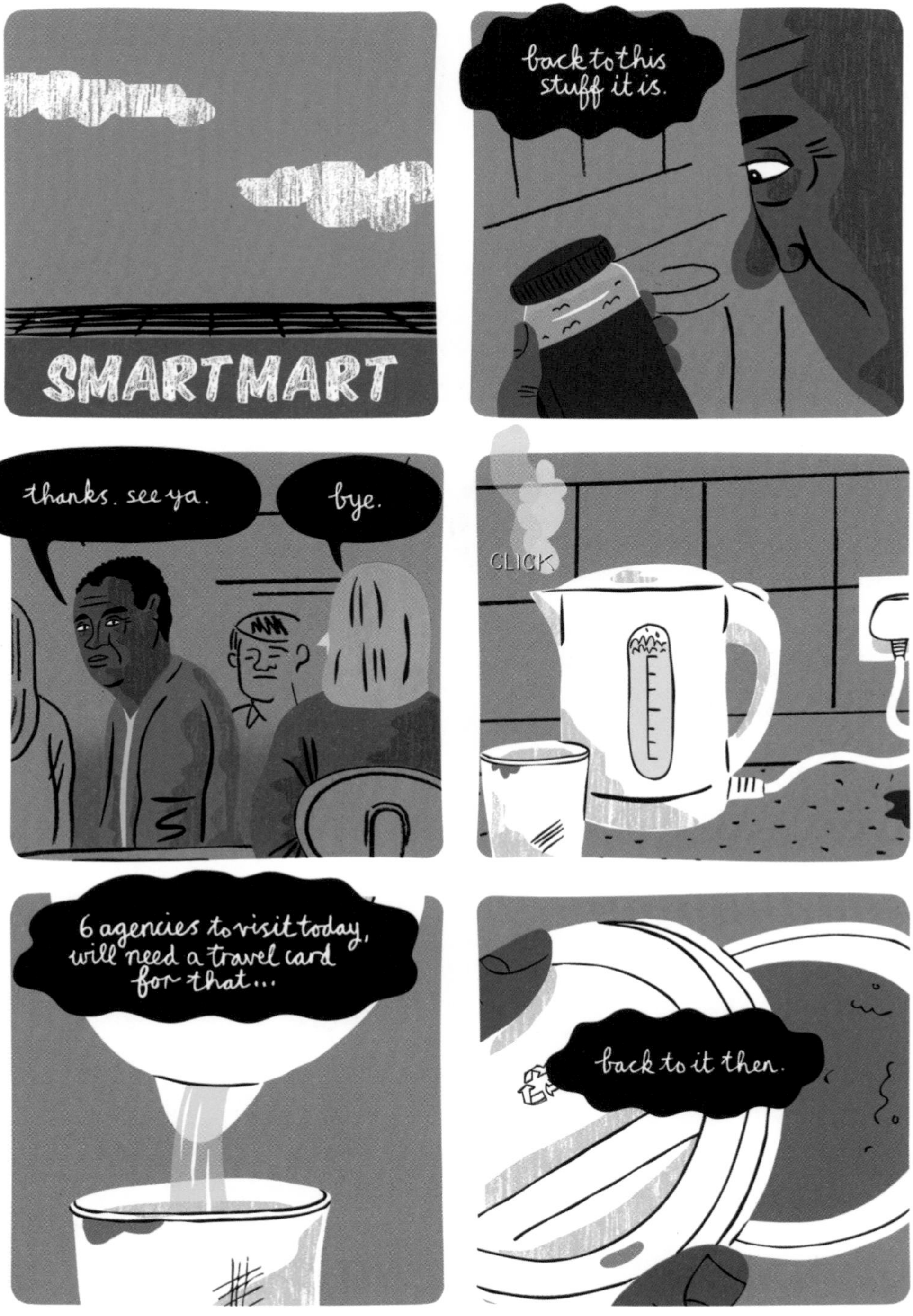
SMARTMART
back to this stuff it is.
thanks. see ya.
bye.
CLICK
6 agencies to visit today, will need a travel card for that...
back to it then.

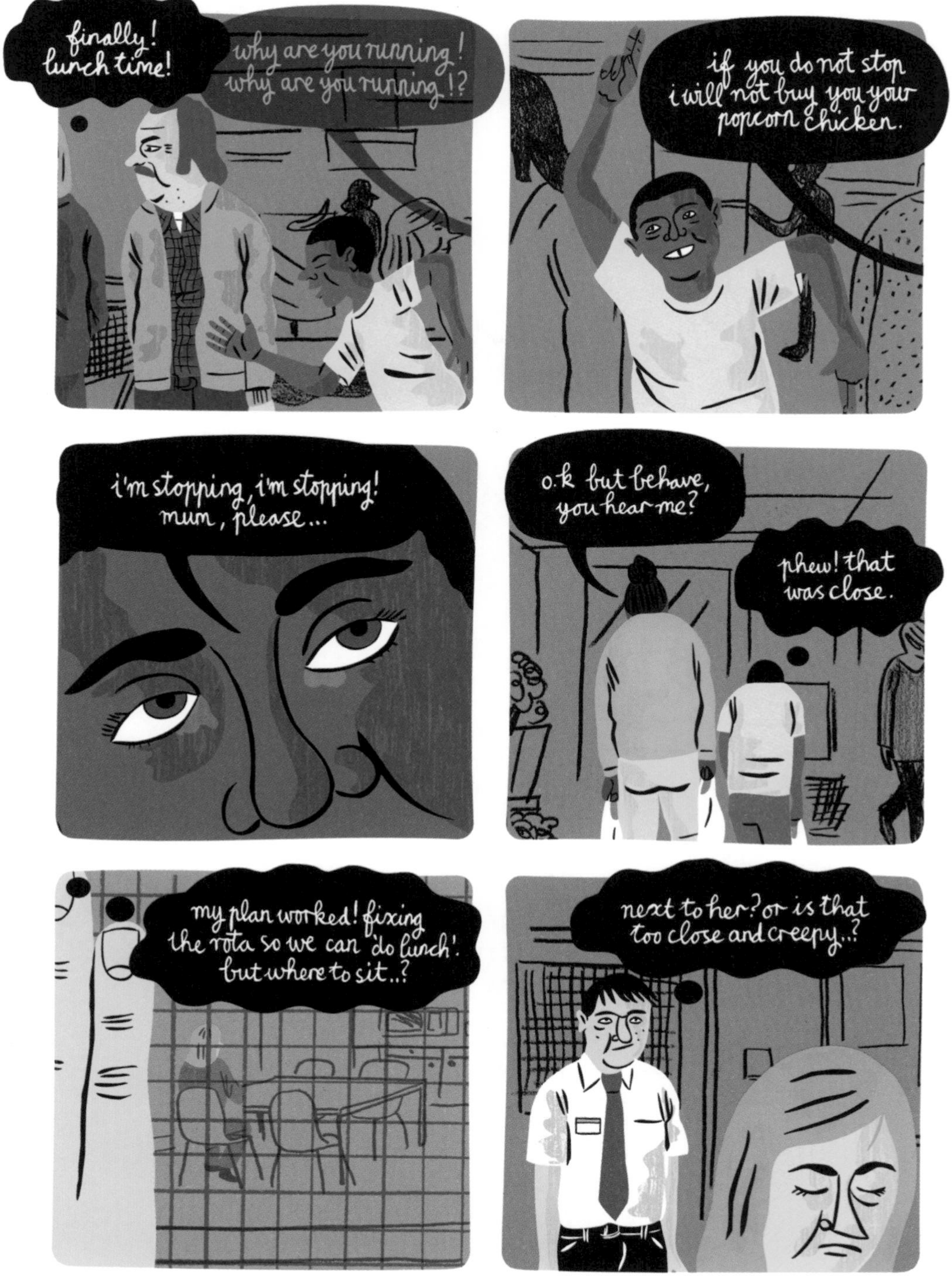
finally! lunch time!
why are you running! why are you running!?
if you do not stop i will not buy you your popcorn chicken.
i'm stopping, i'm stopping! mum, please...
o.k but behave, you hear me?
phew! that was close.
my plan worked! fixing the rota so we can 'do lunch'. but where to sit..?
next to her? or is that too close and creepy..?

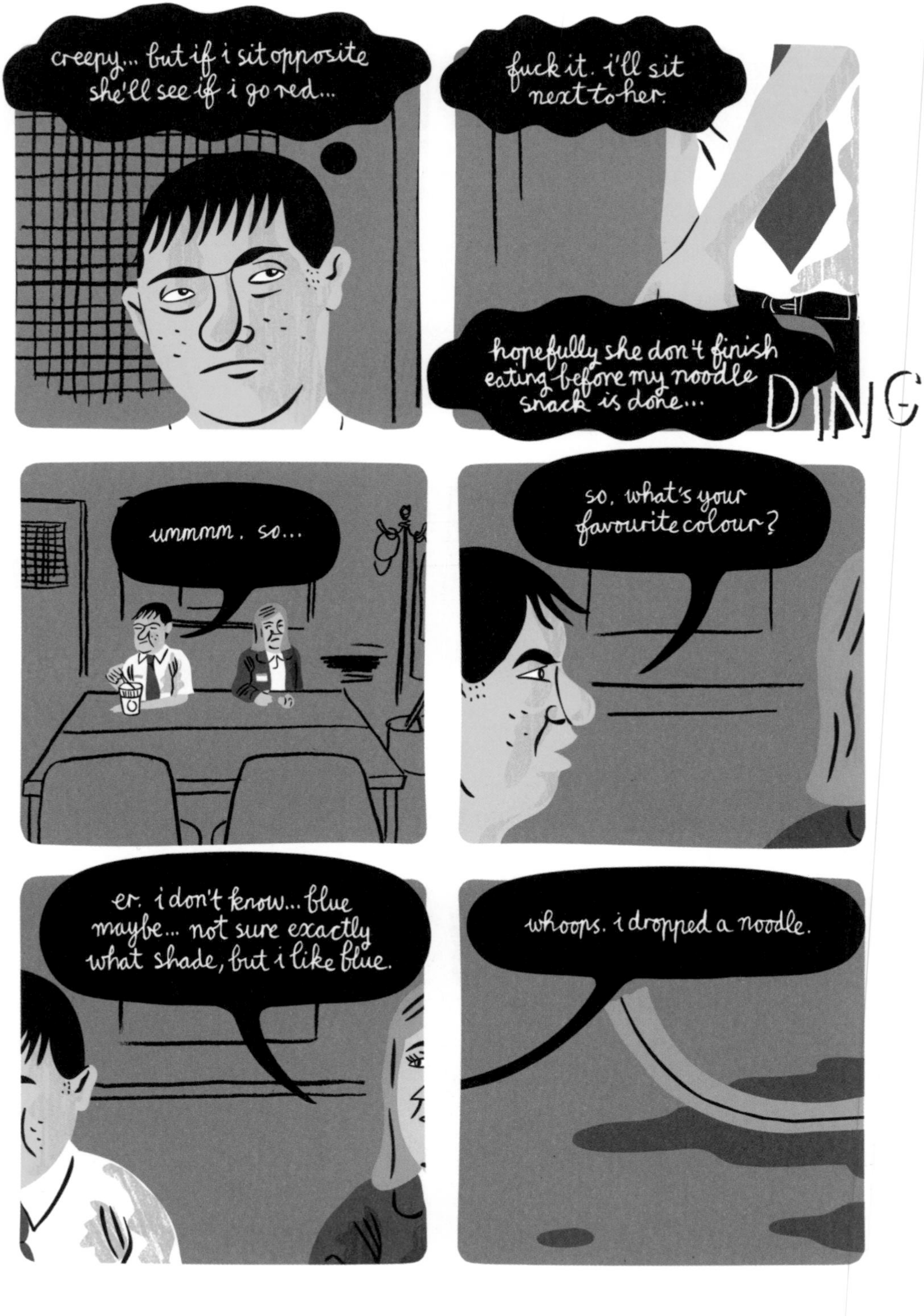
creepy... but if i sit opposite she'll see if i go red...
fuck it. i'll sit next to her.
hopefully she don't finish eating before my noodle snack is done...
DING
ummmm. so...
so, what's your favourite colour?
er. i don't know... blue maybe... not sure exactly what shade, but i like blue.
whoops. i dropped a noodle.

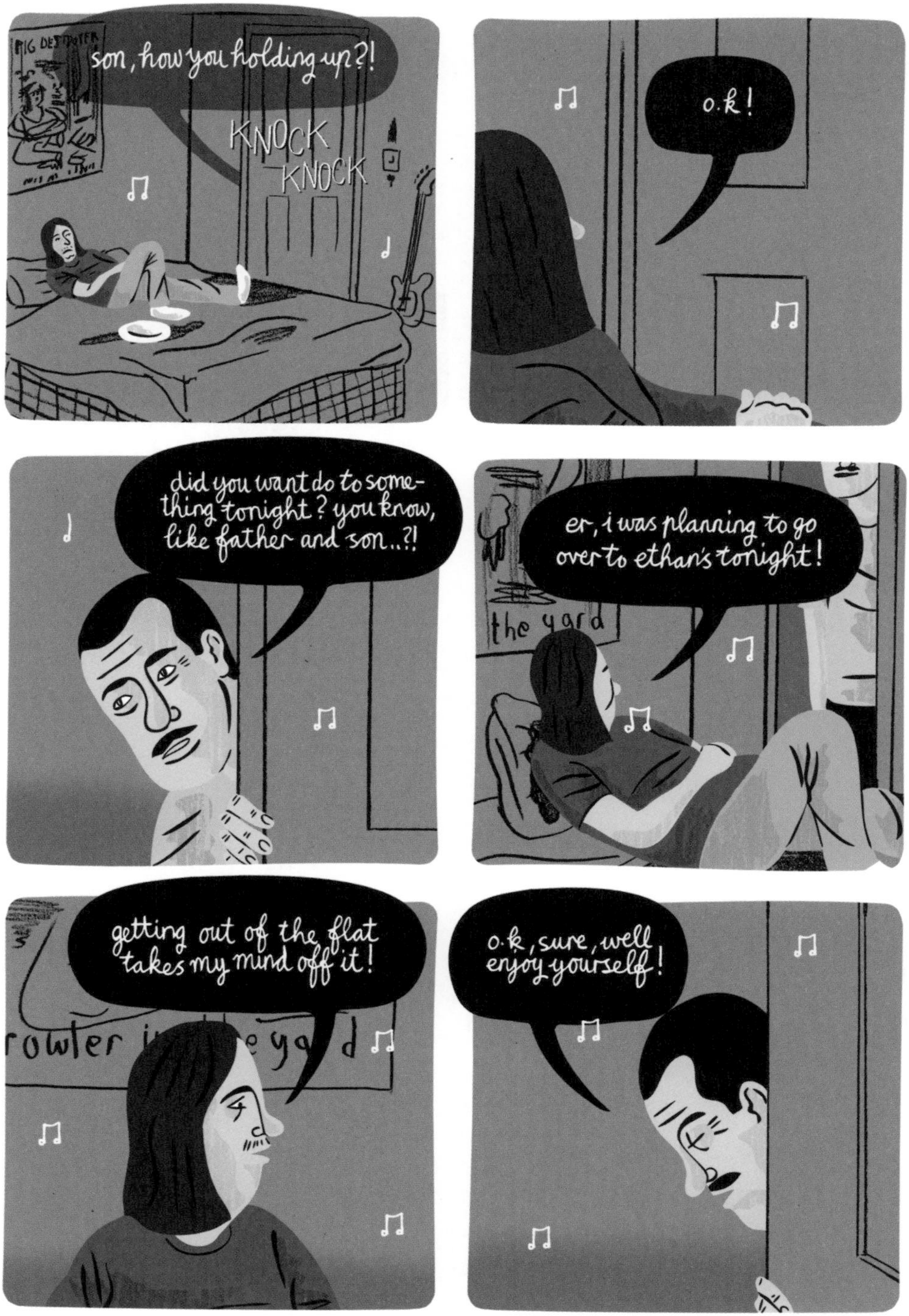
son, how you holding up?!
KNOCK KNOCK
o.k!
did you want do to something tonight? you know, like father and son..?!
er, i was planning to go over to ethan's tonight!
getting out of the flat takes my mind off it!
o.k, sure, well enjoy yourself!

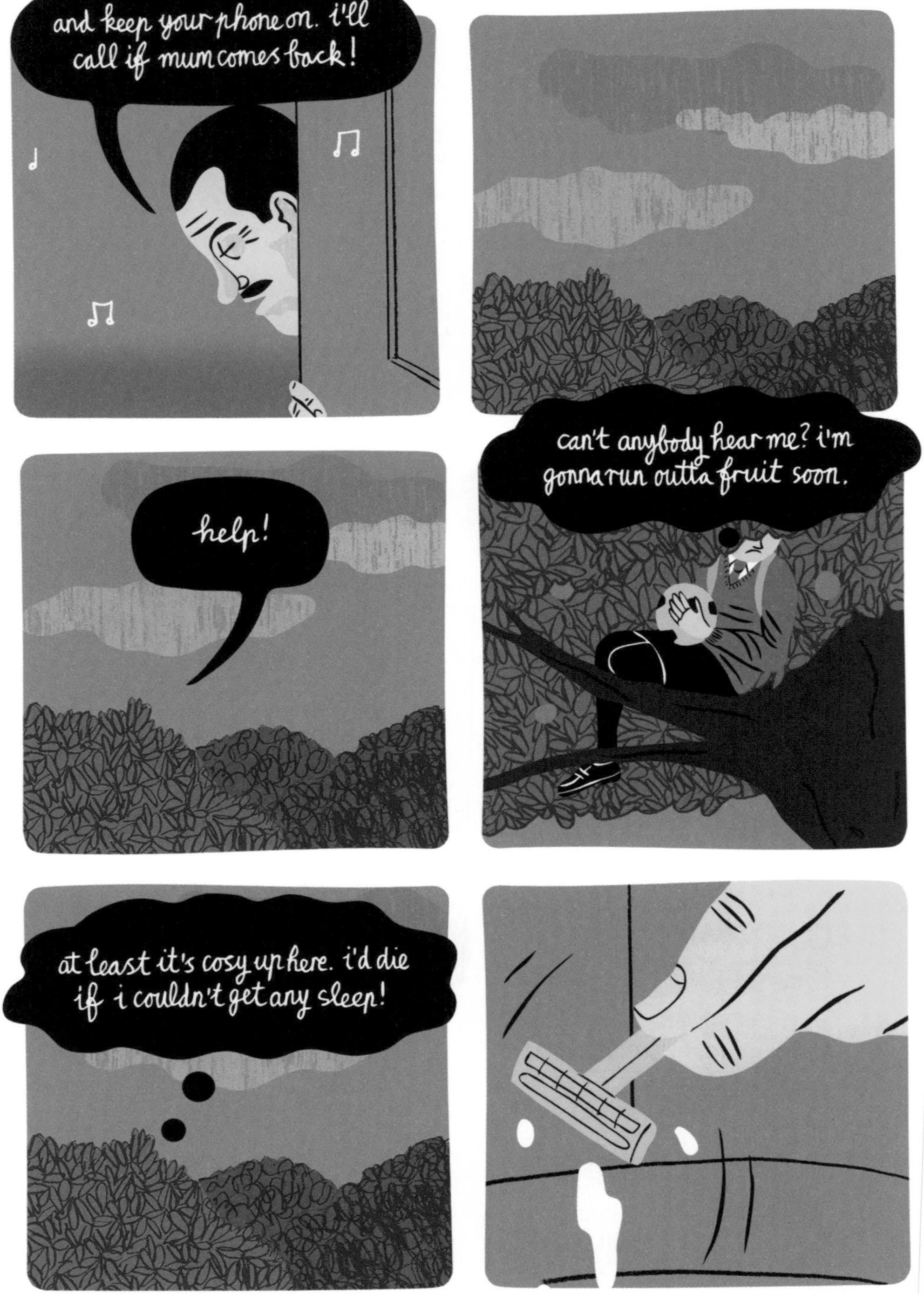
and keep your phone on. i'll call if mum comes back!
help!
can't anybody hear me? i'm gonna run outta fruit soon.
at least it's cosy up here. i'd die if i couldn't get any sleep!

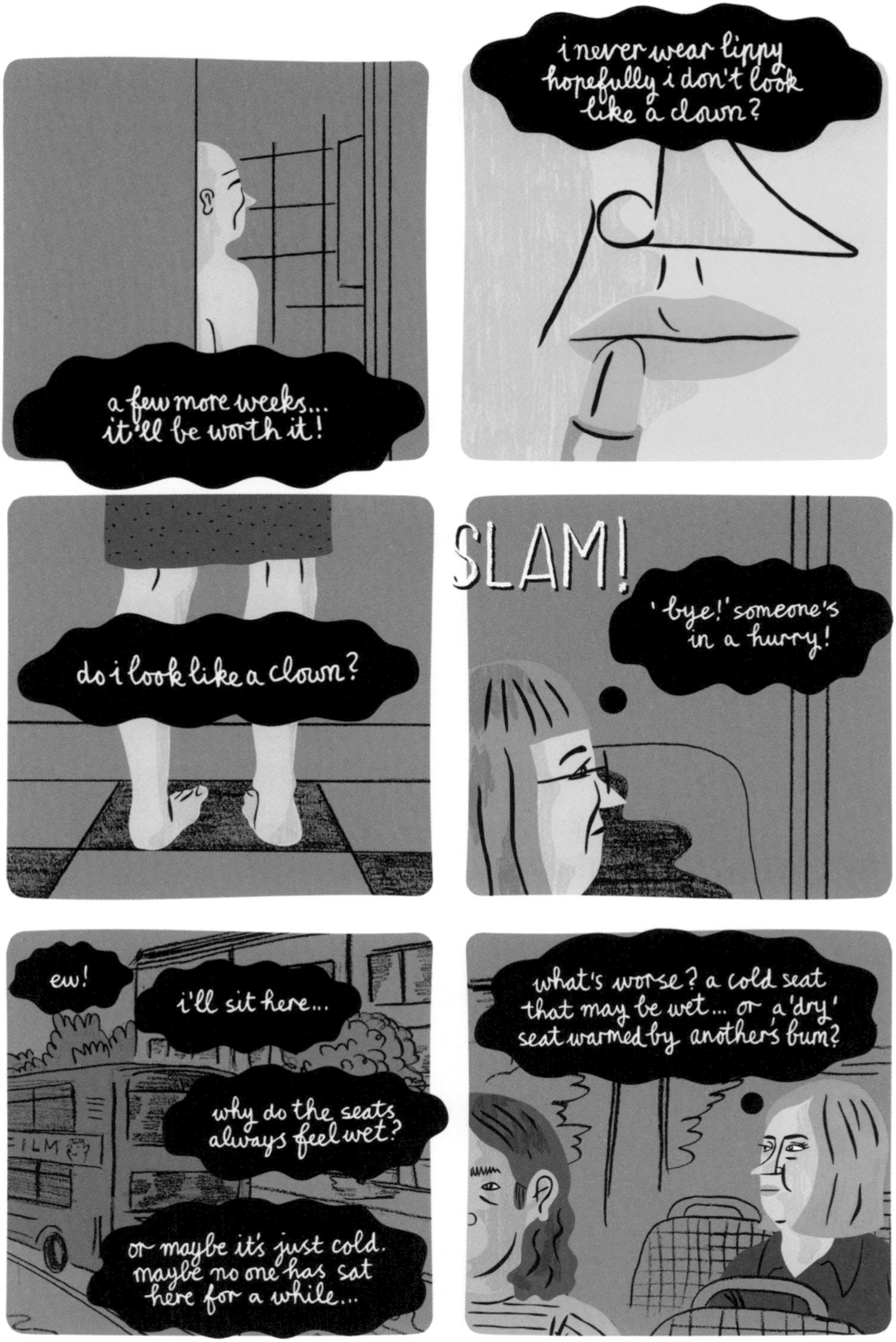
a few more weeks...
it'll be worth it!
i never wear lippy
hopefully i don't look
like a clown?
do i look like a clown?
SLAM!
'bye!' someone's
in a hurry!
ew!
i'll sit here...
why do the seats
always feel wet?
or maybe it's just cold.
maybe no one has sat
here for a while...
what's worse? a cold seat
that may be wet... or a 'dry'
seat warmed by another's bum?

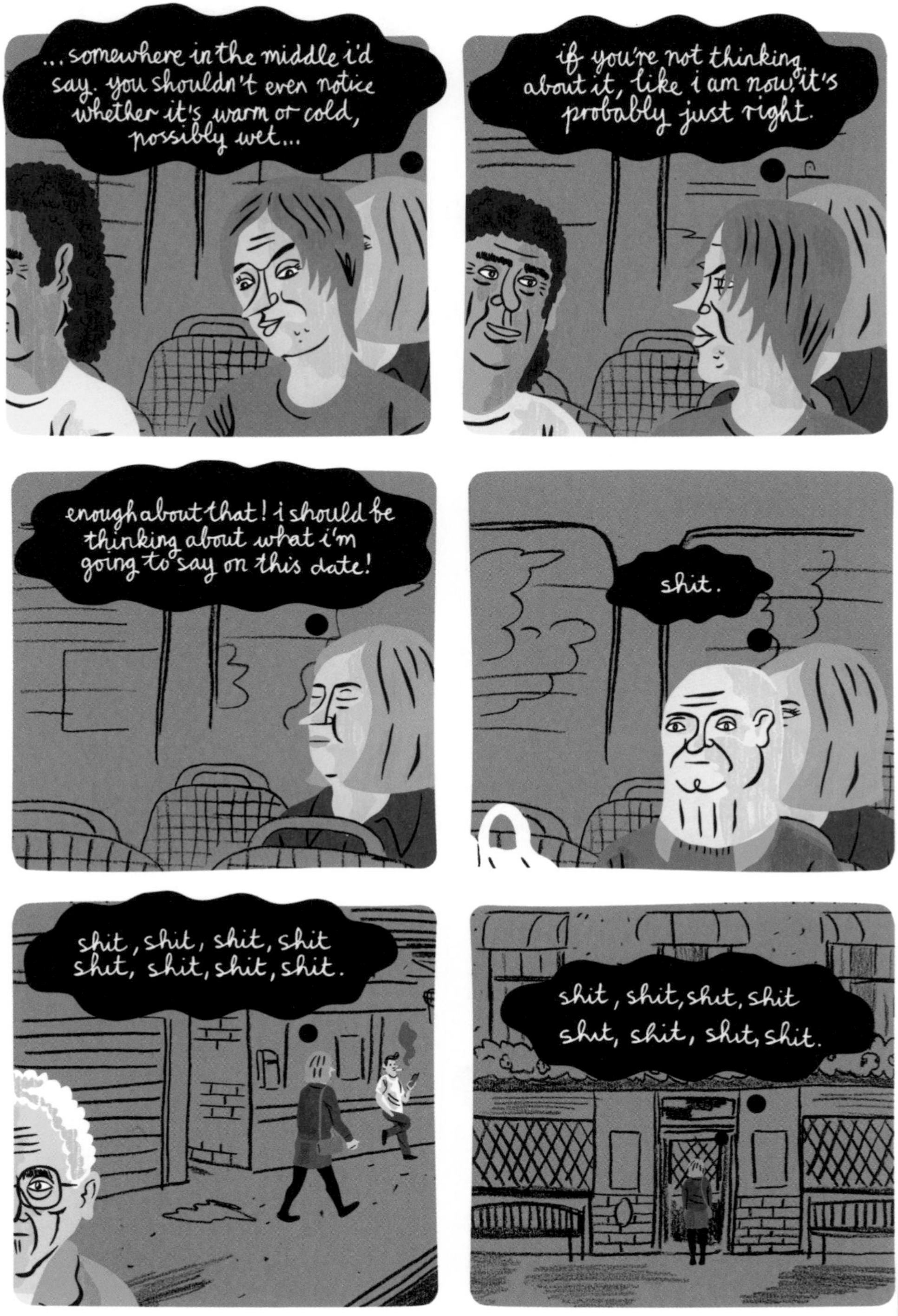
...somewhere in the middle i'd say. you shouldn't even notice whether it's warm or cold, possibly wet...
if you're not thinking about it, like i am now, it's probably just right.
enough about that! i should be thinking about what i'm going to say on this date!
shit.
shit, shit, shit, shit shit, shit, shit, shit.
shit, shit, shit, shit shit, shit, shit, shit.

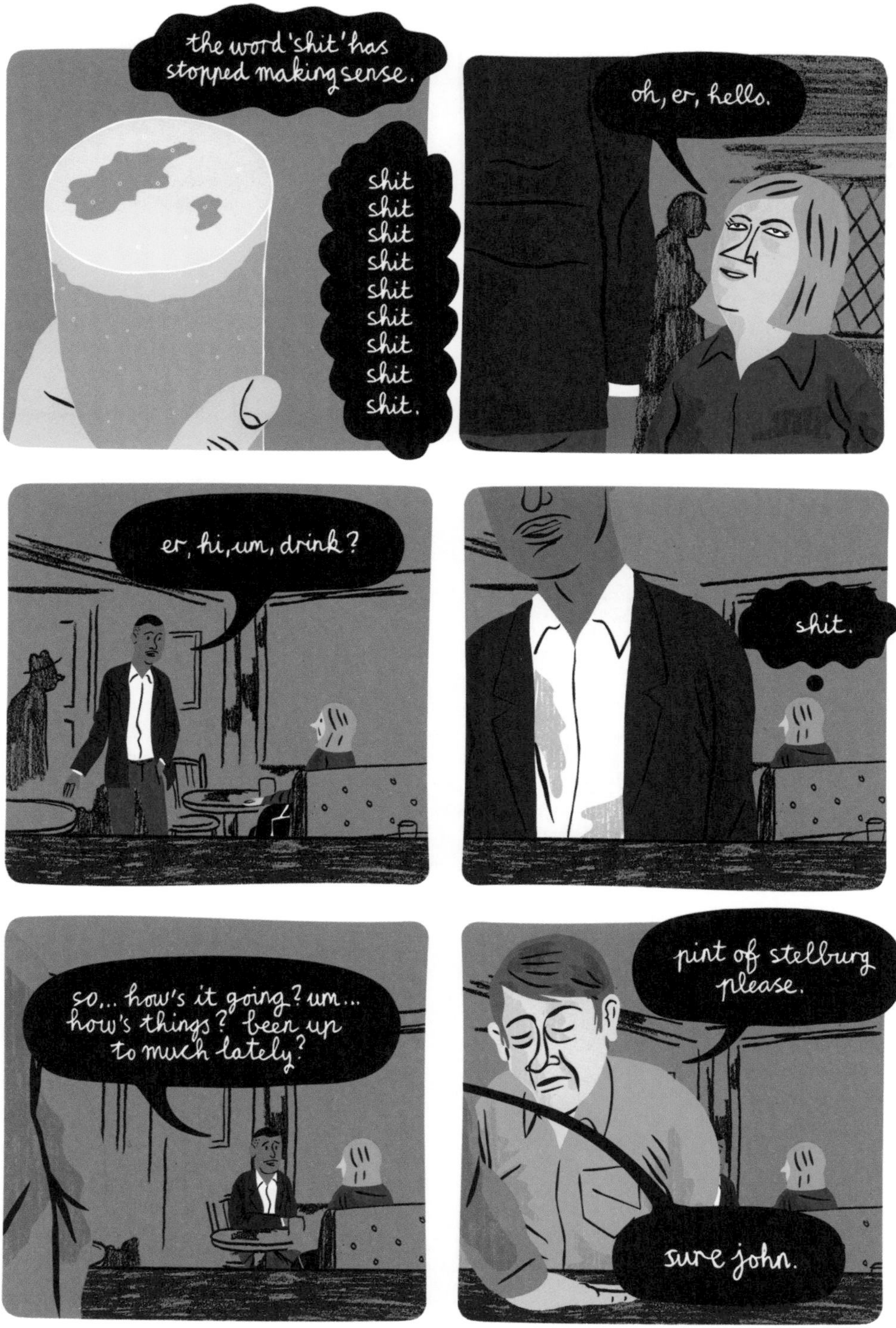

the word 'shit' has stopped making sense.
shit shit shit shit shit shit shit shit shit.
oh, er, hello.
er, hi, um, drink?
shit.
so... how's it going? um... how's things? been up to much lately?
pint of stelburg please.
sure john.

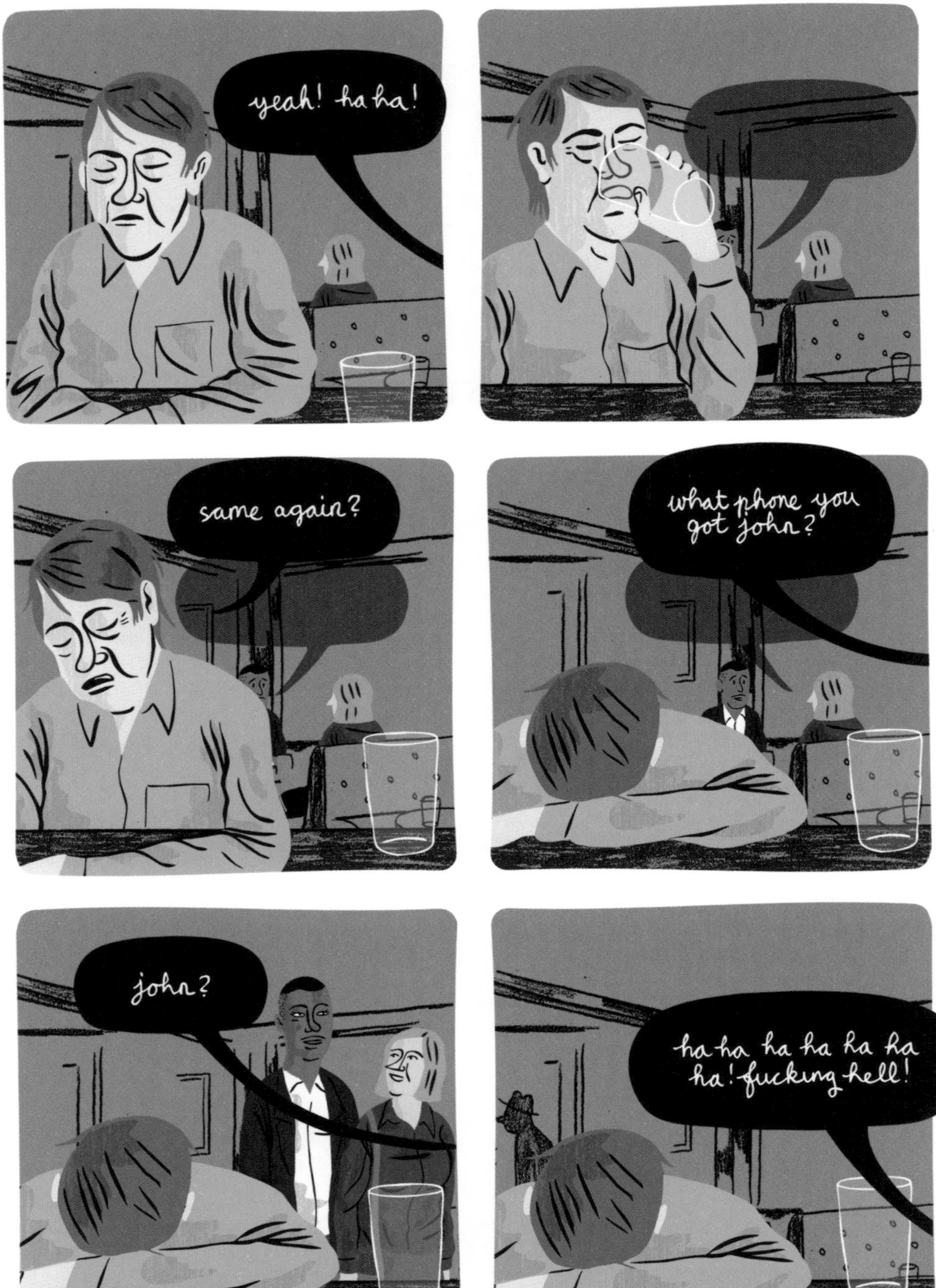
yeah! ha ha!
same again?
what phone you got john?
john?
ha ha ha ha ha ha ha! fucking hell!

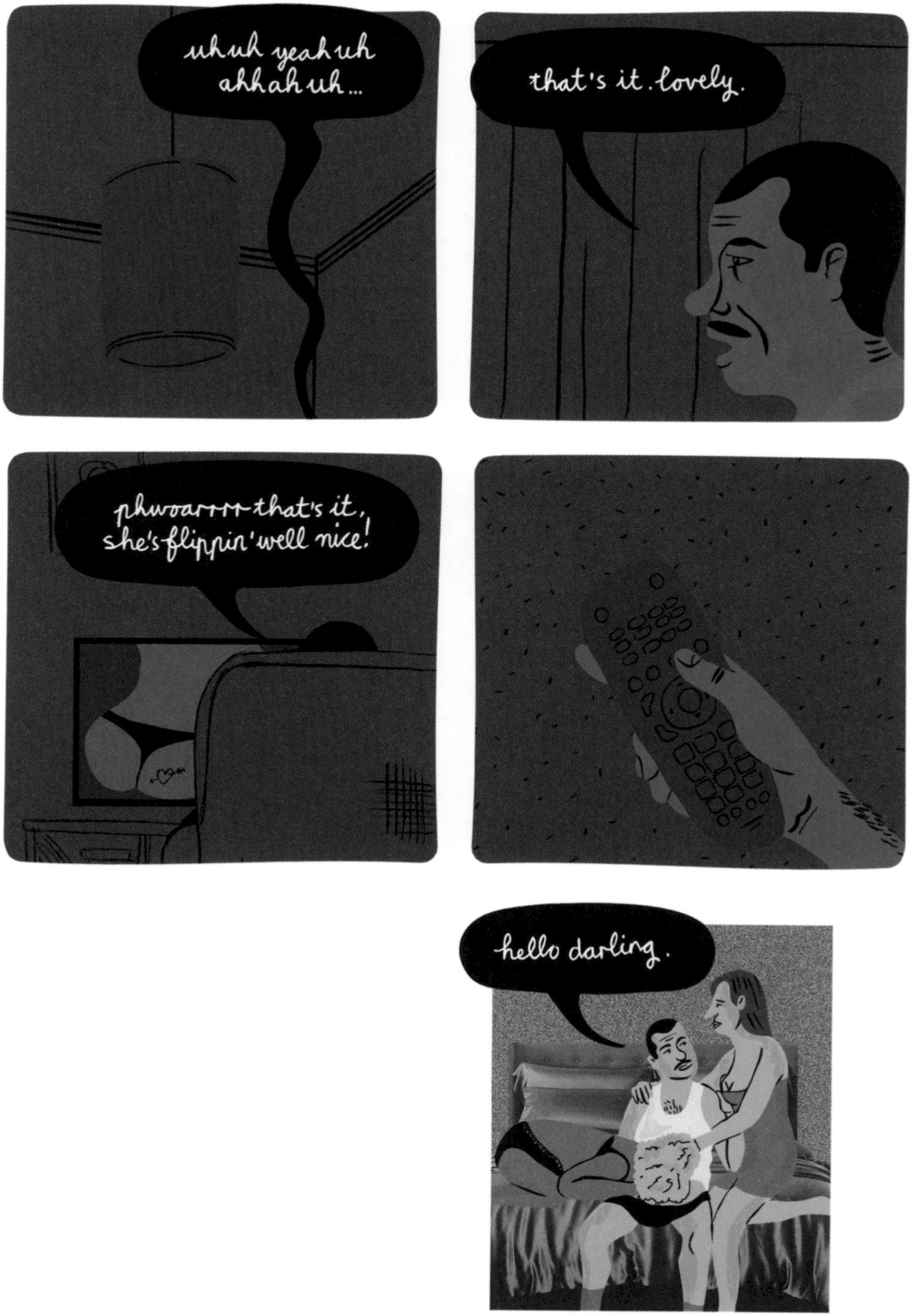
uhuh yeahuh ahhahuh...
that's it. lovely.
phwoarrrr that's it, she's flippin' well nice!
hello darling.

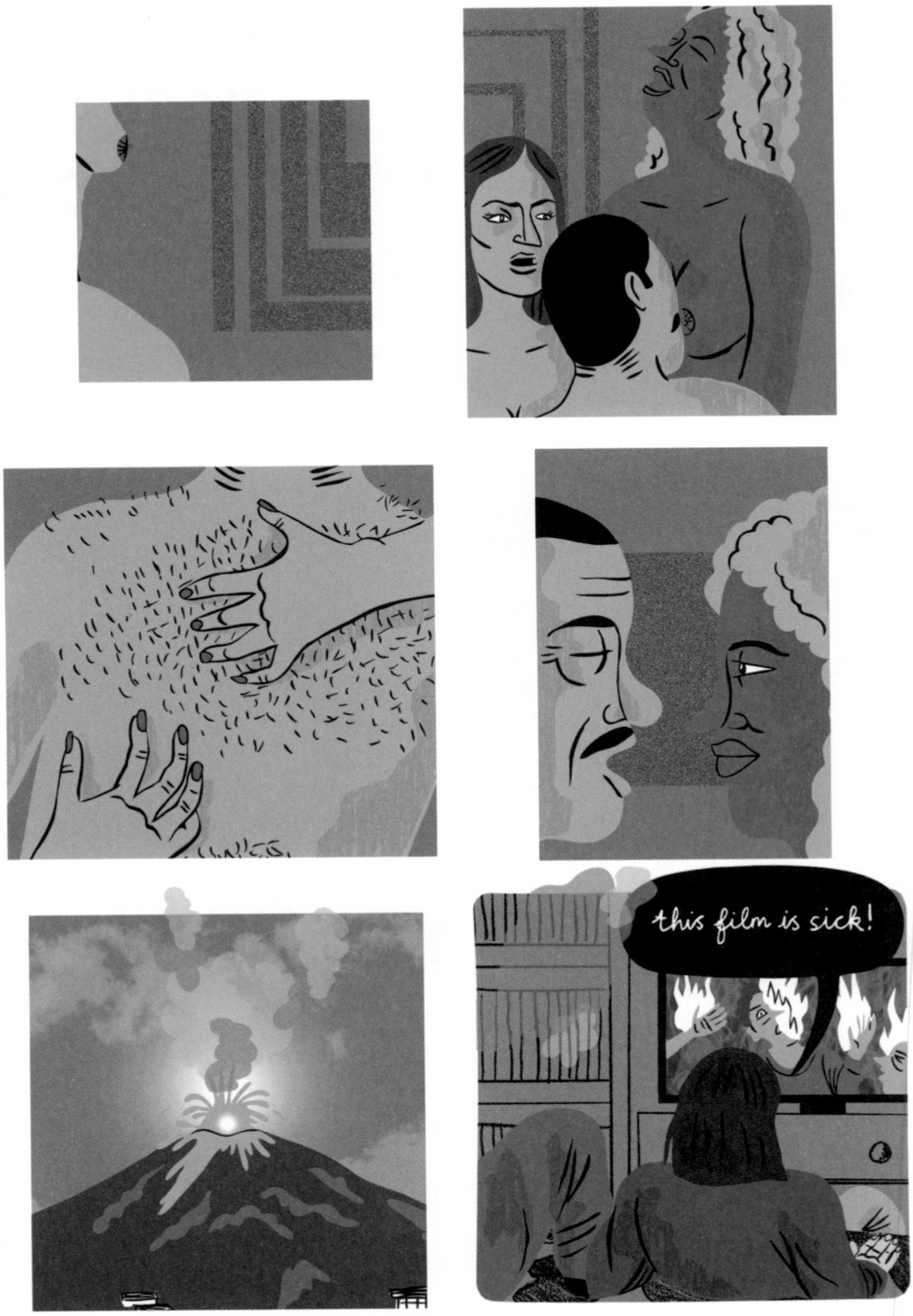
this film is sick!

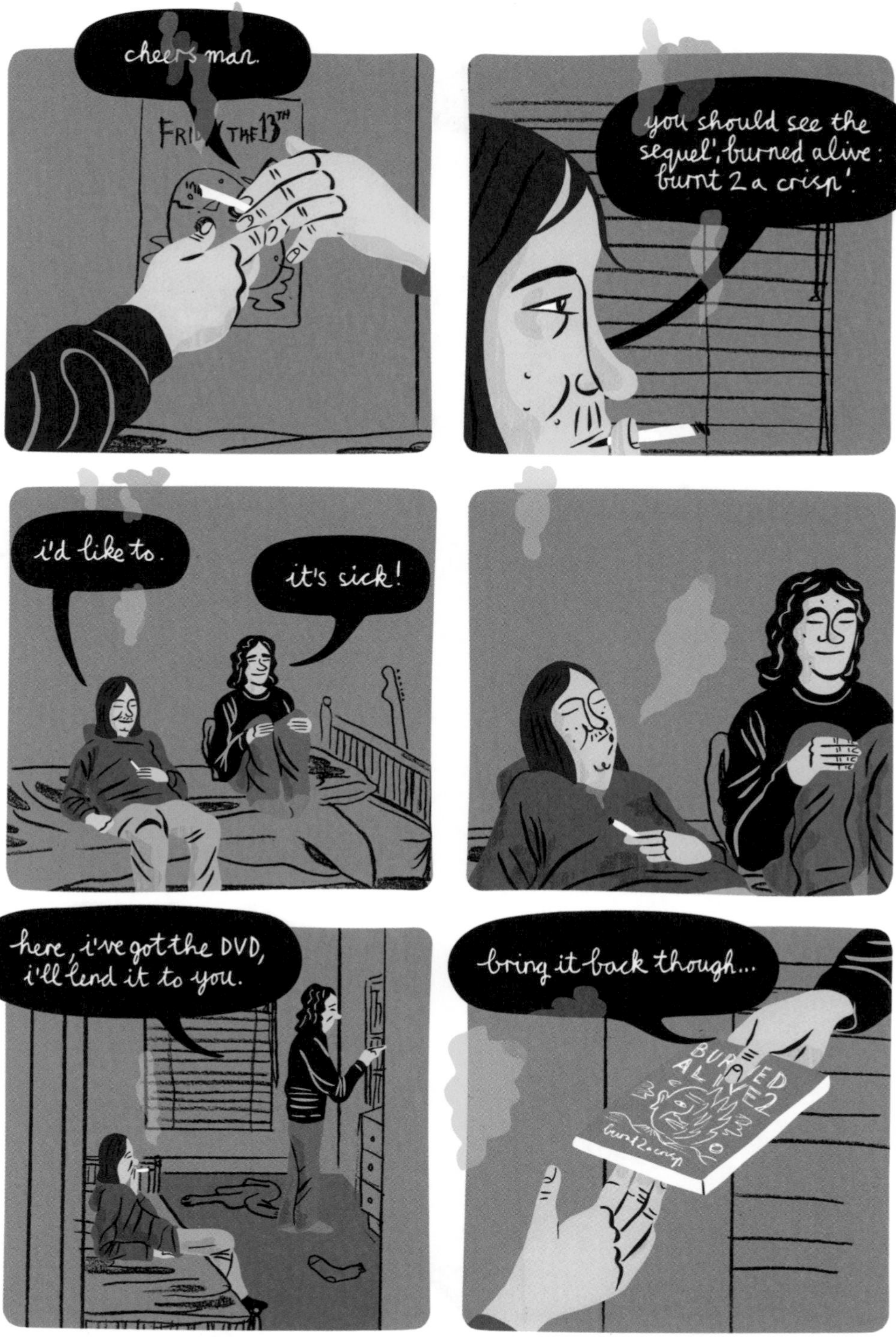
cheers man.
FRIDAY THE 13TH
you should see the sequel', burned alive: burnt 2 a crisp'.
i'd like to.
it's sick!
here, i've got the DVD, i'll lend it to you.
bring it back though...
BURNED ALIVE 2
burnt 2 a crisp

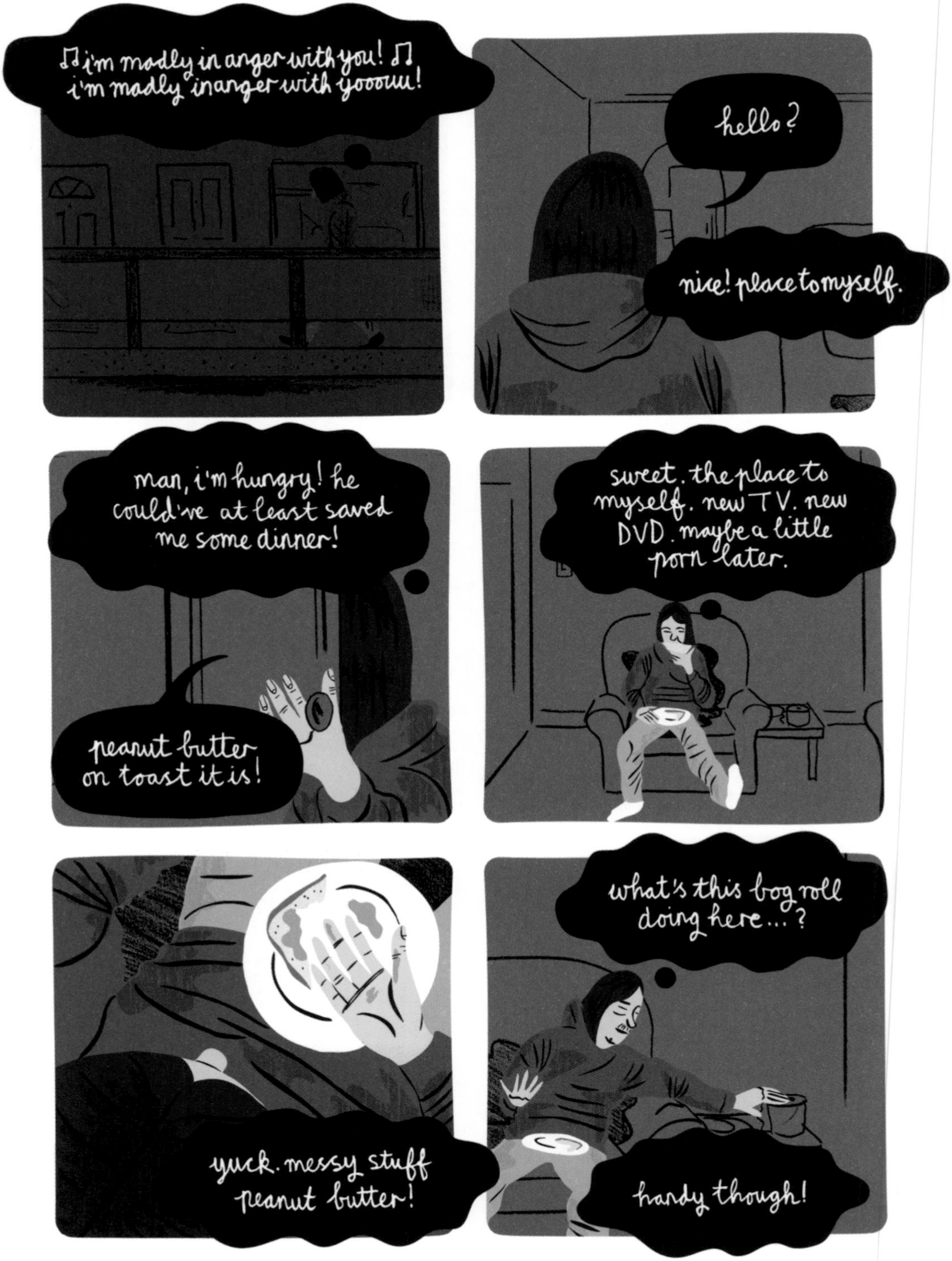
♫ i'm madly in anger with you! ♫ i'm madly in anger with yooouu!
hello?
nice! place to myself.
man, i'm hungry! he could've at least saved me some dinner!
peanut butter on toast it is!
sweet. the place to myself. new TV. new DVD. maybe a little porn later.
yuck. messy stuff peanut butter!
what's this bog roll doing here...?
handy though!

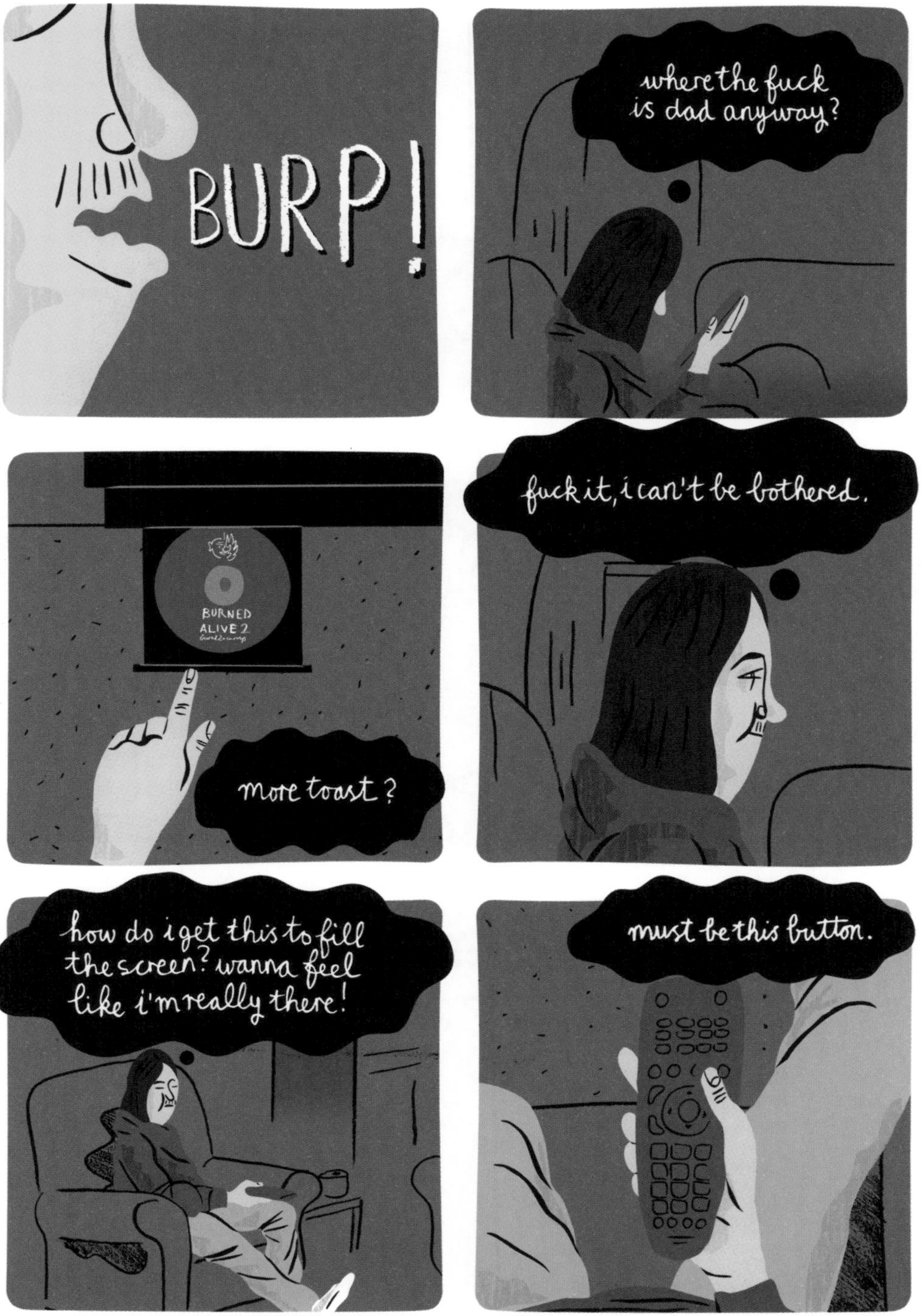
BURP!
where the fuck is dad anyway?
BURNED ALIVE 2
more toast?
fuck it, i can't be bothered.
how do i get this to fill the screen? wanna feel like i'm really there!
must be this button.

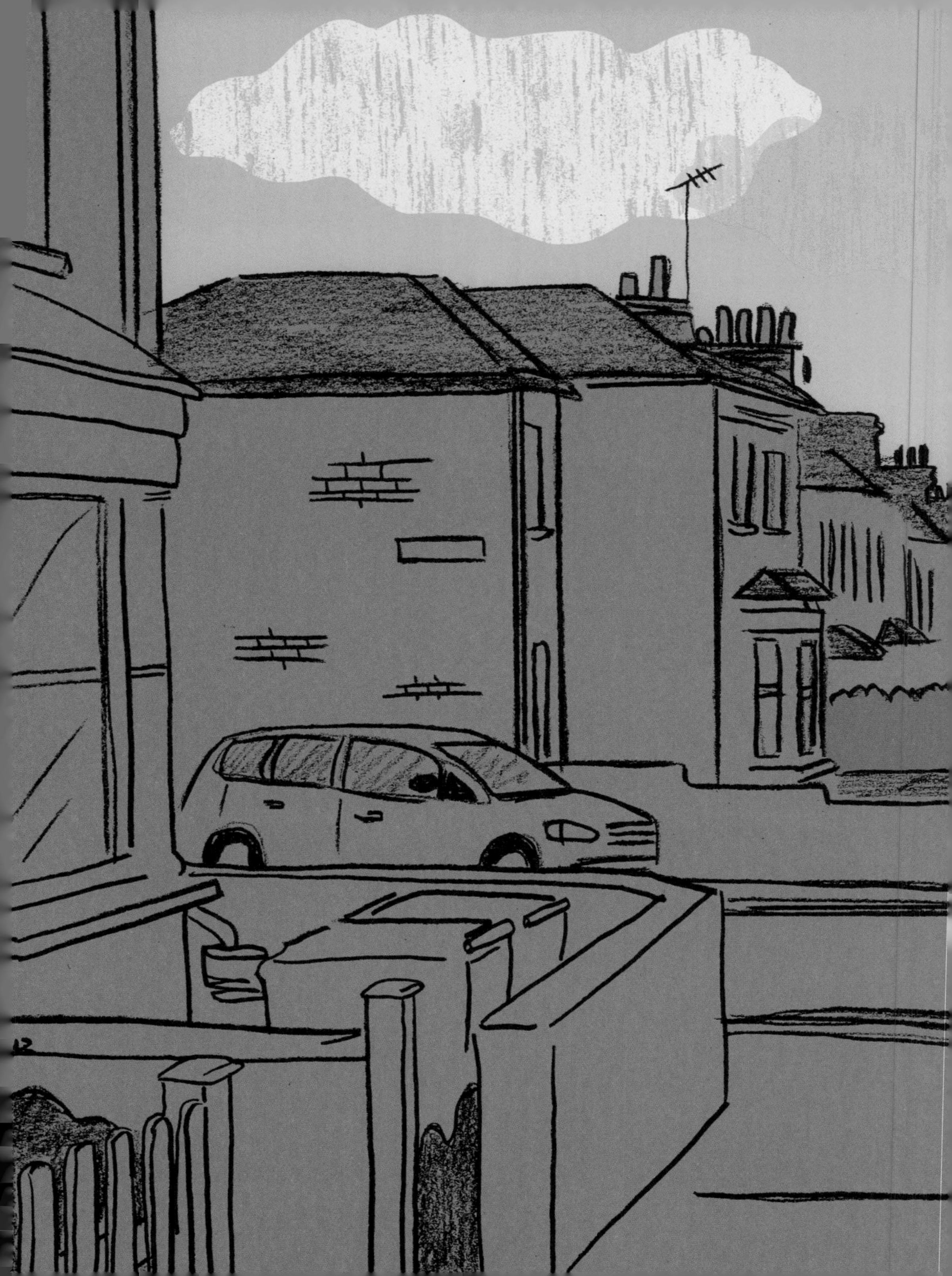

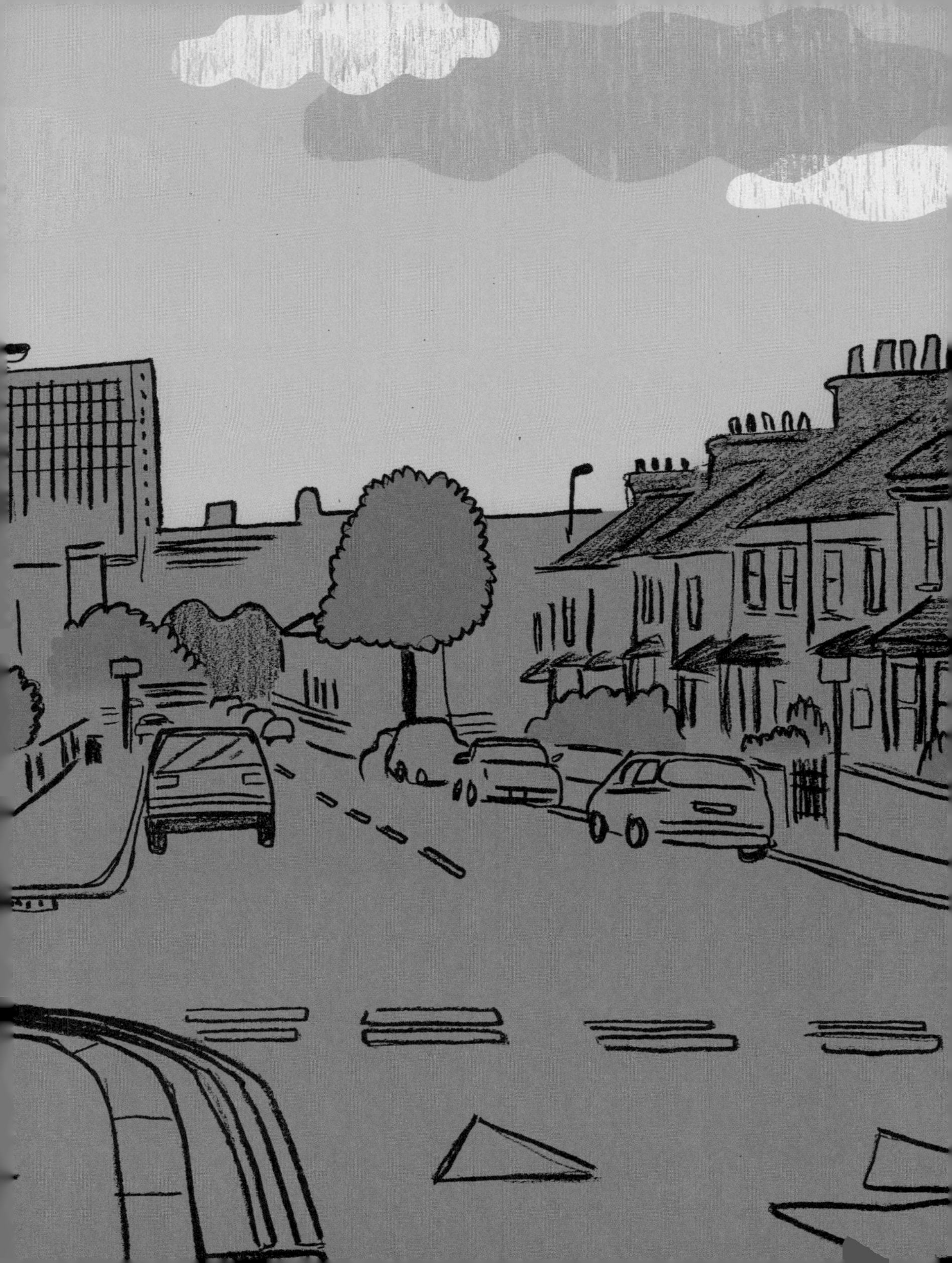

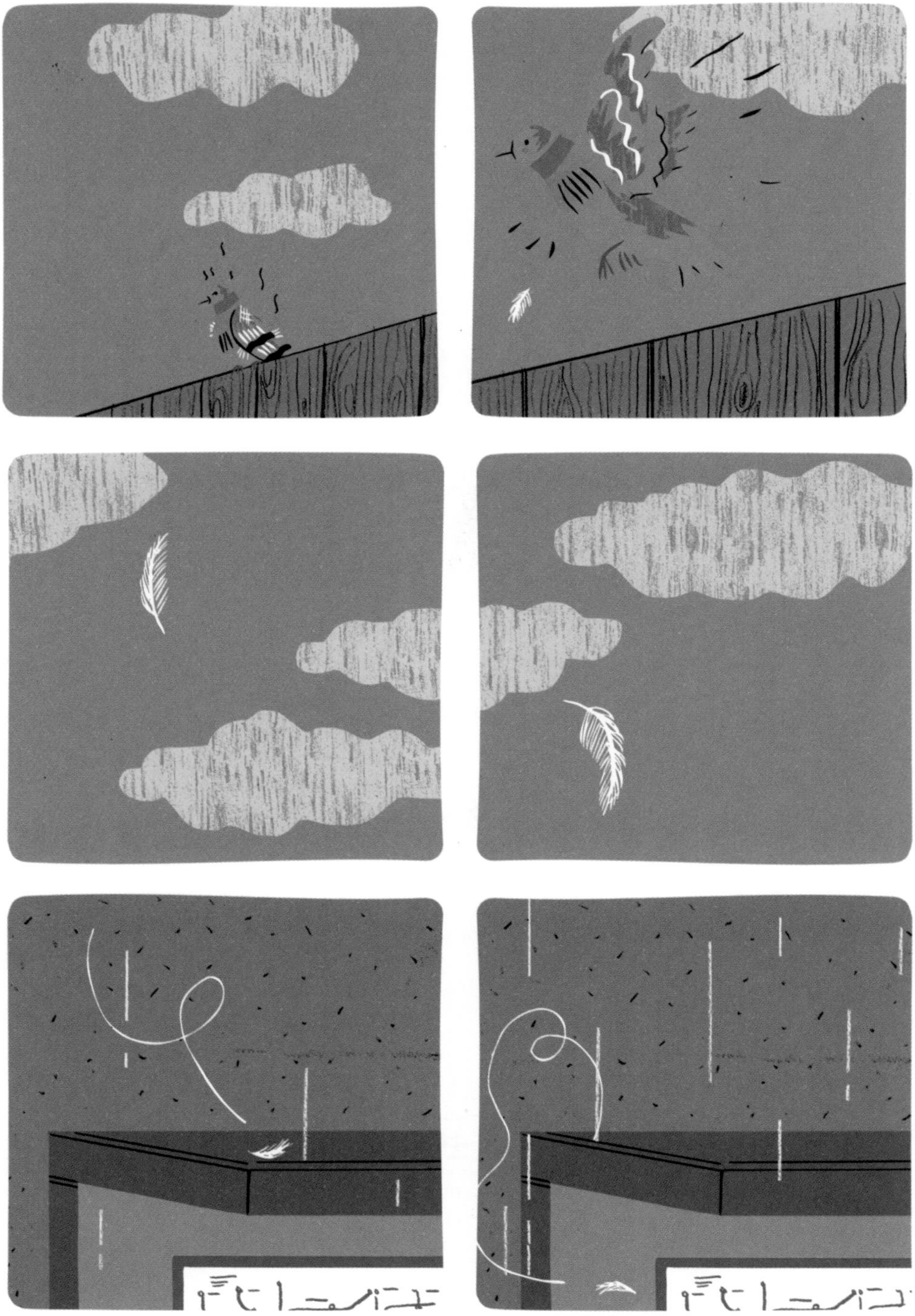

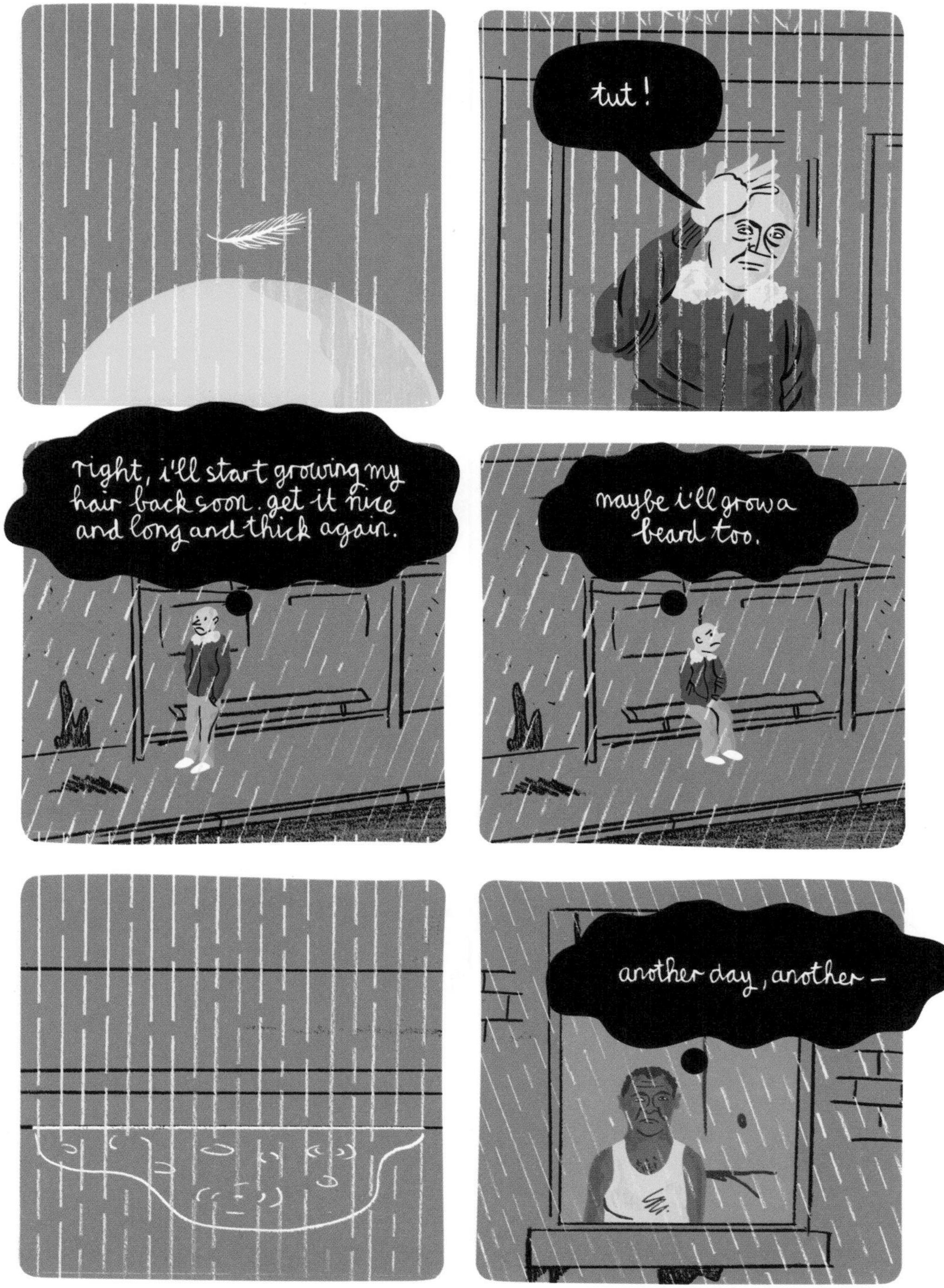
tut!
right, i'll start growing my hair back soon. get it nice and long and thick again.
maybe i'll grow a beard too.
another day, another –

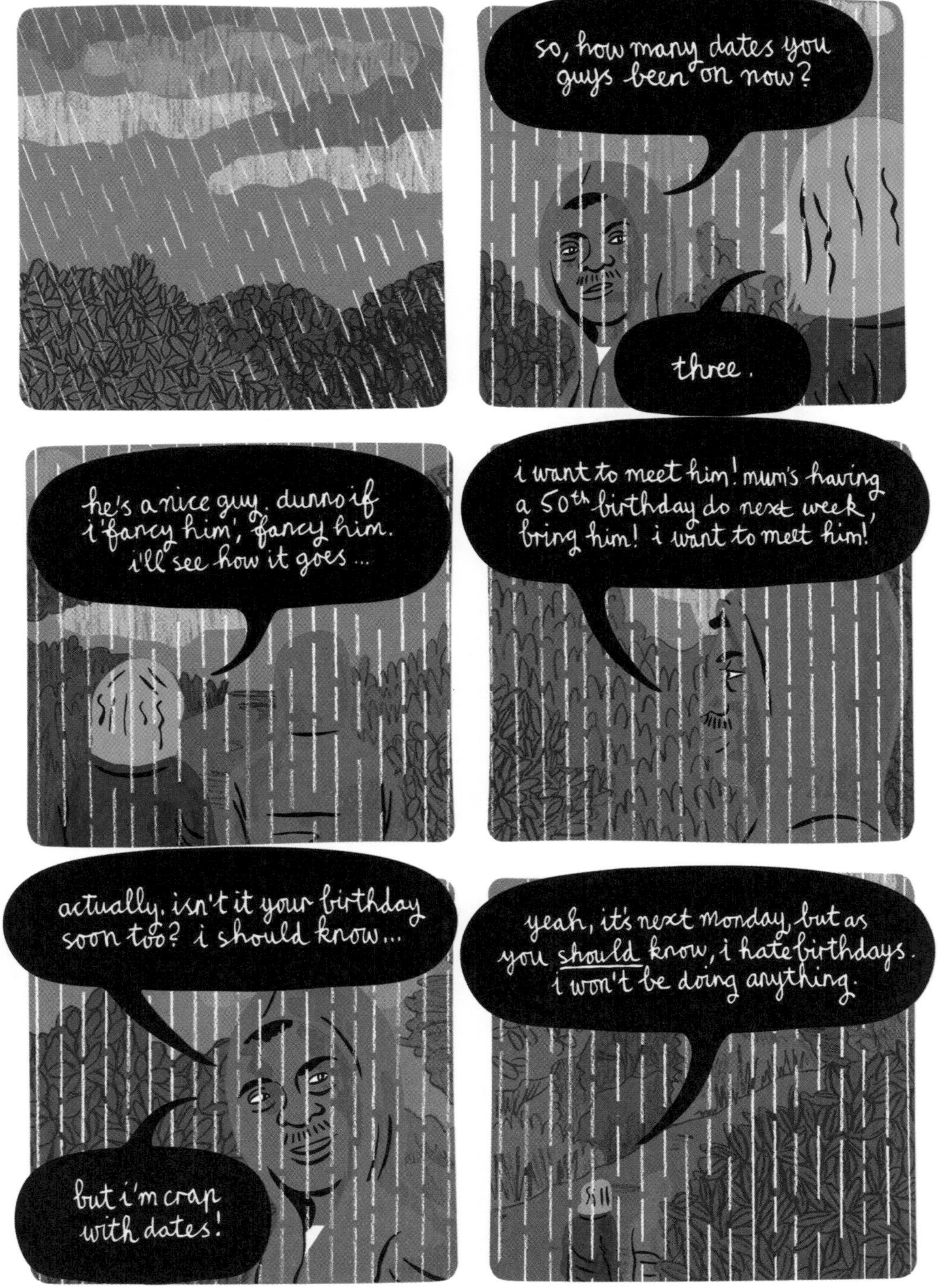
so, how many dates you guys been on now?
three.
he's a nice guy. dunno if i 'fancy him', fancy him. i'll see how it goes...
i want to meet him! mum's having a 50th birthday do next week, bring him! i want to meet him!
actually, isn't it your birthday soon too? i should know...
but i'm crap with dates!
yeah, it's next monday, but as you should know, i hate birthdays. i won't be doing anything.

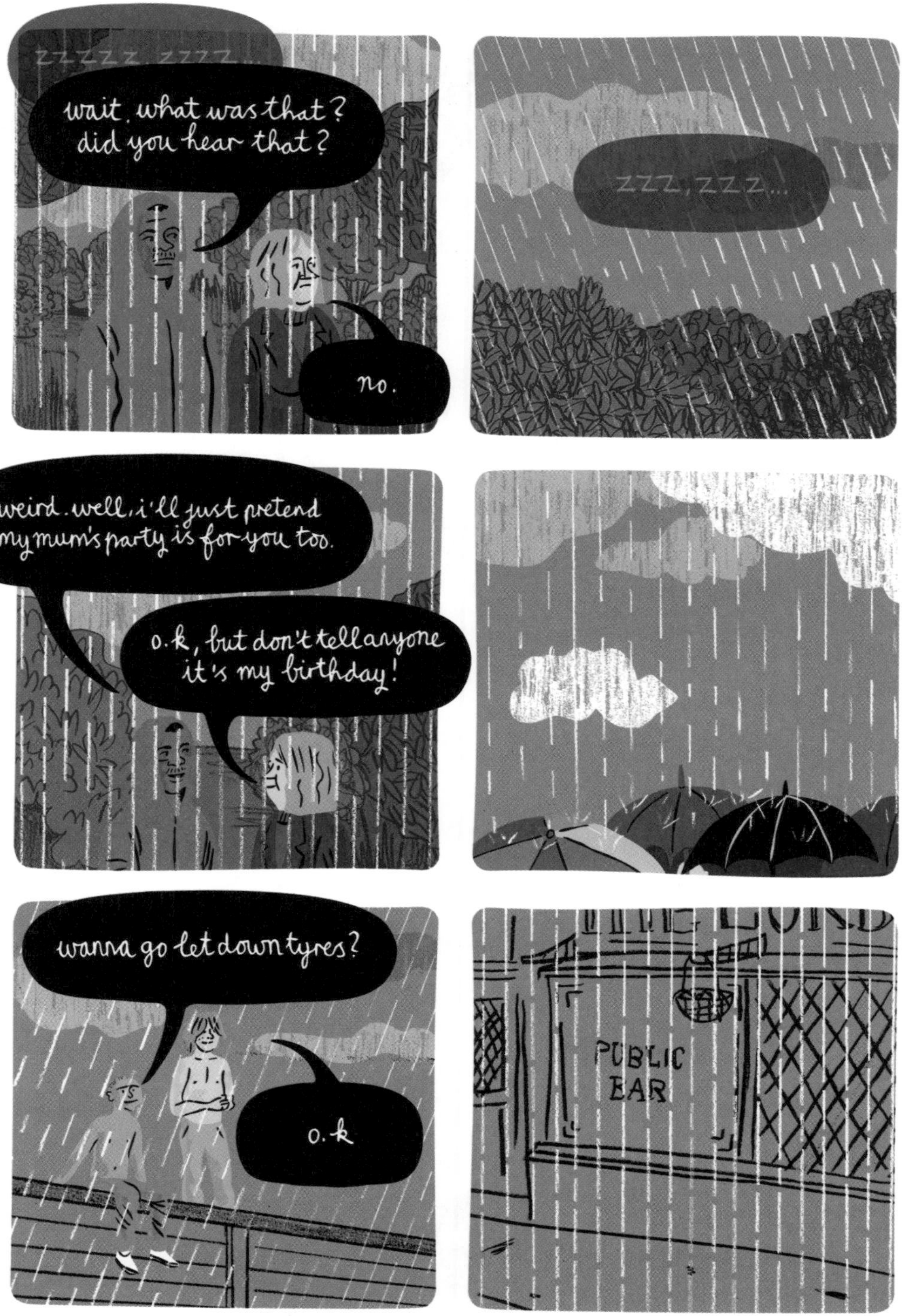
ZZZZZ ZZZZ
wait, what was that? did you hear that?
no.
zzz, zzz...
weird. well, i'll just pretend my mum's party is for you too.
o.k, but don't tell anyone it's my birthday!
wanna go let down tyres?
o.k
PUBLIC BAR

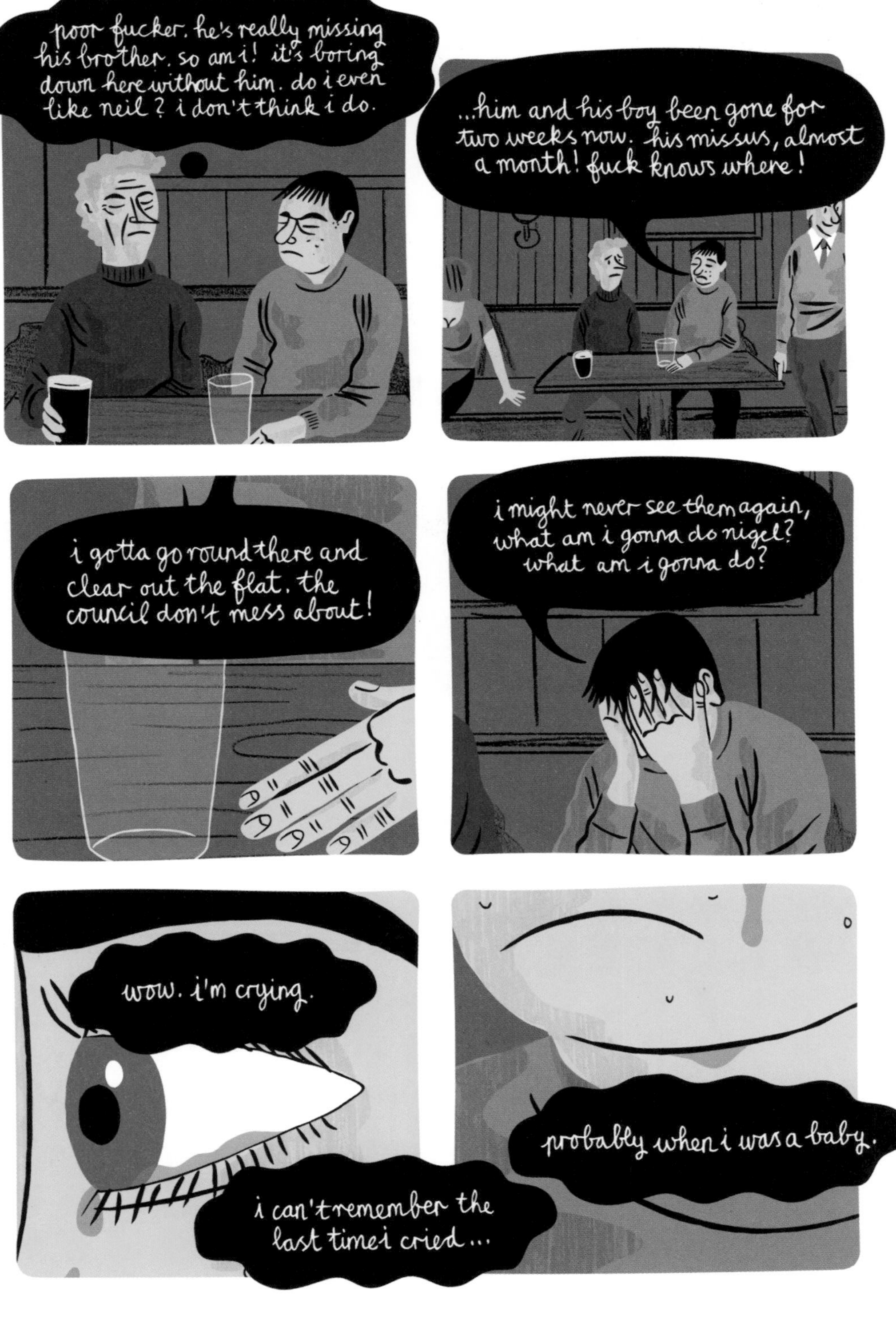

poor fucker. he's really missing his brother. so am i! it's boring down here without him. do i even like neil? i don't think i do.
...him and his boy been gone for two weeks now. his missus, almost a month! fuck knows where!
i gotta go round there and clear out the flat. the council don't mess about!
i might never see them again, what am i gonna do nigel? what am i gonna do?
wow. i'm crying.
i can't remember the last time i cried...
probably when i was a baby.

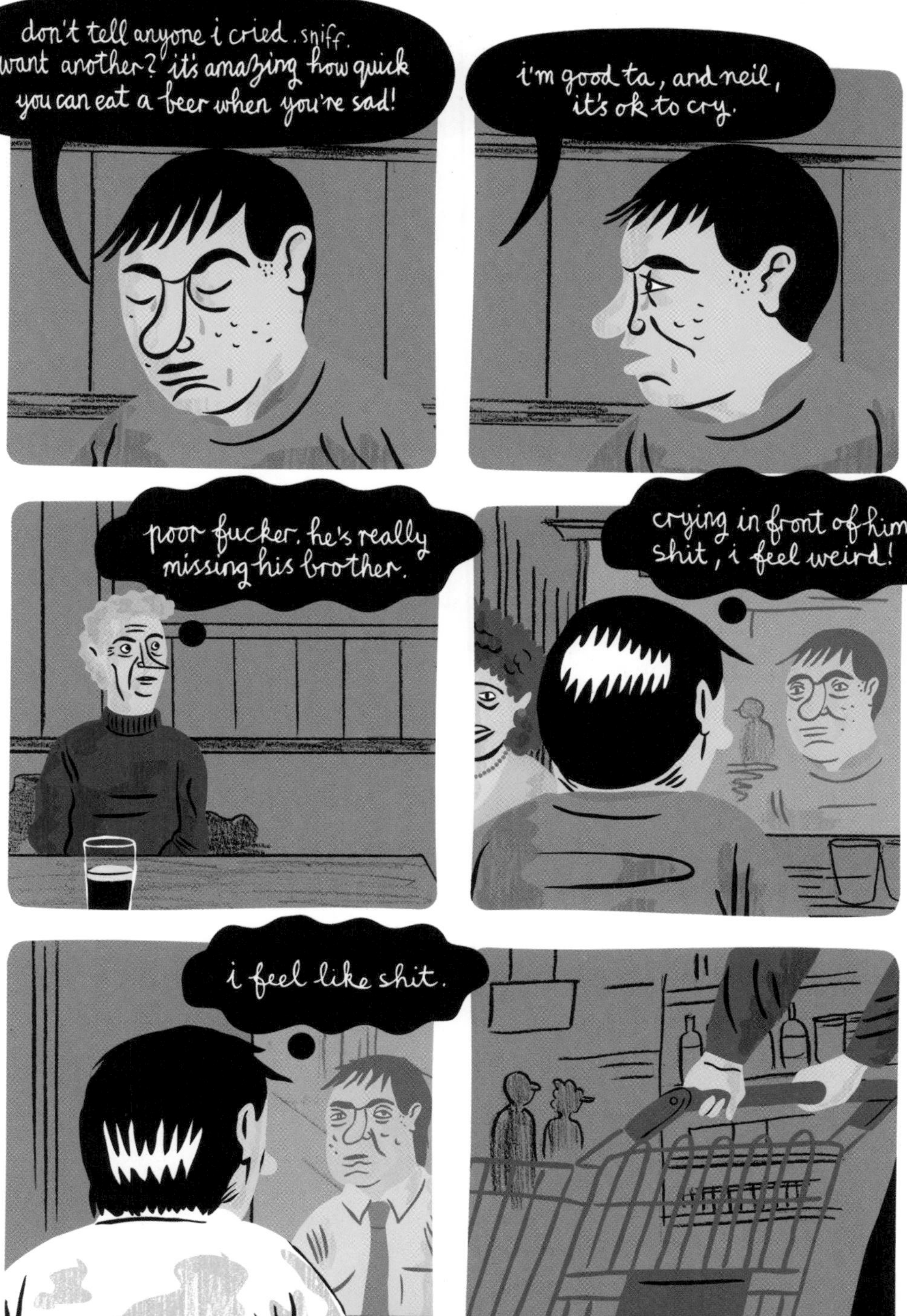
don't tell anyone i cried. sniff. want another? it's amazing how quick you can eat a beer when you're sad!
i'm good ta, and neil, it's ok to cry.
poor fucker. he's really missing his brother.
crying in front of him. shit, i feel weird!
i feel like shit.

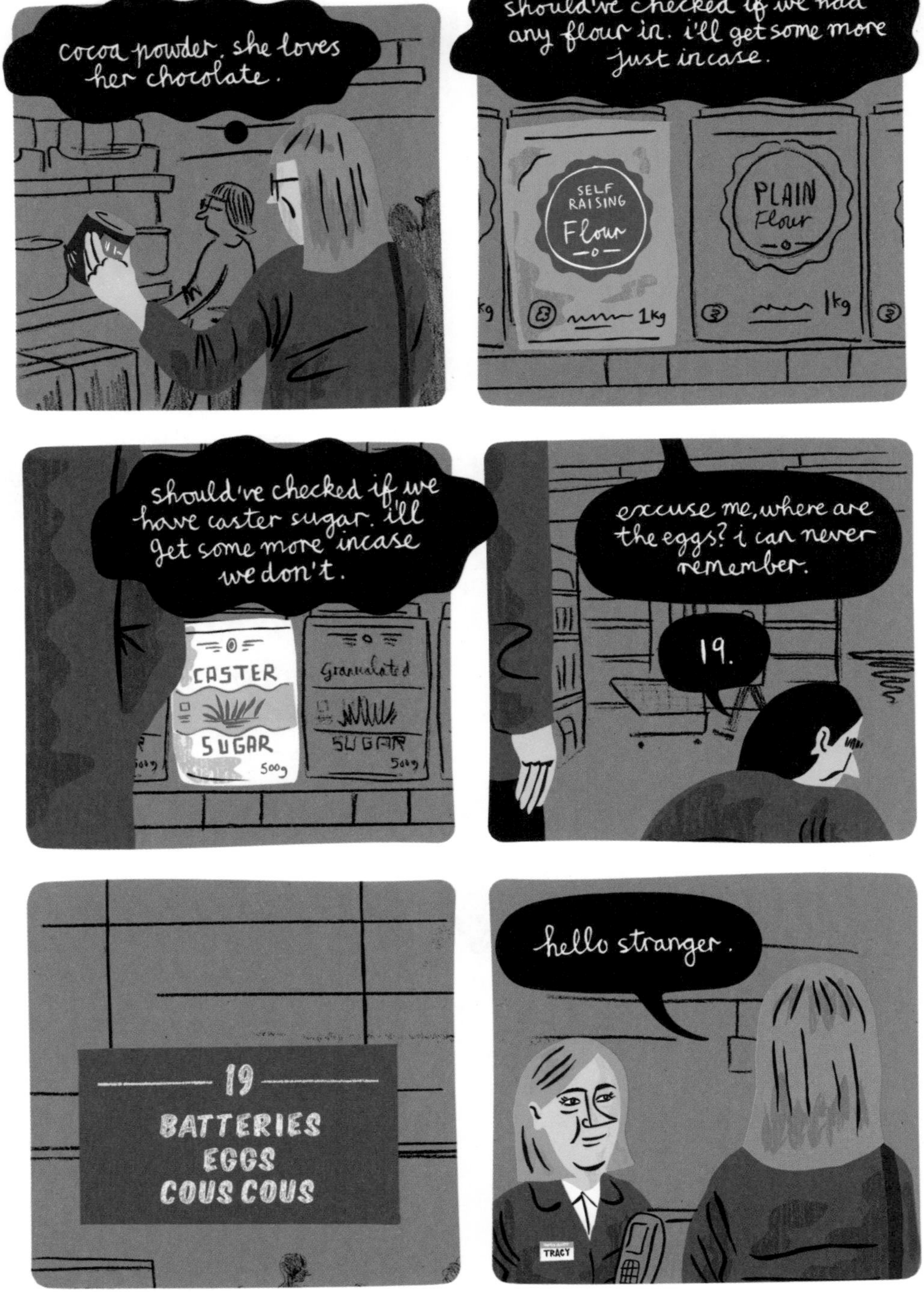
cocoa powder. she loves her chocolate.
should've checked if we had any flour in. i'll get some more just incase.
SELF RAISING Flour
1kg
PLAIN Flour
1kg
should've checked if we have caster sugar. i'll get some more incase we don't.
CASTER SUGAR
500g
Granulated SUGAR
500g
excuse me, where are the eggs? i can never remember.
19.
19
BATTERIES
EGGS
COUS COUS
hello stranger.
TRACY

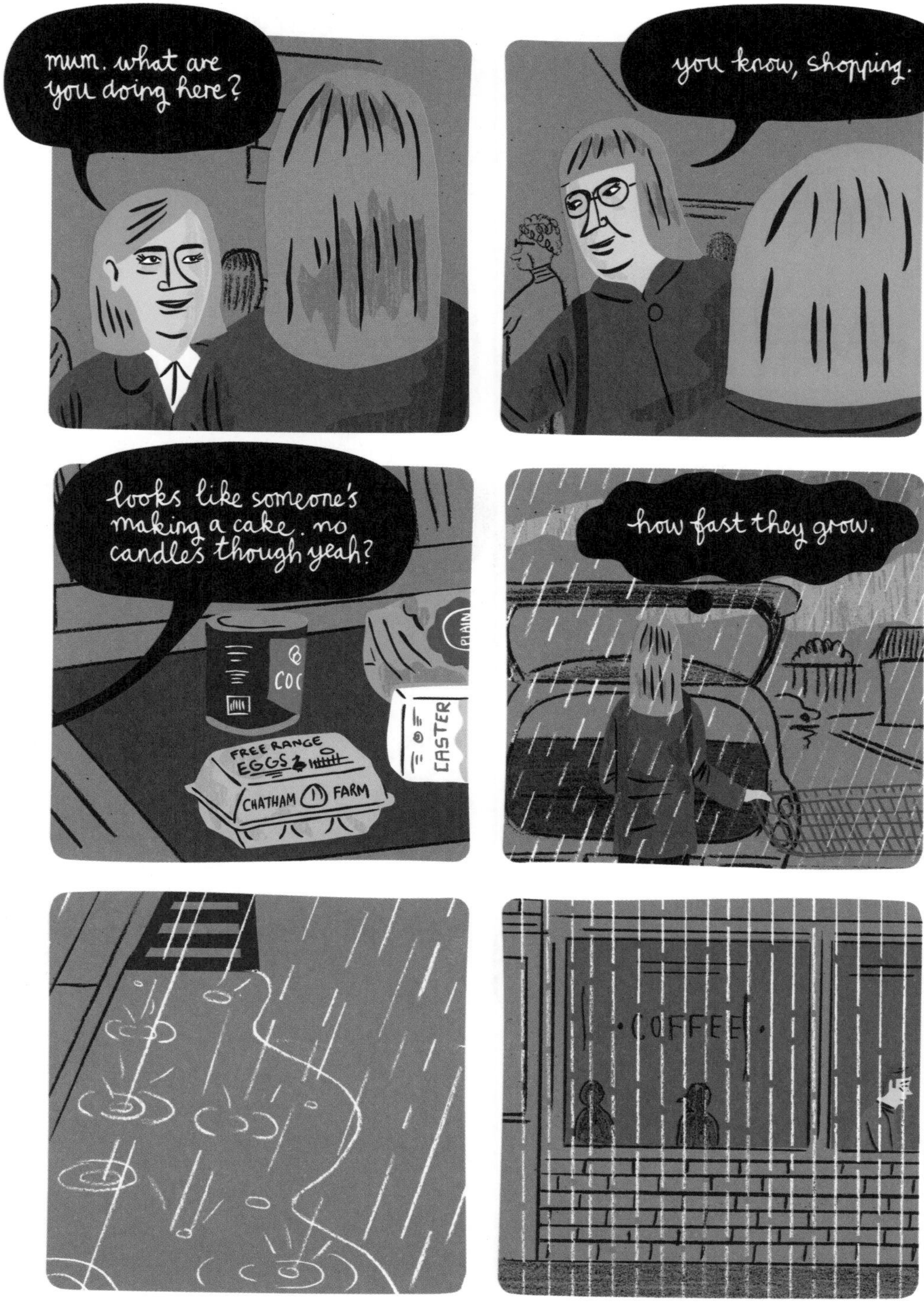
mum. what are you doing here?
you know, shopping.
looks like someone's making a cake. no candles though yeah?
CO
PLAIN
FREE RANGE EGGS
CHATHAM FARM
CASTER
how fast they grow.
COFFEE

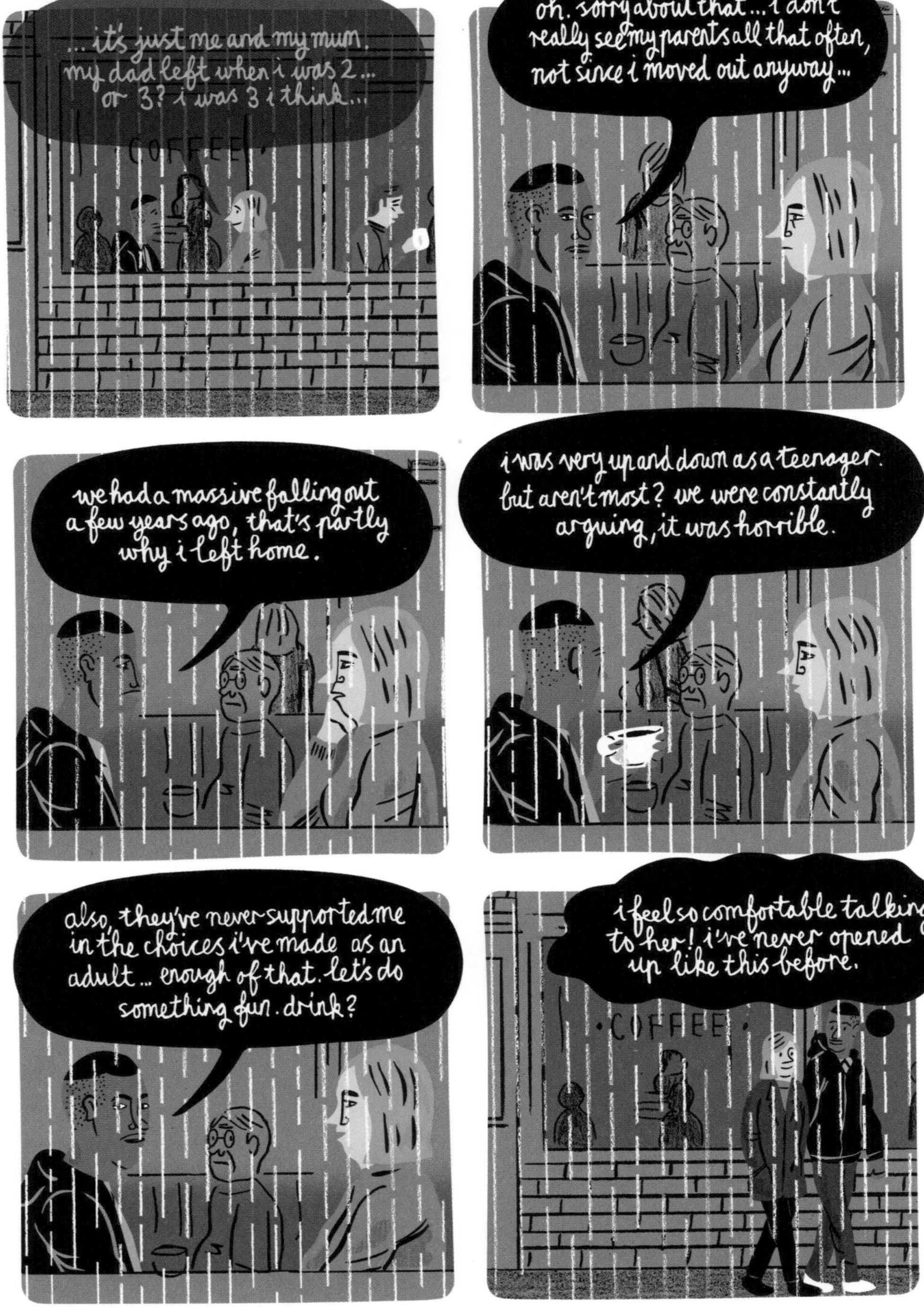
... it's just me and my mum, my dad left when i was 2... or 3? i was 3 i think...
COFFEE
oh. sorry about that... i don't really see my parents all that often, not since i moved out anyway...
we had a massive falling out a few years ago, that's partly why i left home.
i was very up and down as a teenager. but aren't most? we were constantly arguing, it was horrible.
also, they've never supported me in the choices i've made as an adult... enough of that. let's do something fun. drink?
i feel so comfortable talking to her! i've never opened up like this before.
COFFEE

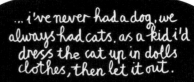
... i've never had a dog, we always had cats, as a kid i'd dress the cat up in dolls clothes, then let it out.

i liked the idea of other people spotting a cat wandering around in a party dress.

ha ha ha!

ha ha!

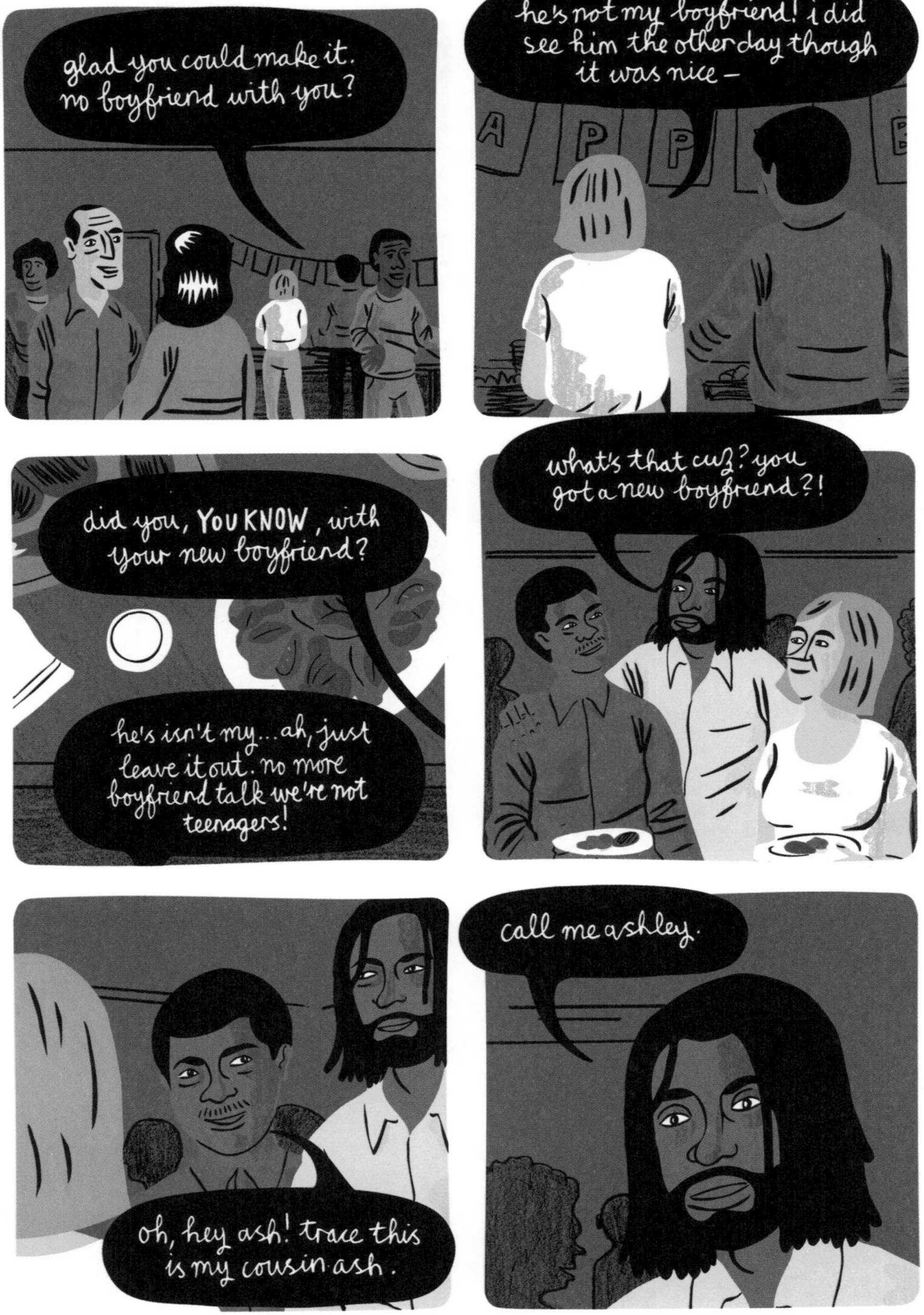
glad you could make it. no boyfriend with you?
he's not my boyfriend! i did see him the other day though it was nice –
did you, YOU KNOW, with your new boyfriend?
he's isn't my... ah, just leave it out. no more boyfriend talk we're not teenagers!
what's that cuz? you got a new boyfriend?!
oh, hey ash! trace this is my cousin ash.
call me ashley.

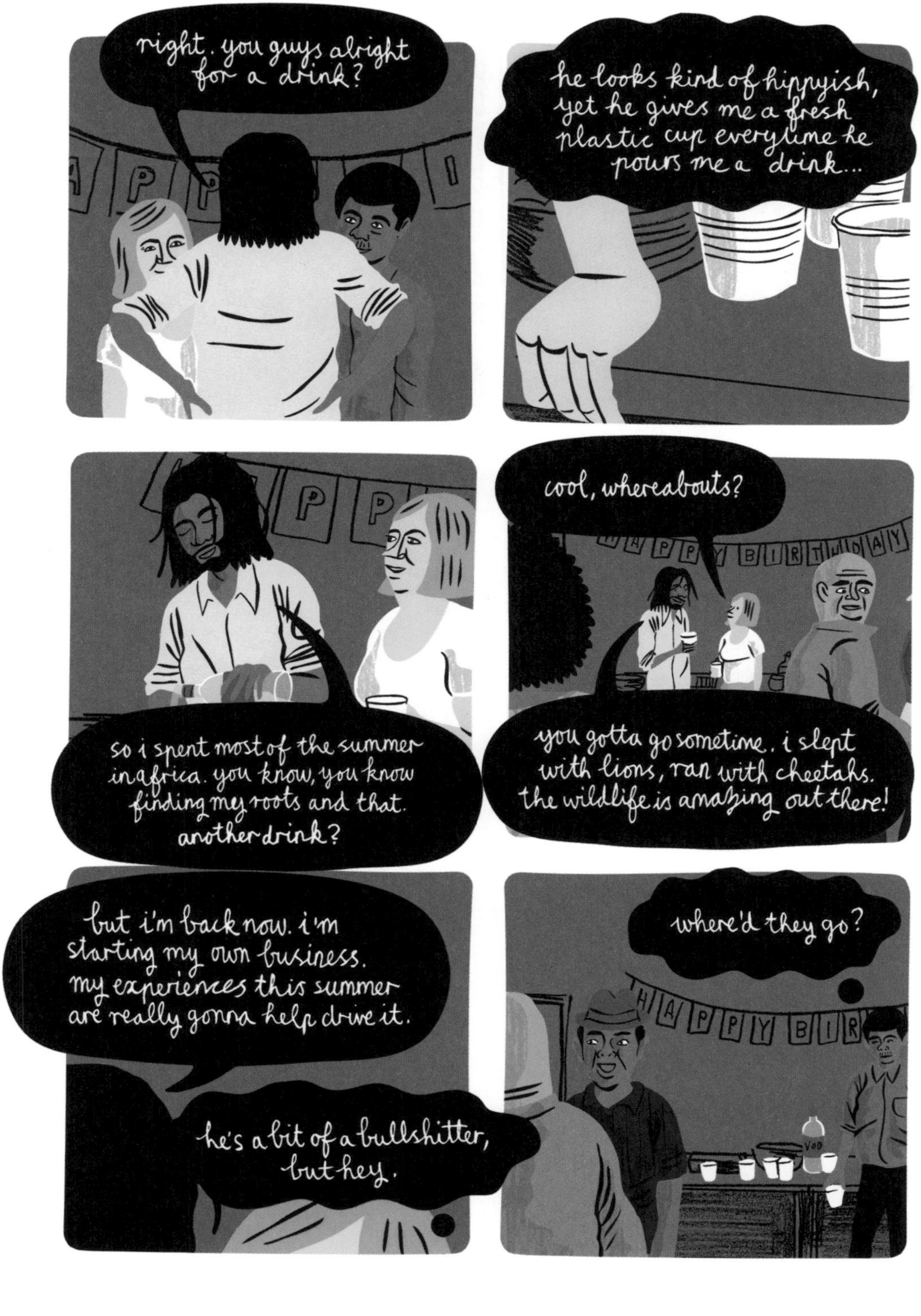
right. you guys alright for a drink?
he looks kind of hippyish, yet he gives me a fresh plastic cup everytime he pours me a drink...
so i spent most of the summer in africa. you know, you know finding my roots and that. another drink?
cool, whereabouts?
you gotta go sometime. i slept with lions, ran with cheetahs. the wildlife is amazing out there!
but i'm back now. i'm starting my own business. my experiences this summer are really gonna help drive it.
he's a bit of a bullshitter, but hey.
where'd they go?

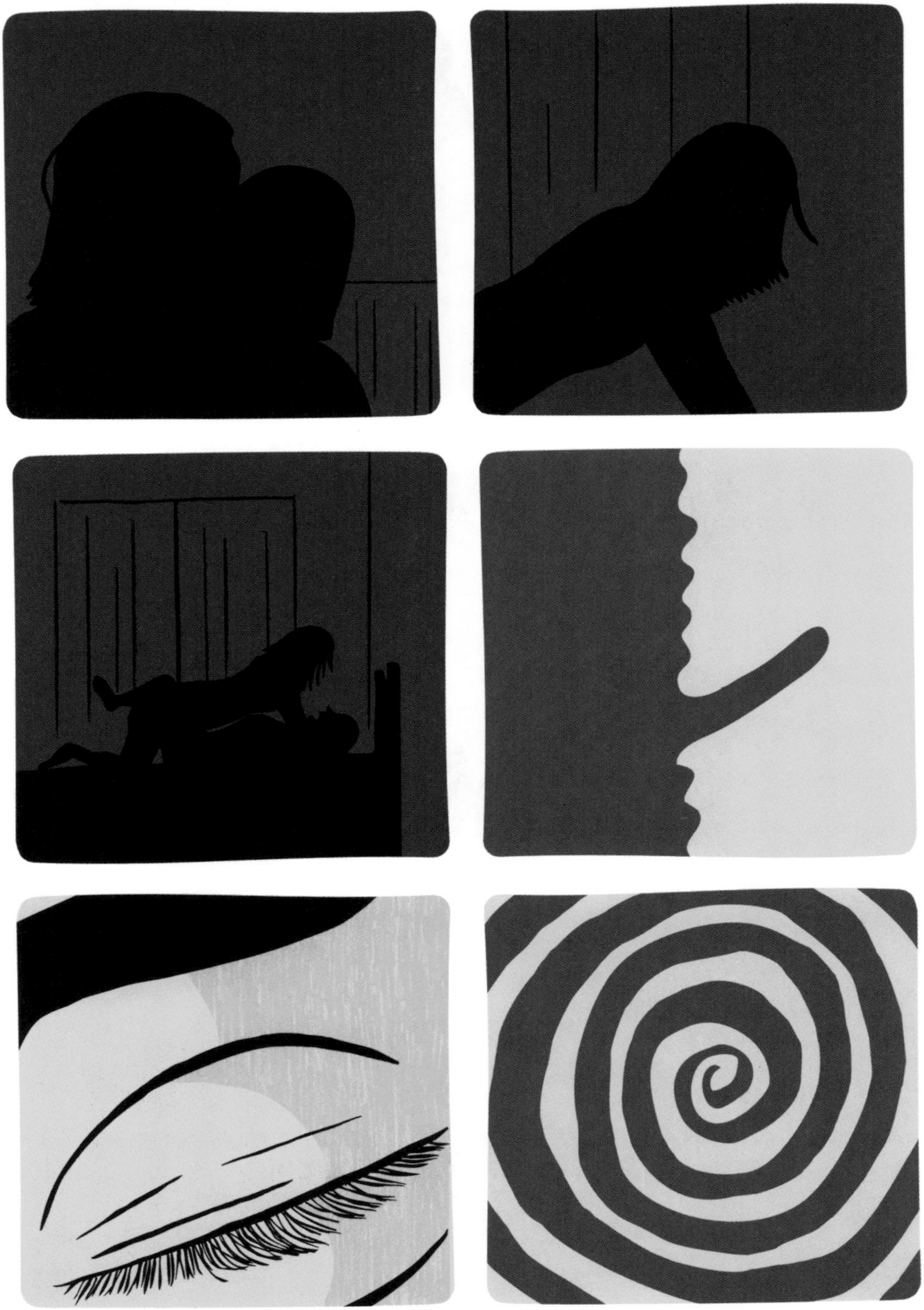

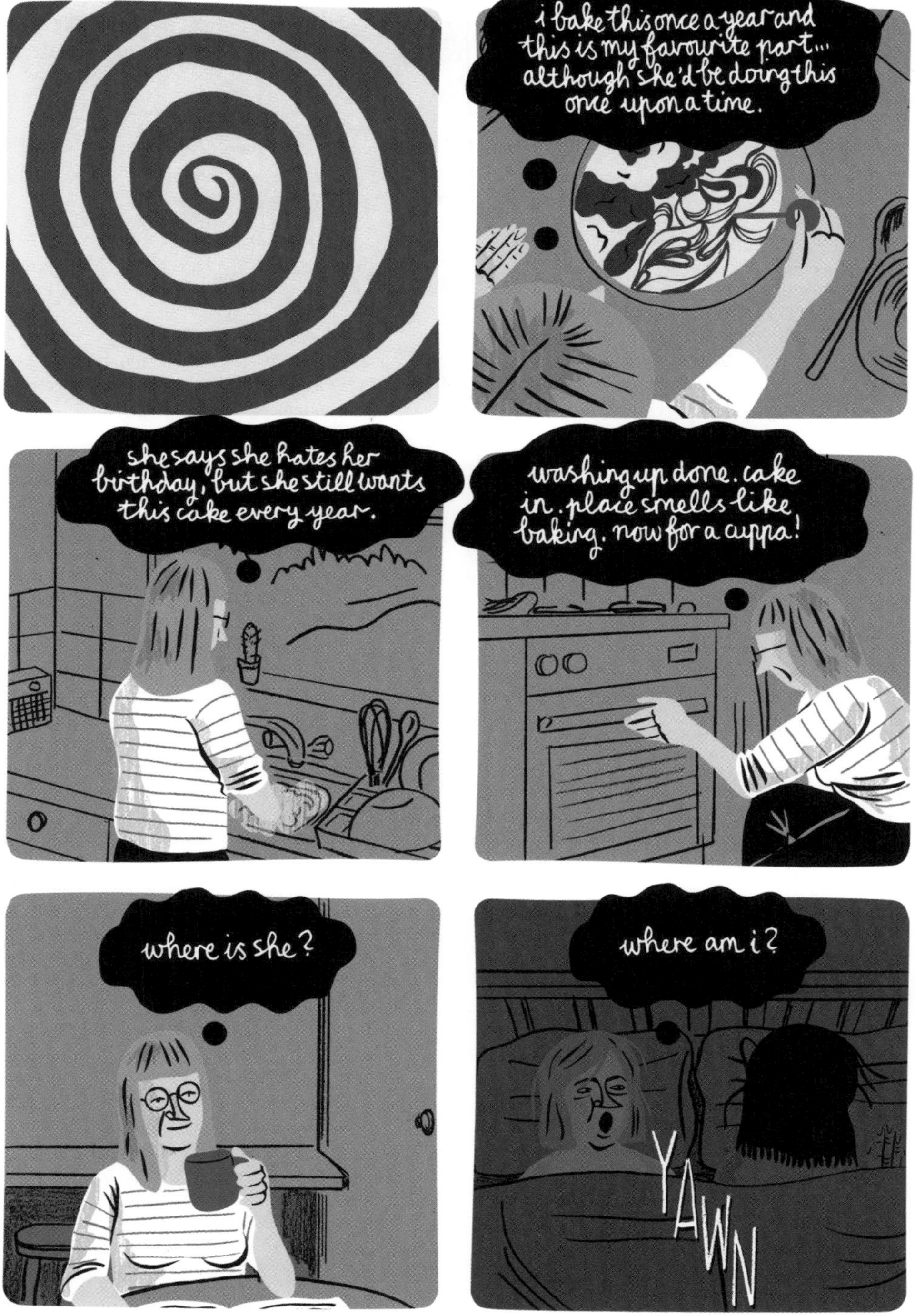
i bake this once a year and this is my favourite part... although she'd be doing this once upon a time.
she says she hates her birthday, but she still wants this cake every year.
washing up done. cake in. place smells like baking. now for a cuppa!
where is she?
where am i?
YAWN

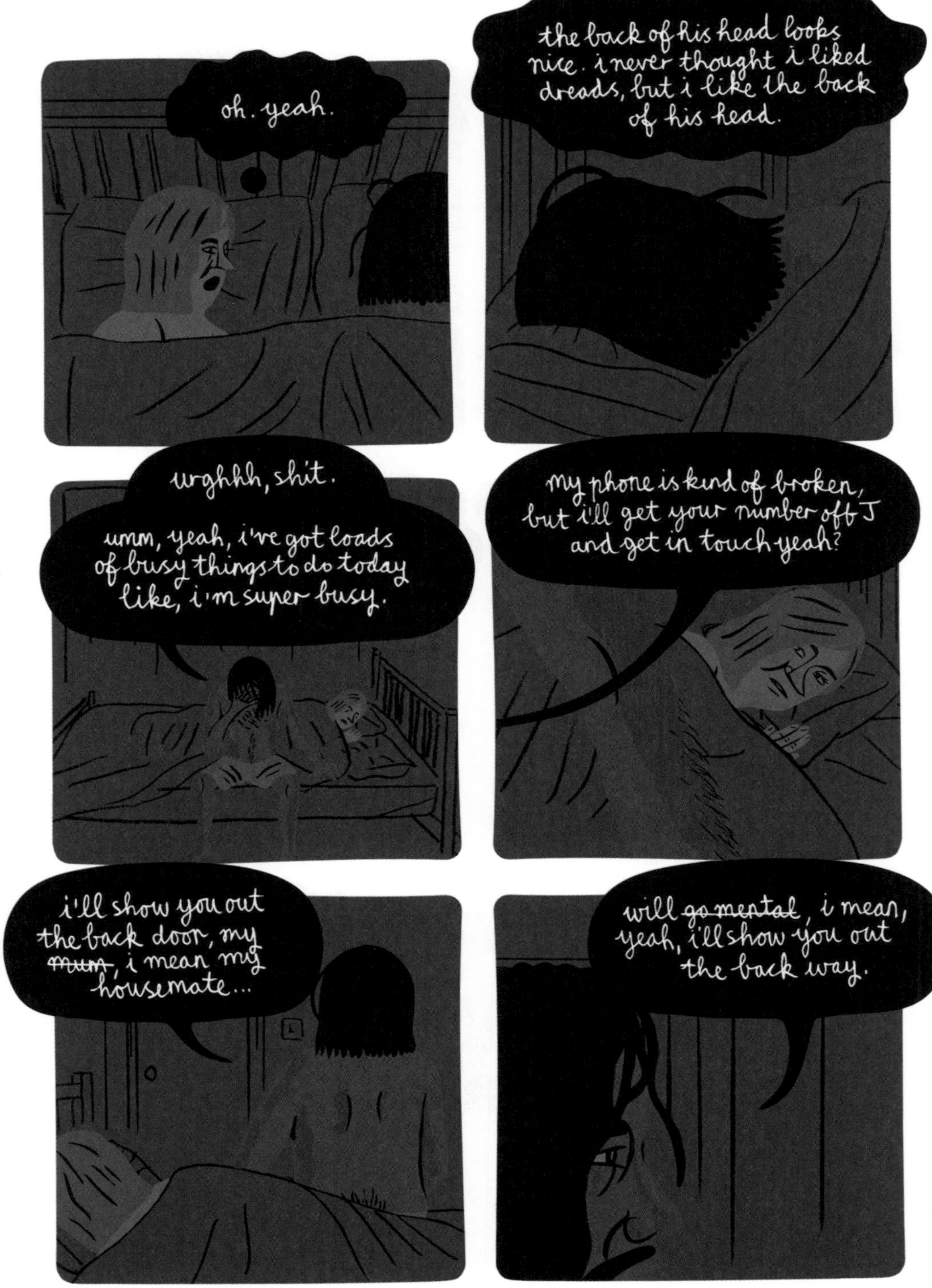

oh. yeah.
the back of his head looks nice. i never thought i liked dreads, but i like the back of his head.
urghhh, shit.
umm, yeah, i've got loads of busy things to do today like, i'm super busy.
my phone is kind of broken, but i'll get your number off J and get in touch yeah?
i'll show you out the back door, my ~~mum~~, i mean my housemate...
will ~~go mental~~, i mean, yeah, i'll show you out the back way.

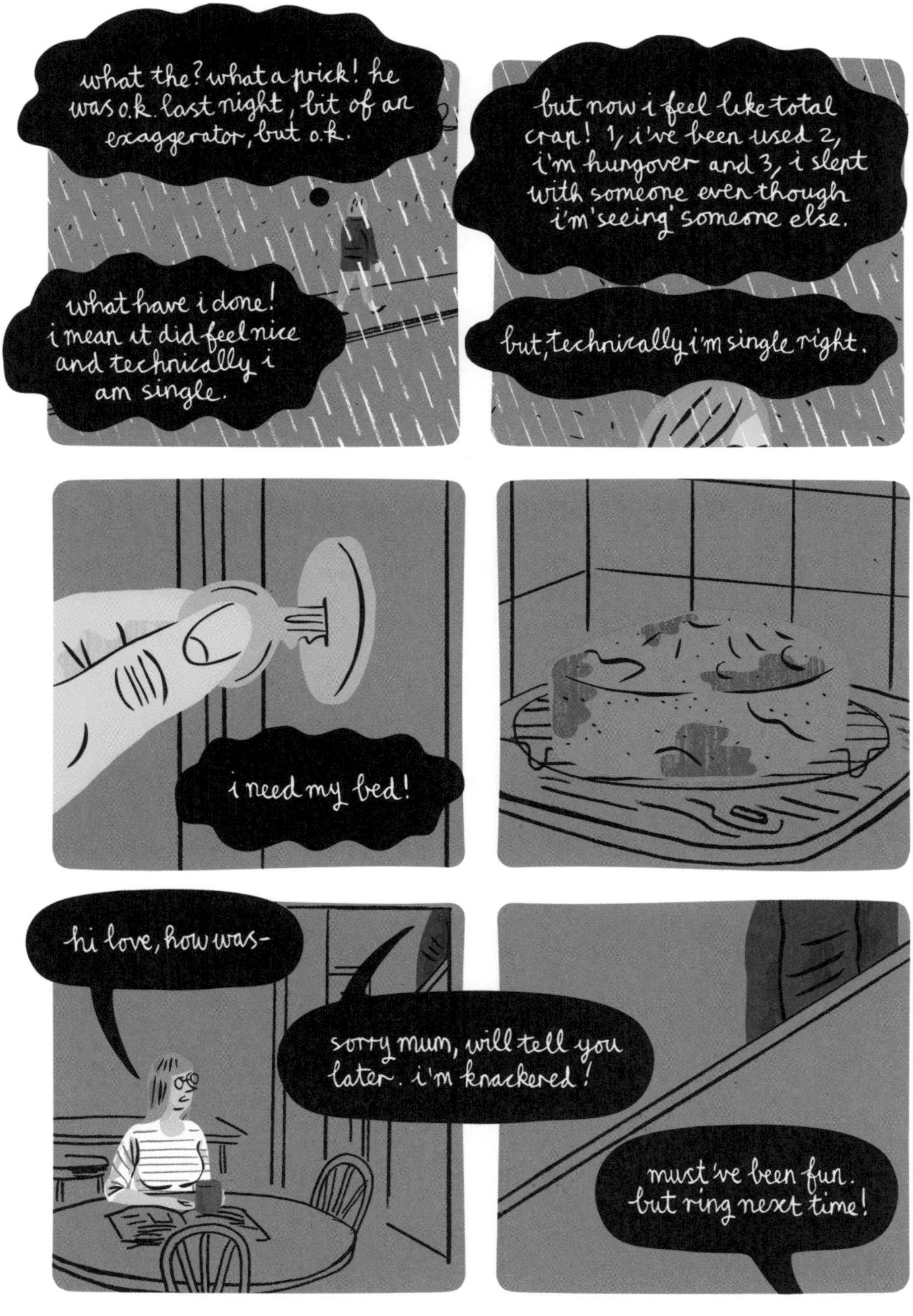
what the? what a prick! he was o.k. last night, bit of an exaggerator, but o.k.
what have i done! i mean it did feel nice and technically i am single.
but now i feel like total crap! 1, i've been used 2, i'm hungover and 3, i slept with someone even though i'm 'seeing' someone else.
but, technically i'm single right.
i need my bed!
hi love, how was-
sorry mum, will tell you later. i'm knackered!
must've been fun. but ring next time!

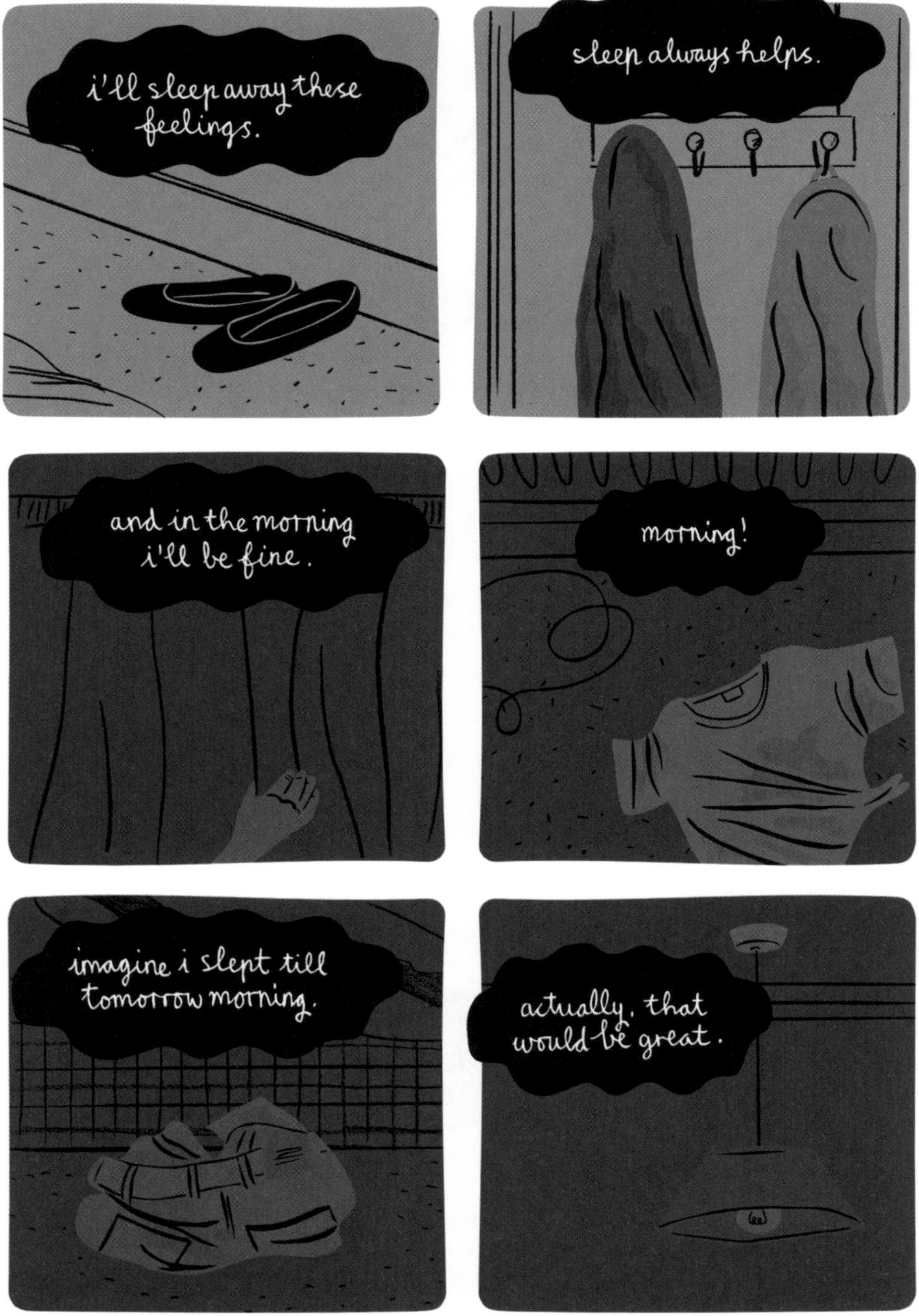
i'll sleep away these feelings.
sleep always helps.
and in the morning i'll be fine.
morning!
imagine i slept till tomorrow morning.
actually, that would be great.

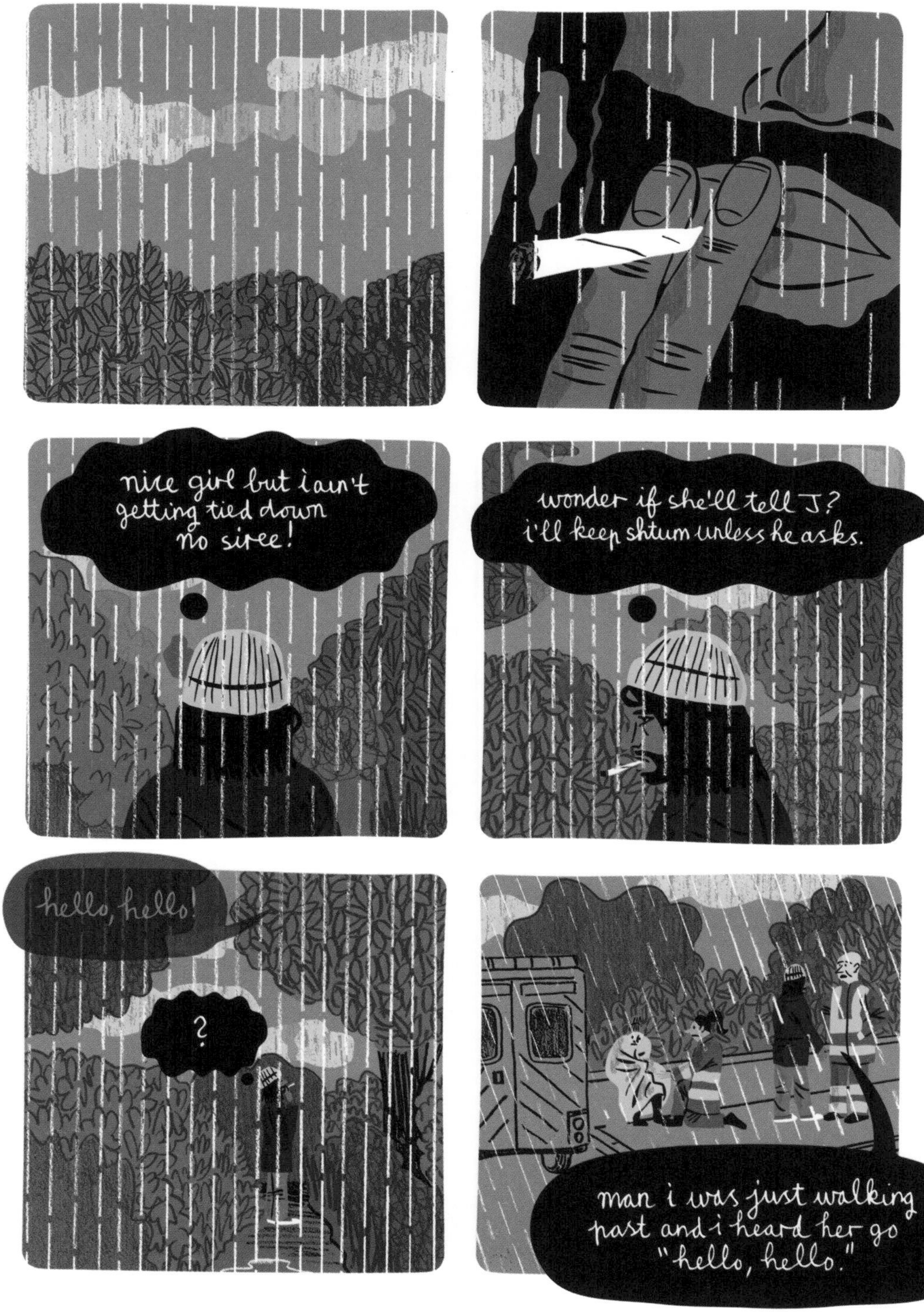
nice girl but i ain't getting tied down no siree!
wonder if she'll tell J? i'll keep shtum unless he asks.
hello, hello!
?
man i was just walking past and i heard her go "hello, hello."

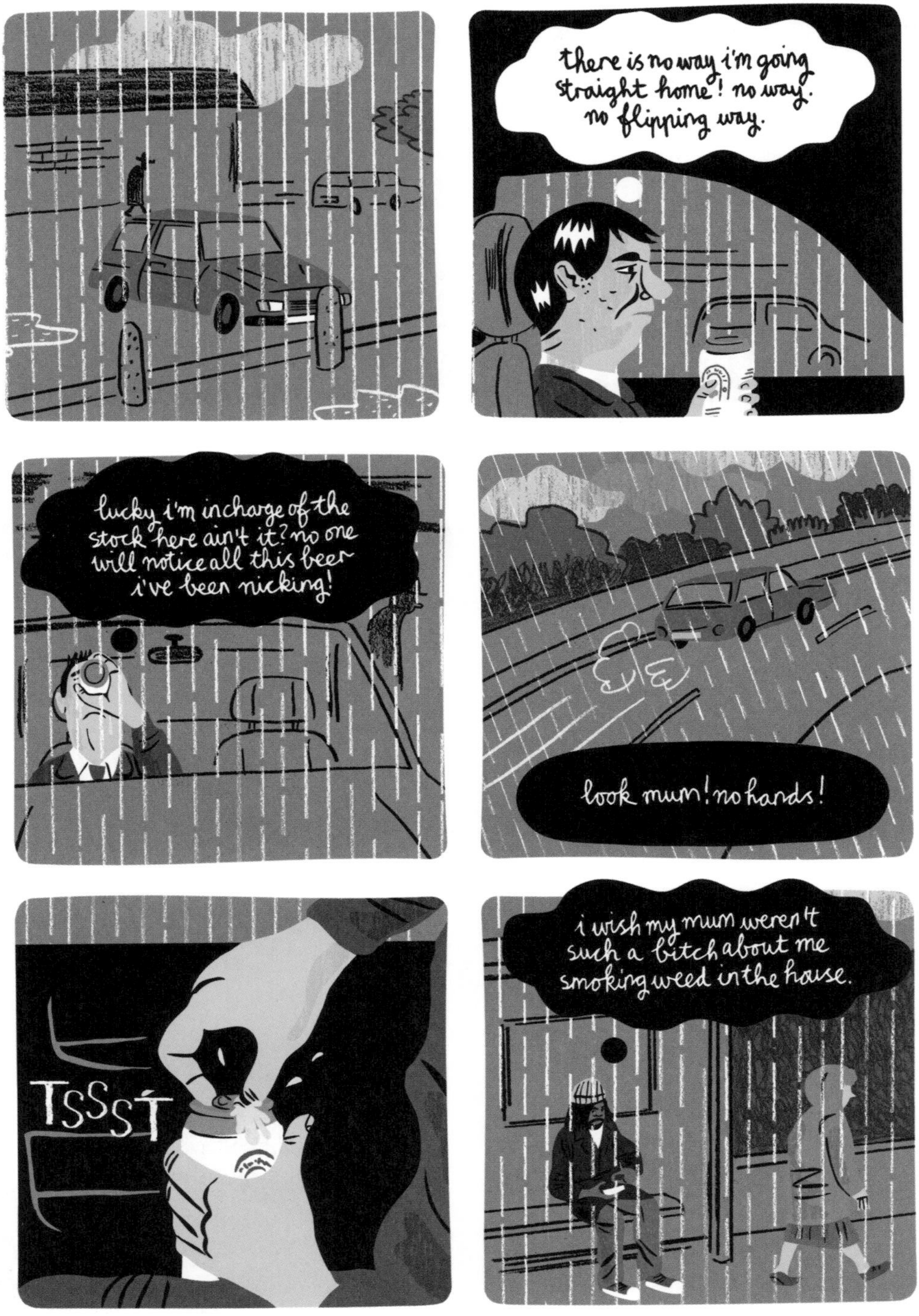
there is no way i'm going straight home! no way. no flipping way.
lucky i'm incharge of the stock here ain't it? no one will notice all this beer i've been nicking!
look mum! no hands!
TSSST
i wish my mum weren't such a bitch about me smoking weed in the house.

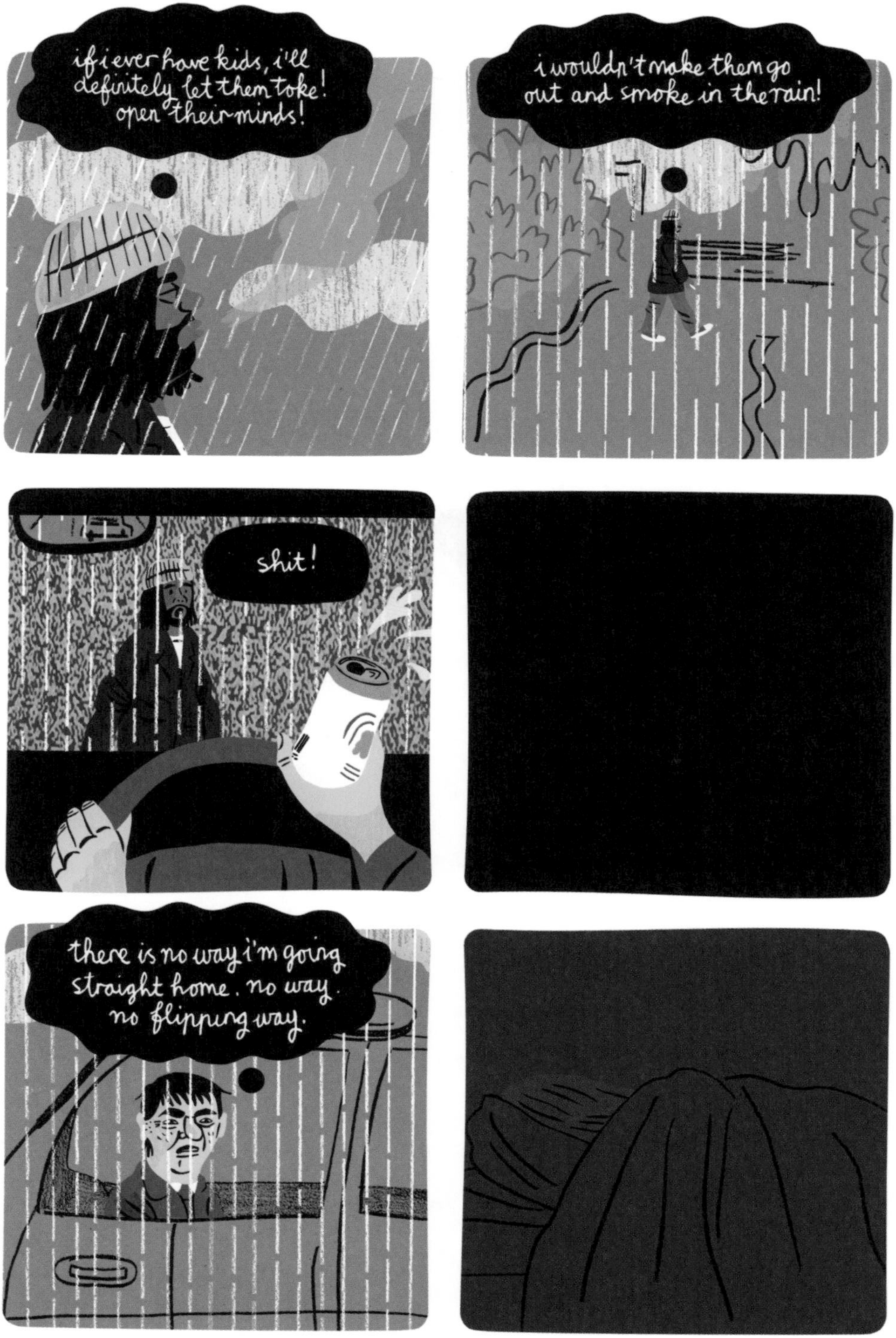
if i ever have kids, i'll definitely let them toke! open their minds!
i wouldn't make them go out and smoke in the rain!
shit!
there is no way i'm going straight home. no way. no flipping way.

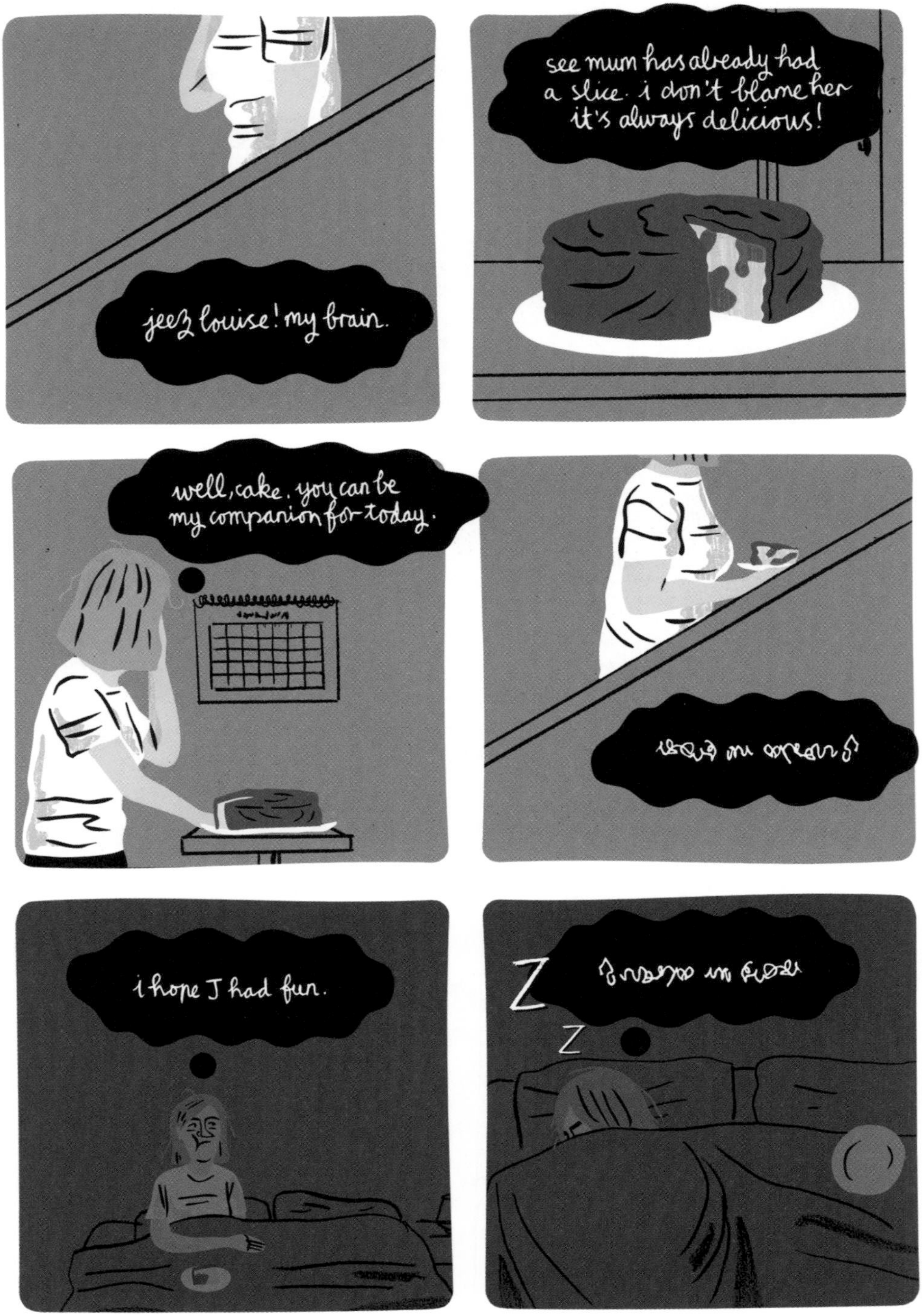

jeez louise! my brain.
see mum has already had a slice. i don't blame her it's always delicious!
well, cake. you can be my companion for today.
i hope J had fun.
Z
Z

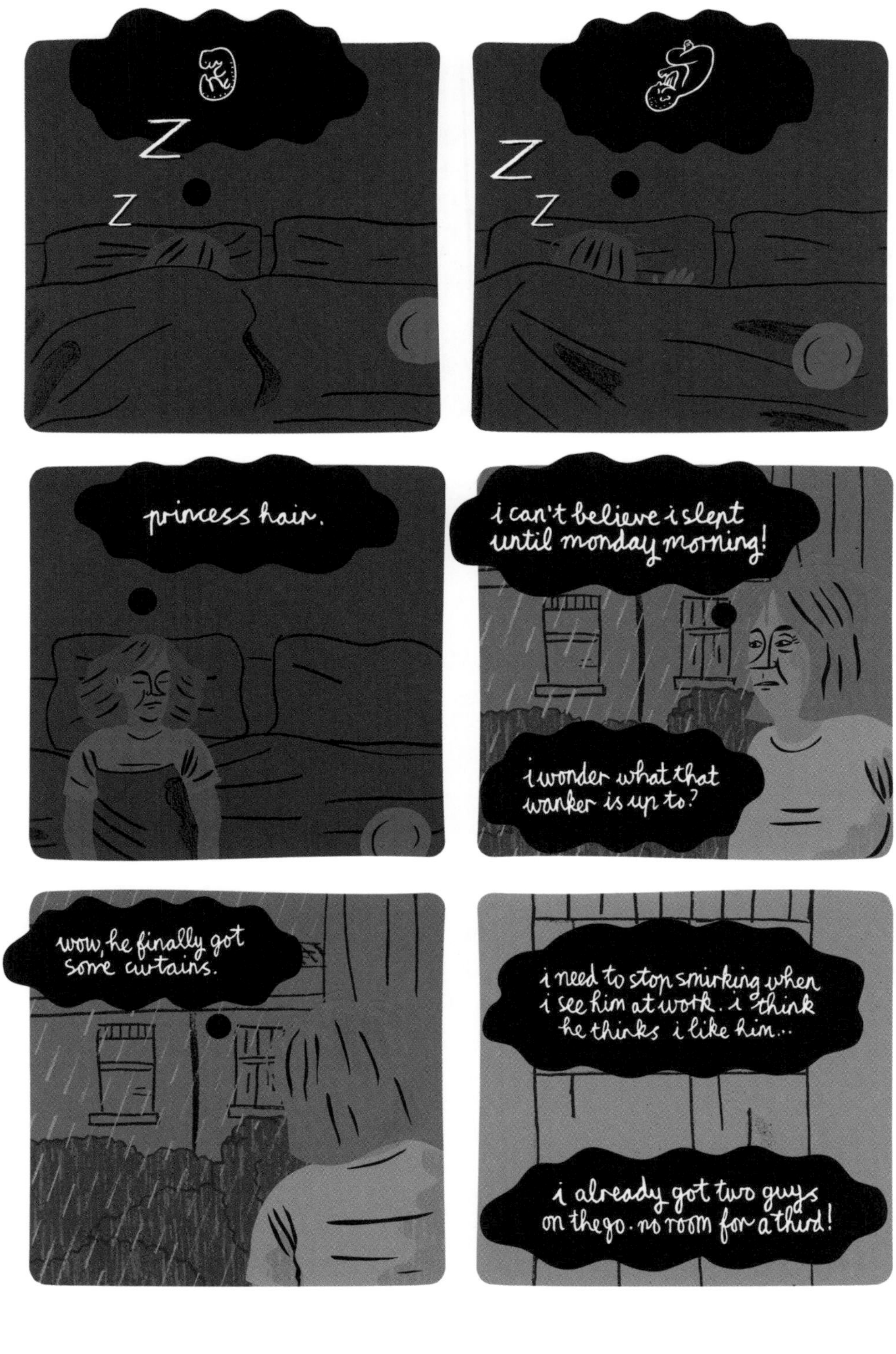
Z
Z
Z
Z
princess hair.
i can't believe i slept until monday morning!
i wonder what that wanker is up to?
wow, he finally got some curtains.
i need to stop smirking when i see him at work. i think he thinks i like him...
i already got two guys on the go. no room for a third!

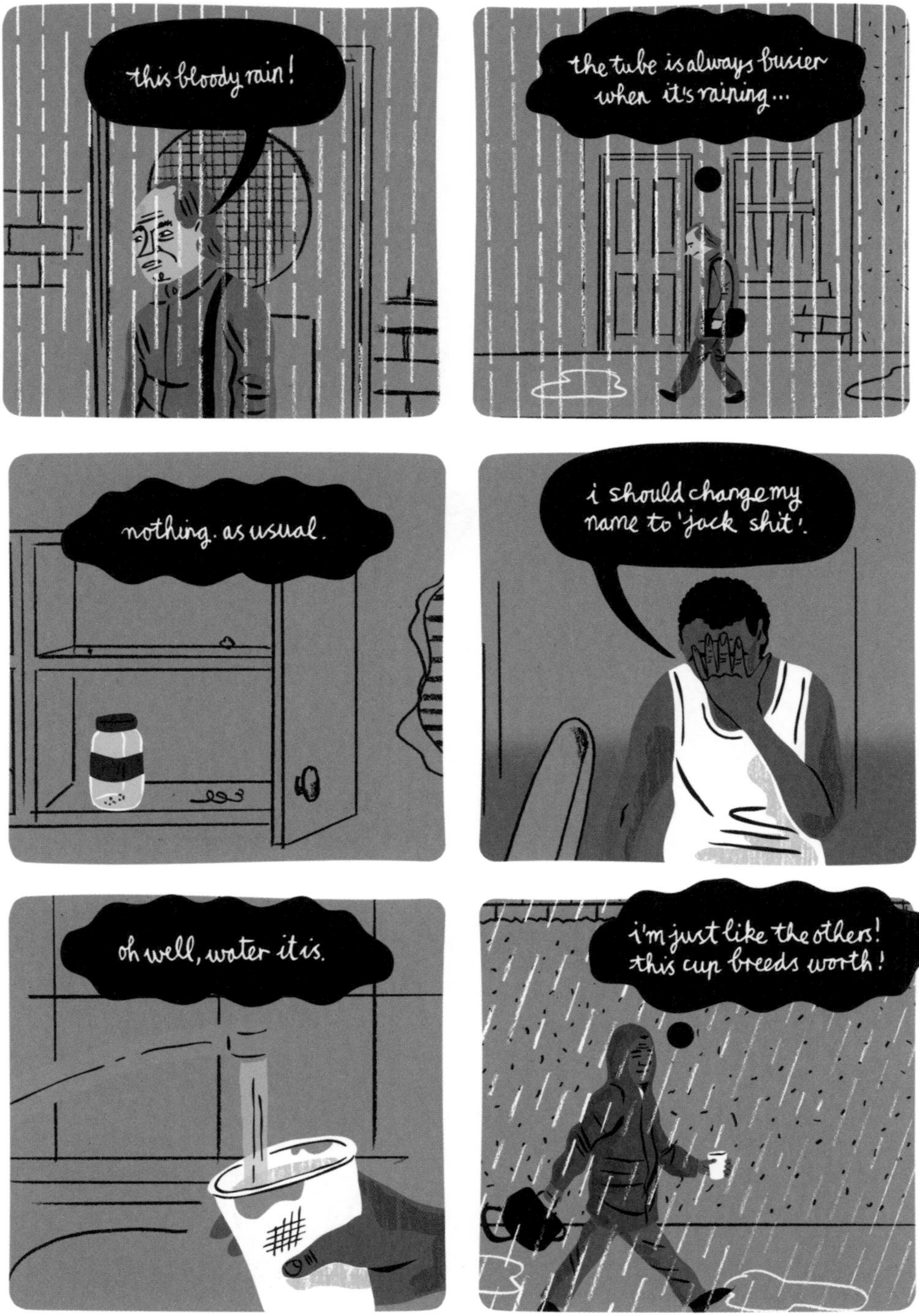
this bloody rain!
the tube is always busier when it's raining...
nothing. as usual.
i should change my name to 'jack shit'.
oh well, water it is.
i'm just like the others! this cup breeds worth!

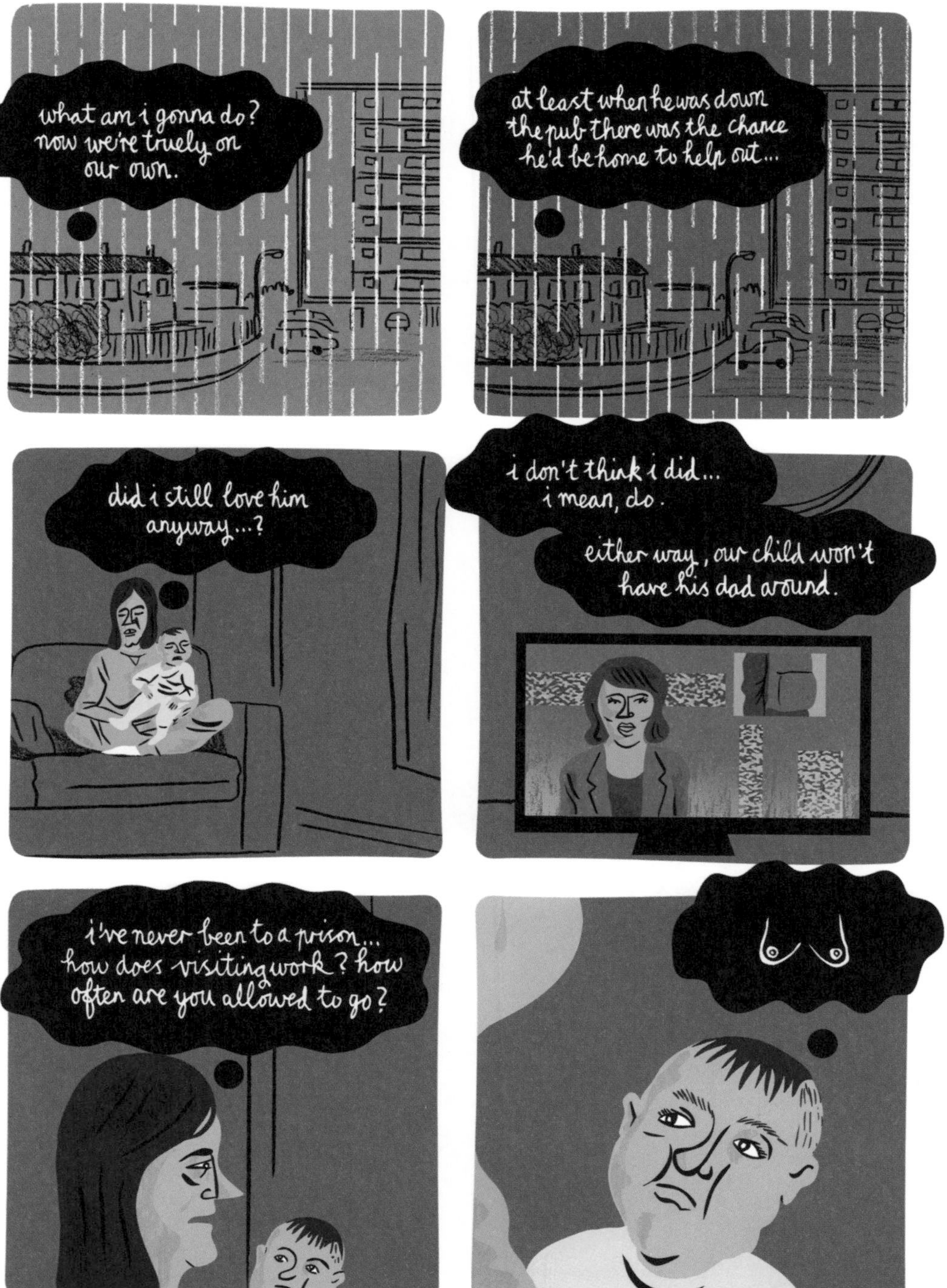
what am i gonna do? now we're truely on our own.
at least when he was down the pub there was the chance he'd be home to help out...
did i still love him anyway...?
i don't think i did... i mean, do.
either way, our child won't have his dad around.
i've never been to a prison... how does visiting work? how often are you allowed to go?

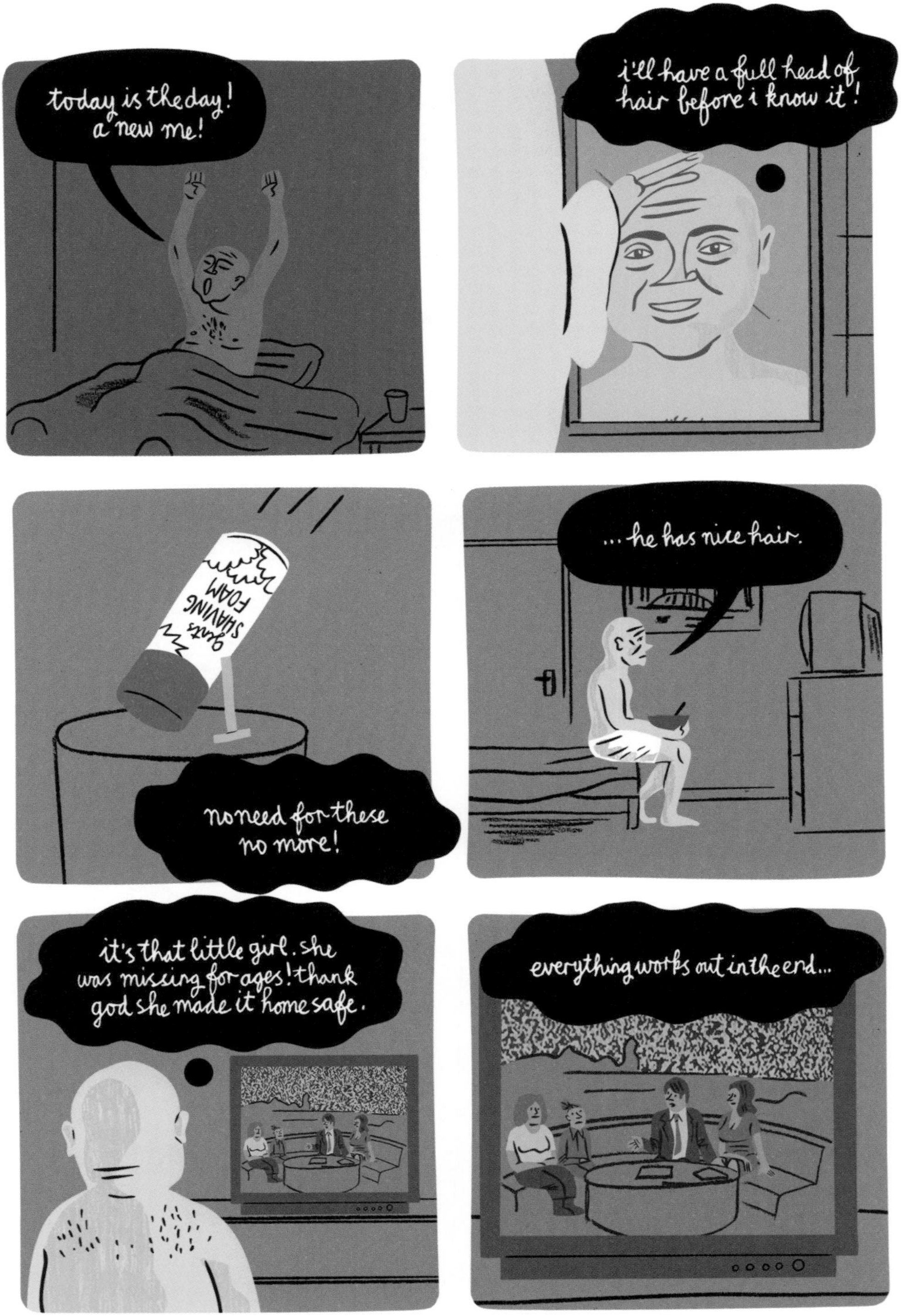
today is the day! a new me!
i'll have a full head of hair before i know it!
gats SHAVING FOAM
no need for these no more!
...he has nice hair.
it's that little girl. she was missing for ages! thank god she made it home safe.
everything works out in the end...

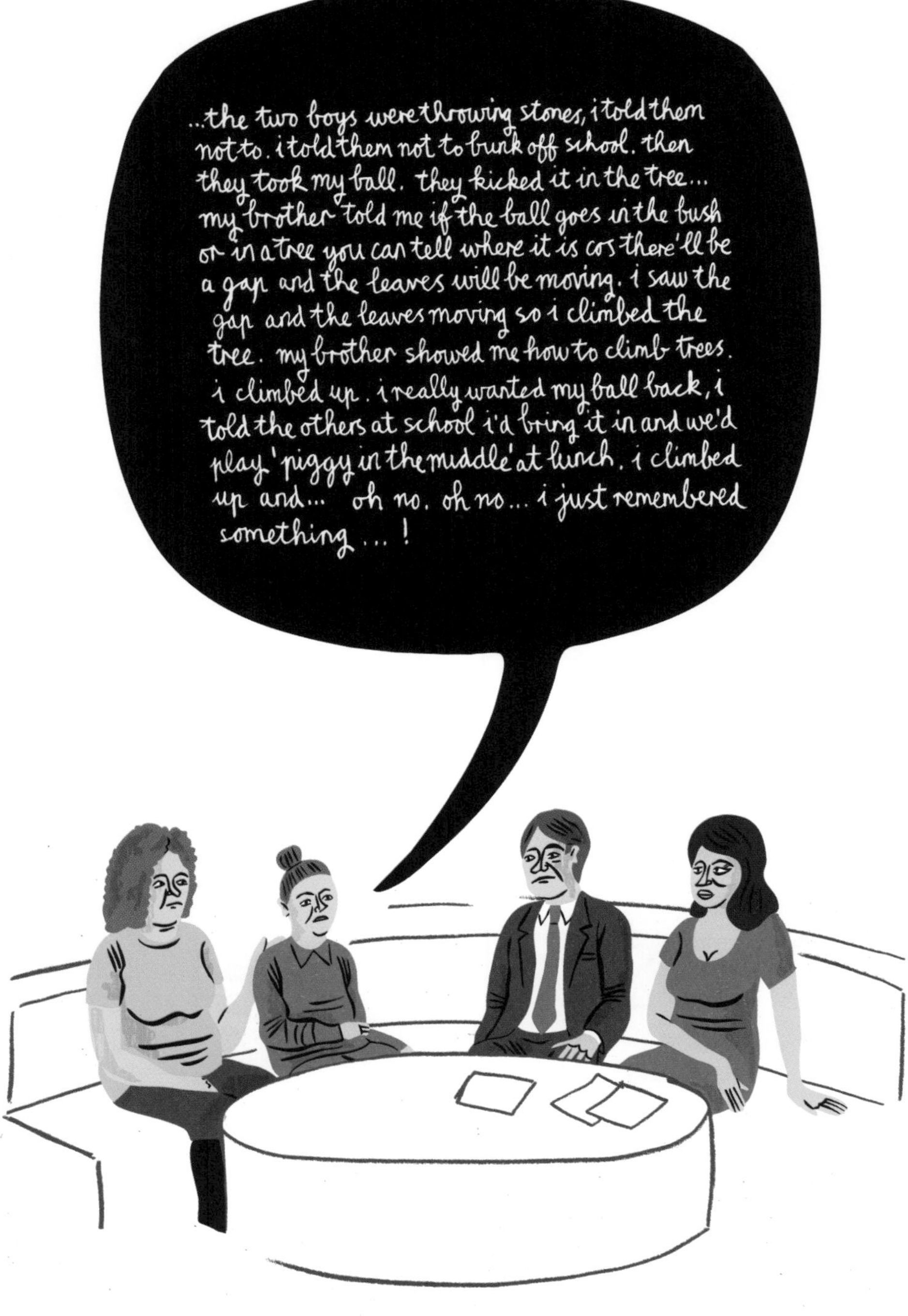
...the two boys were throwing stones, i told them not to. i told them not to bunk off school. then they took my ball. they kicked it in the tree... my brother told me if the ball goes in the bush or in a tree you can tell where it is cos there'll be a gap and the leaves will be moving. i saw the gap and the leaves moving so i climbed the tree. my brother showed me how to climb trees. i climbed up. i really wanted my ball back, i told the others at school i'd bring it in and we'd play 'piggy in the middle' at lunch. i climbed up and... oh no. oh no... i just remembered something... !

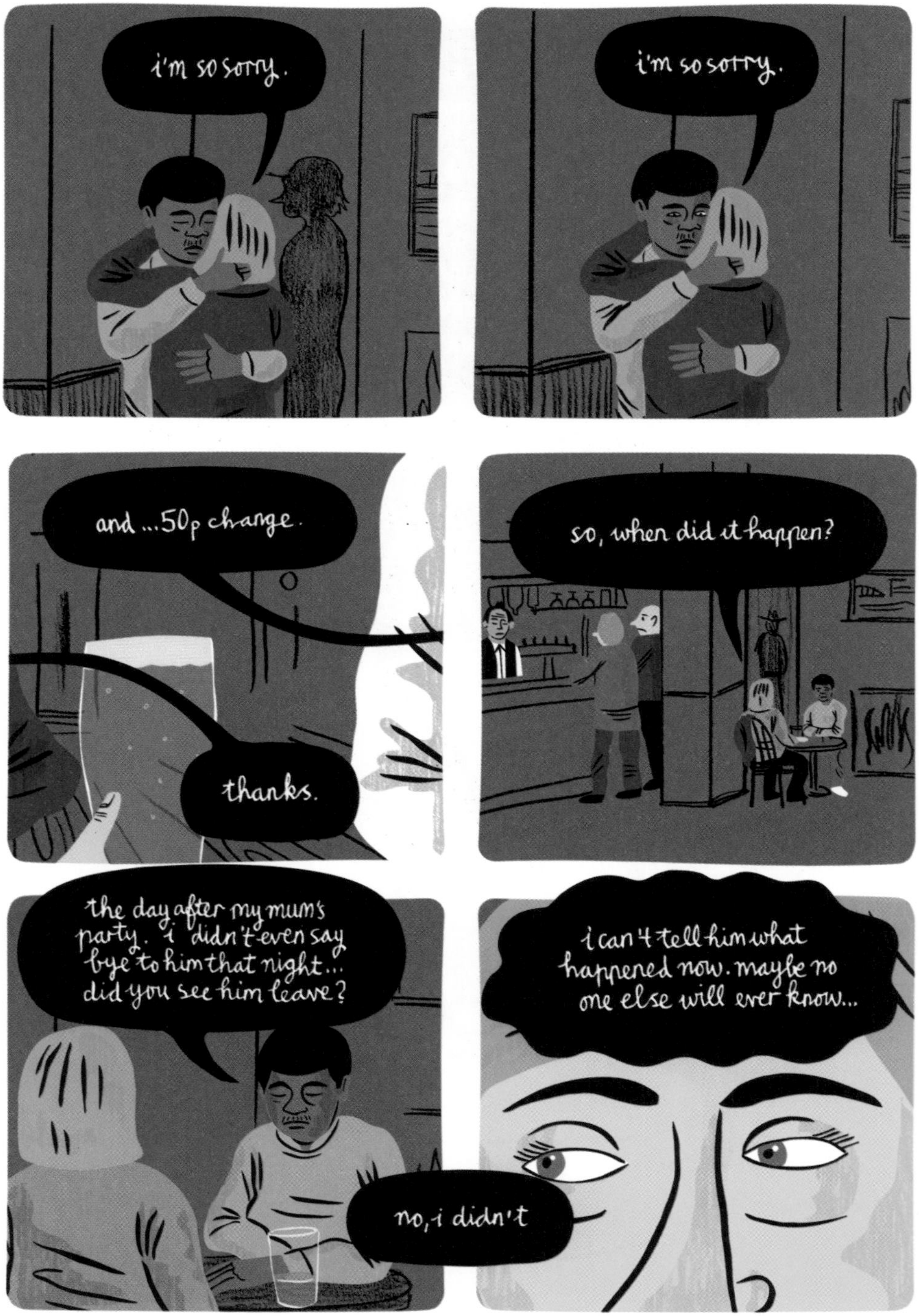
i'm so sorry.
i'm so sorry.
and ...50p change.
thanks.
so, when did it happen?
the day after my mum's party. i didn't even say bye to him that night... did you see him leave?
i can't tell him what happened now. maybe no one else will ever know...
no, i didn't

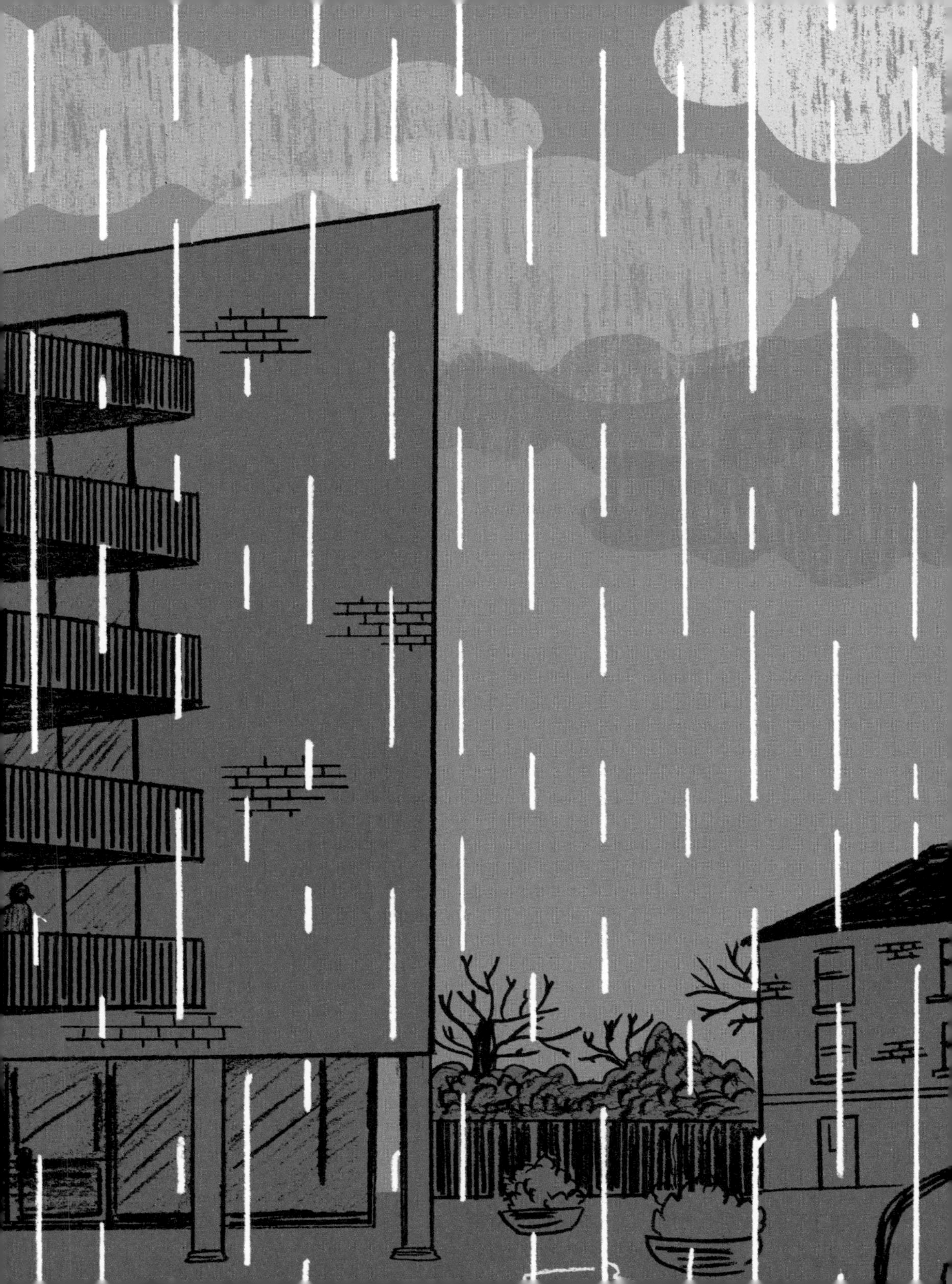

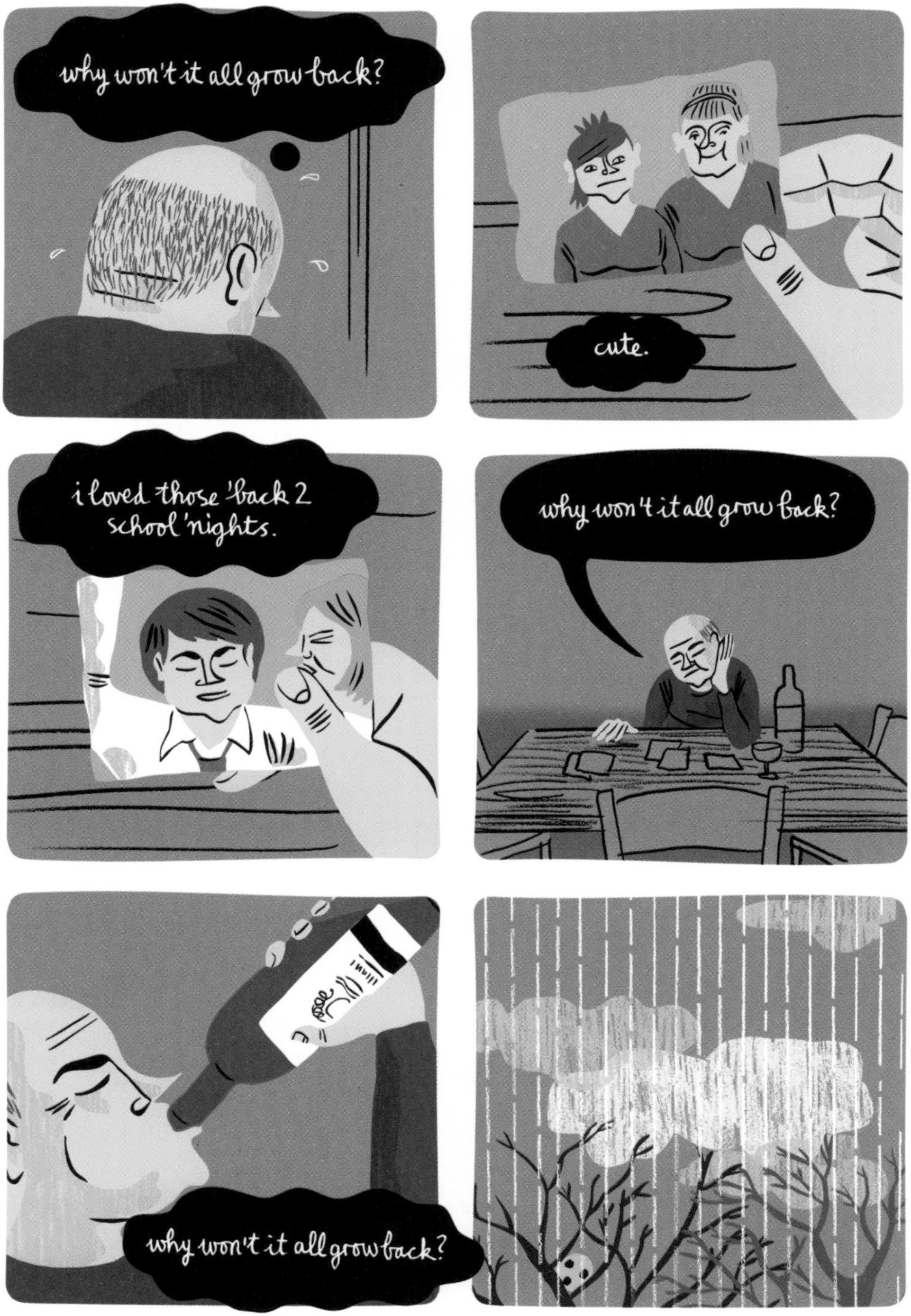
why won't it all grow back?
cute.
i loved those 'back 2 school' nights.
why won't it all grow back?
why won't it all grow back?

CHEMIST 163
usually, i'm like clockwork...
i can't be pregnant.
people try for months...
shit.

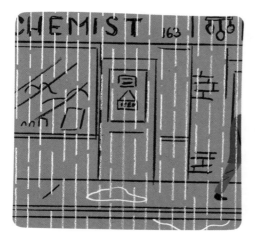

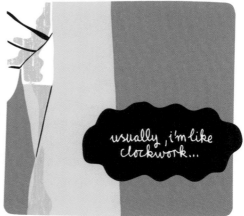

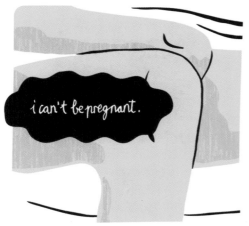

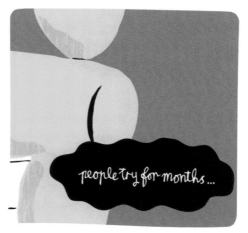

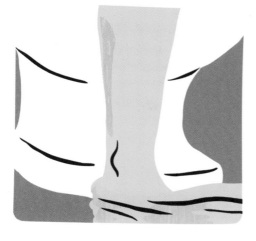

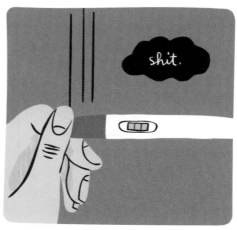

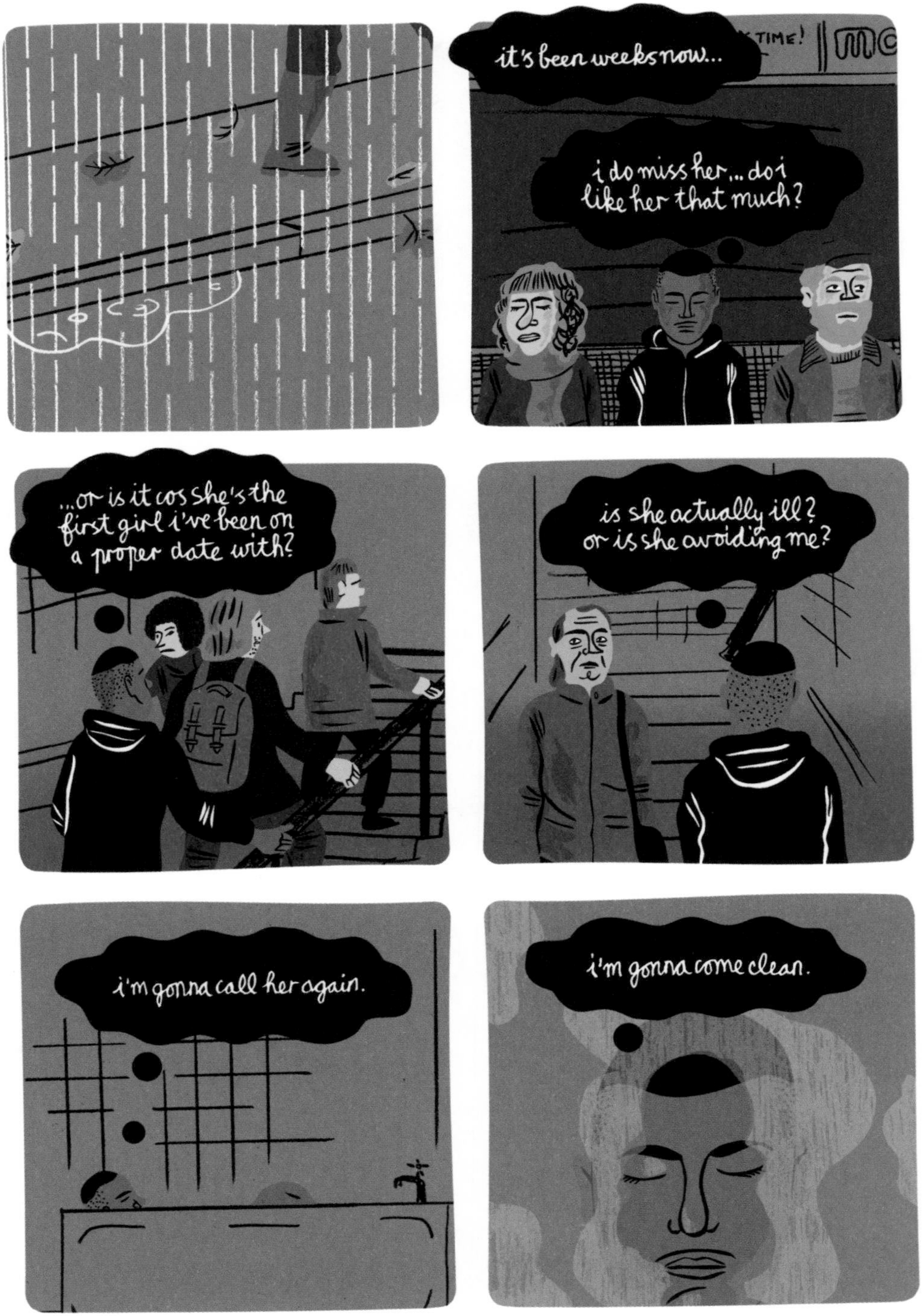
it's been weeks now...
i do miss her... do i like her that much?
...or is it cos she's the first girl i've been on a proper date with?
is she actually ill? or is she avoiding me?
i'm gonna call her again.
i'm gonna come clean.

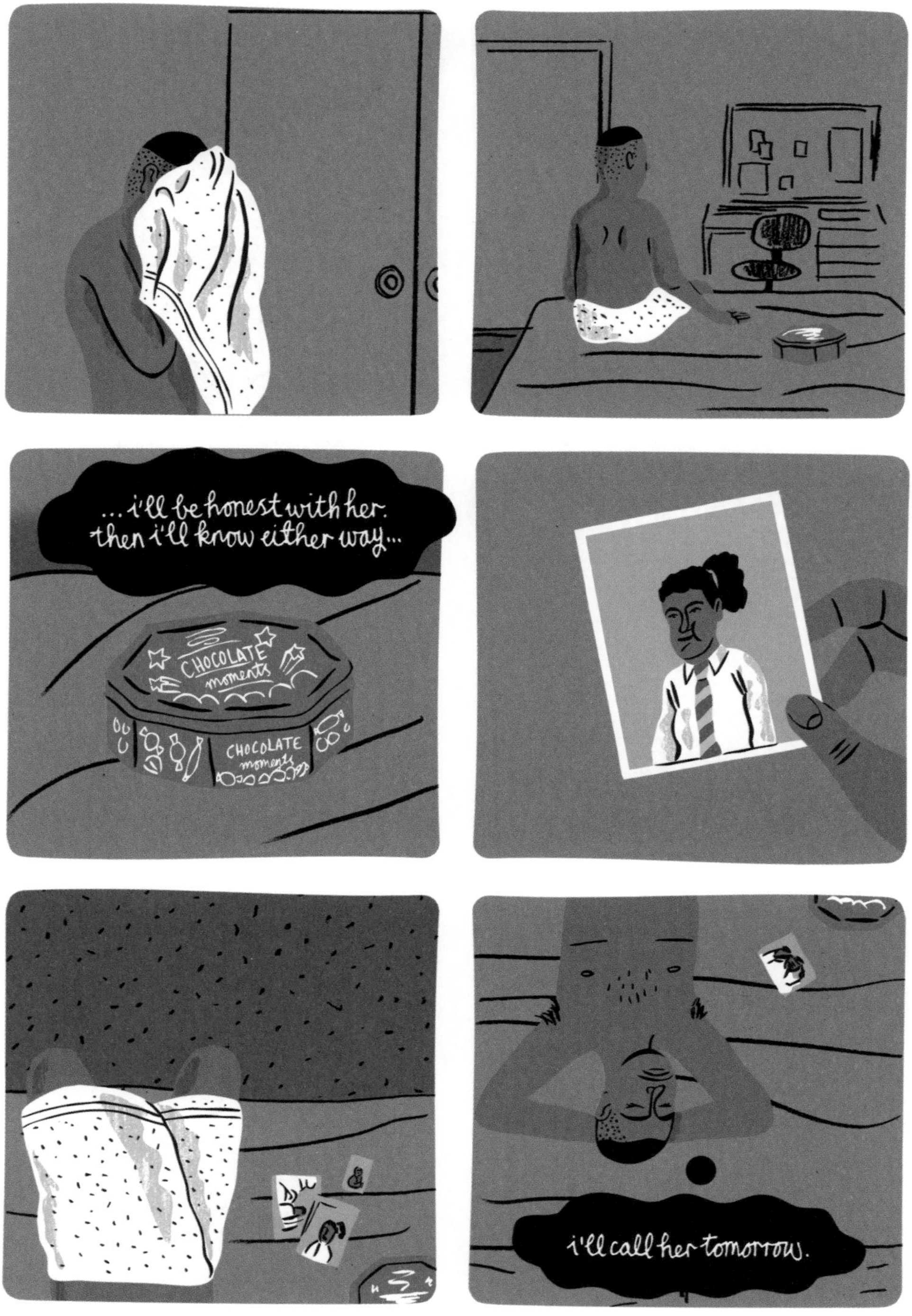
...i'll be honest with her.
then i'll know either way...
CHOCOLATE moments
CHOCOLATE moments
i'll call her tomorrow.

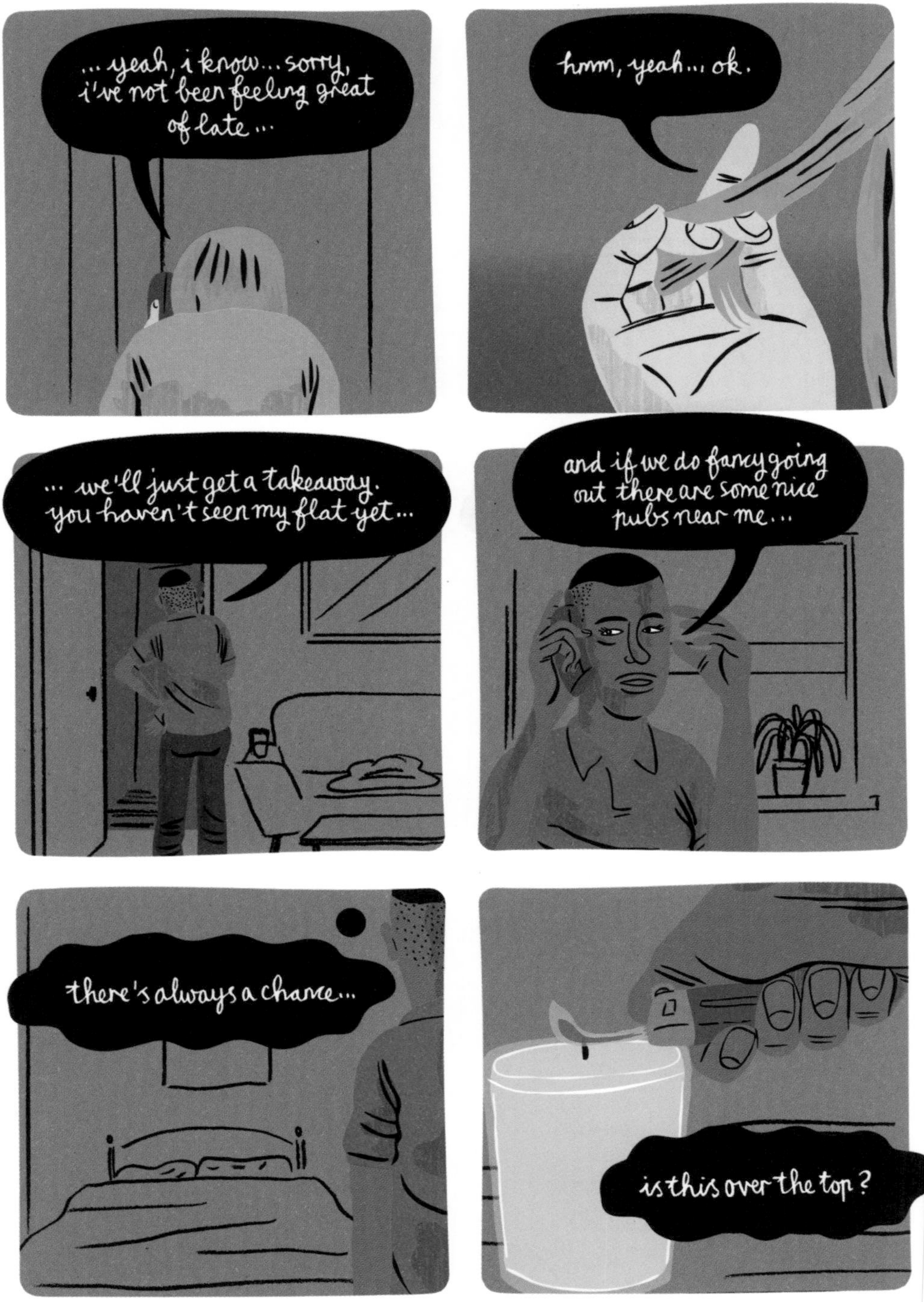
... yeah, i know ... sorry, i've not been feeling great of late ...
hmm, yeah... ok.
... we'll just get a takeaway. you haven't seen my flat yet ...
and if we do fancy going out there are some nice pubs near me ...
there's always a chance ...
is this over the top ?

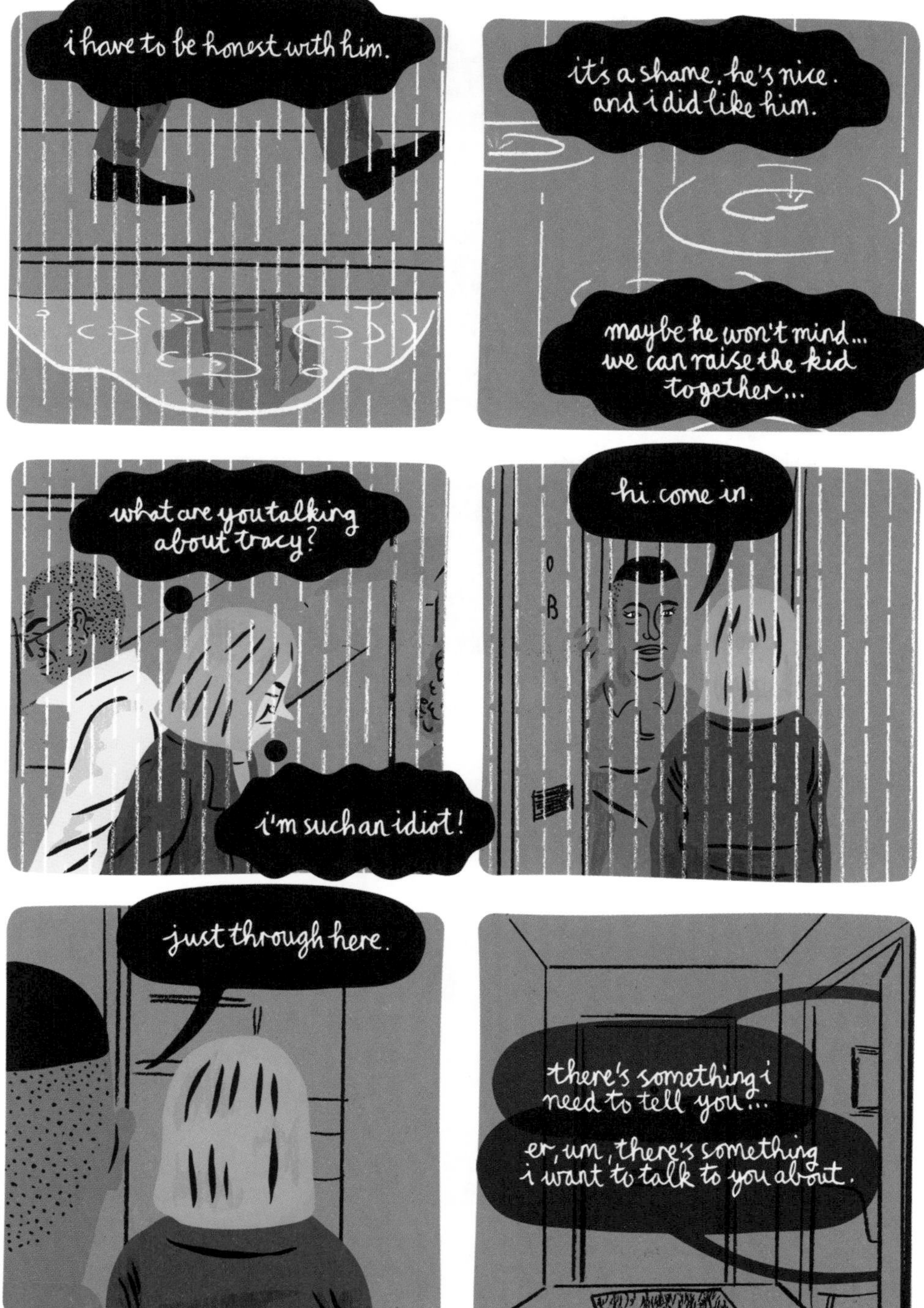
i have to be honest with him.
it's a shame, he's nice. and i did like him.
maybe he won't mind... we can raise the kid together...
what are you talking about tracy?
i'm such an idiot!
hi. come in.
just through here.
there's something i need to tell you...
er, um, there's something i want to talk to you about.

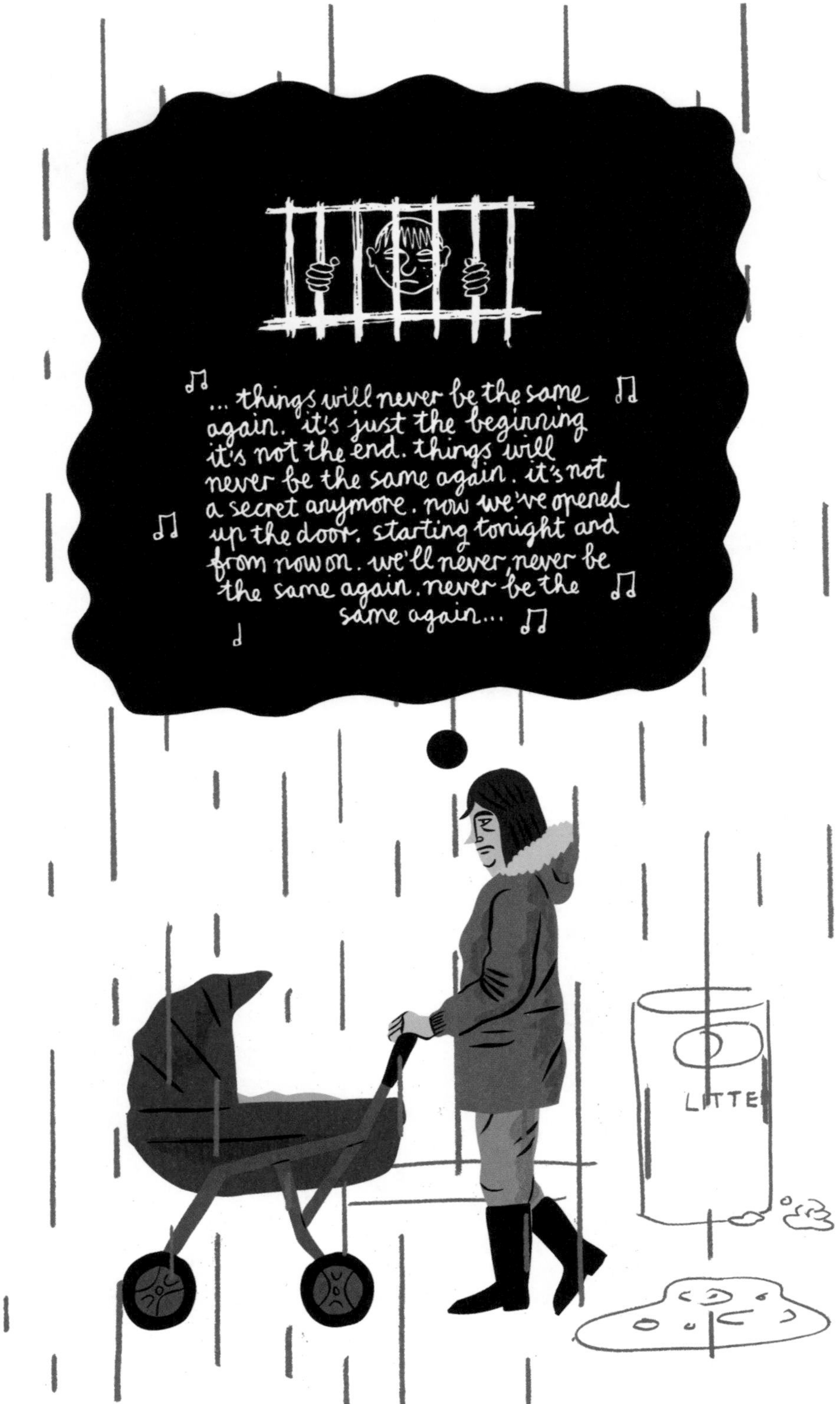
... things will never be the same again. it's just the beginning it's not the end. things will never be the same again. it's not a secret anymore. now we've opened up the door. starting tonight and from now on. we'll never, never be the same again. never be the same again...
LITTE

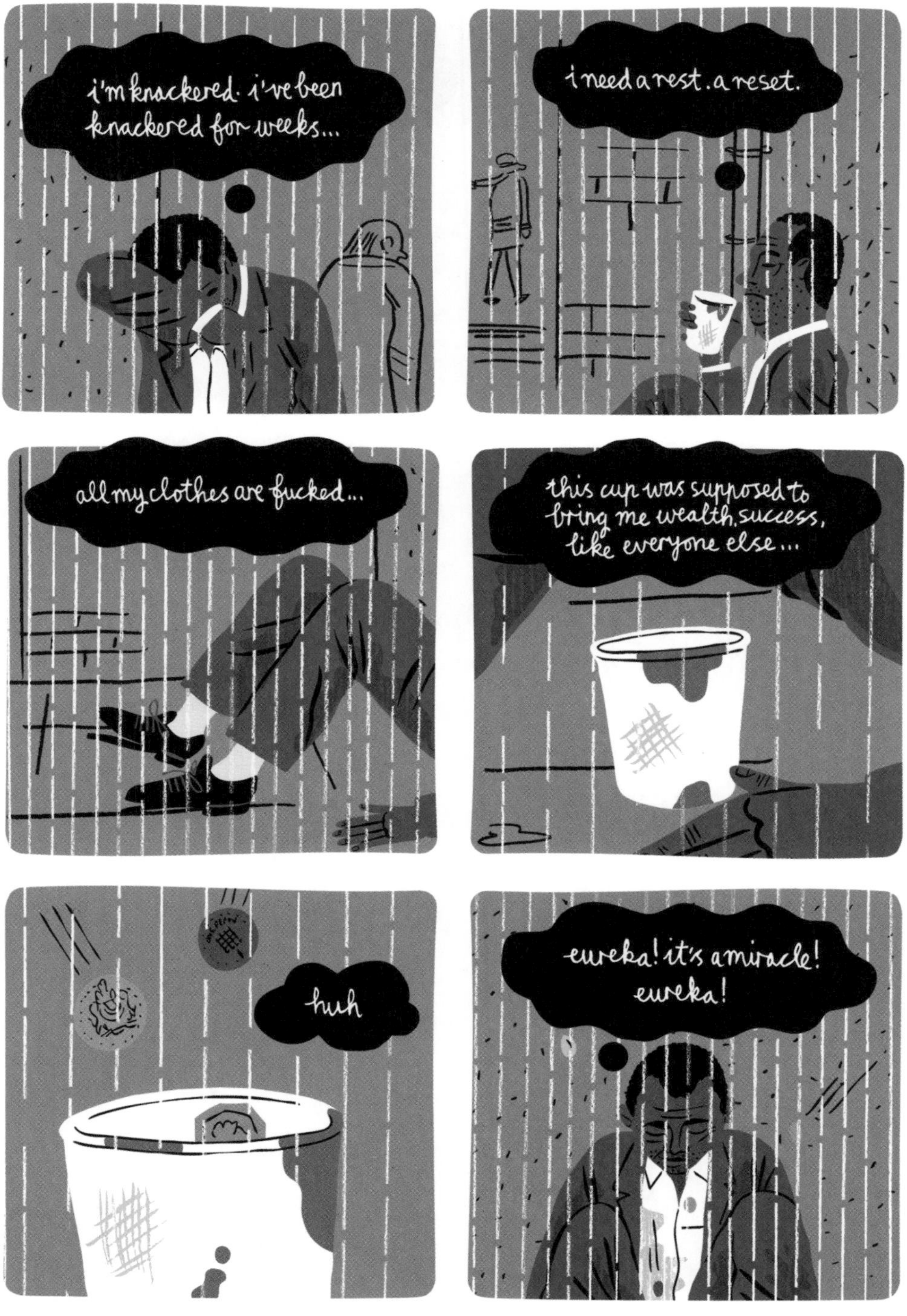
i'm knackered. i've been knackered for weeks...
i need a rest. a reset.
all my clothes are fucked...
this cup was supposed to bring me wealth, success, like everyone else...
huh
eureka! it's a miracle! eureka!

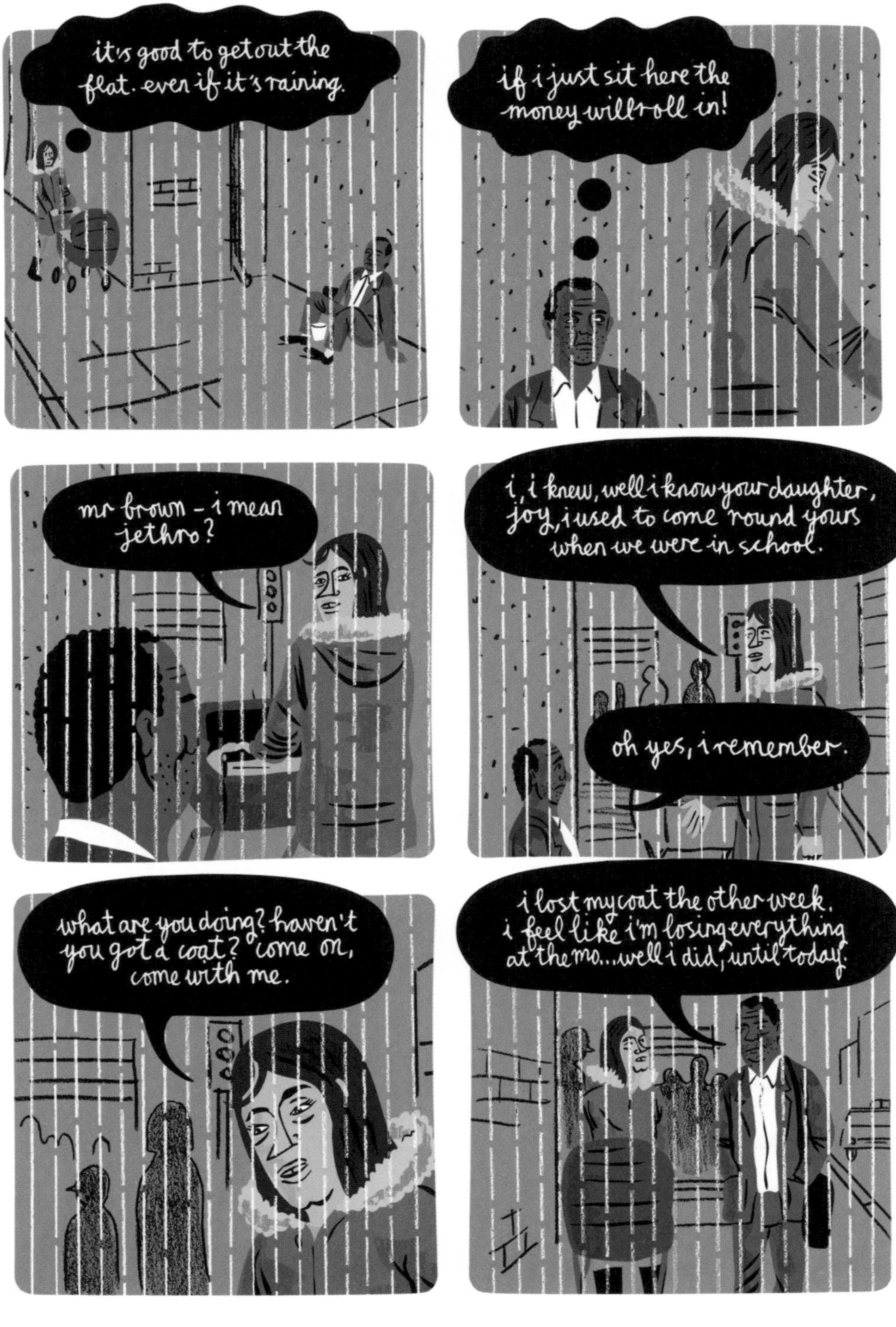
it's good to get out the flat. even if it's raining.
if i just sit here the money will roll in!
mr brown – i mean jethro?
i, i knew, well i know your daughter, joy, i used to come round yours when we were in school.
oh yes, i remember.
what are you doing? haven't you got a coat? come on, come with me.
i lost my coat the other week. i feel like i'm losing everything at the mo... well i did, until today.

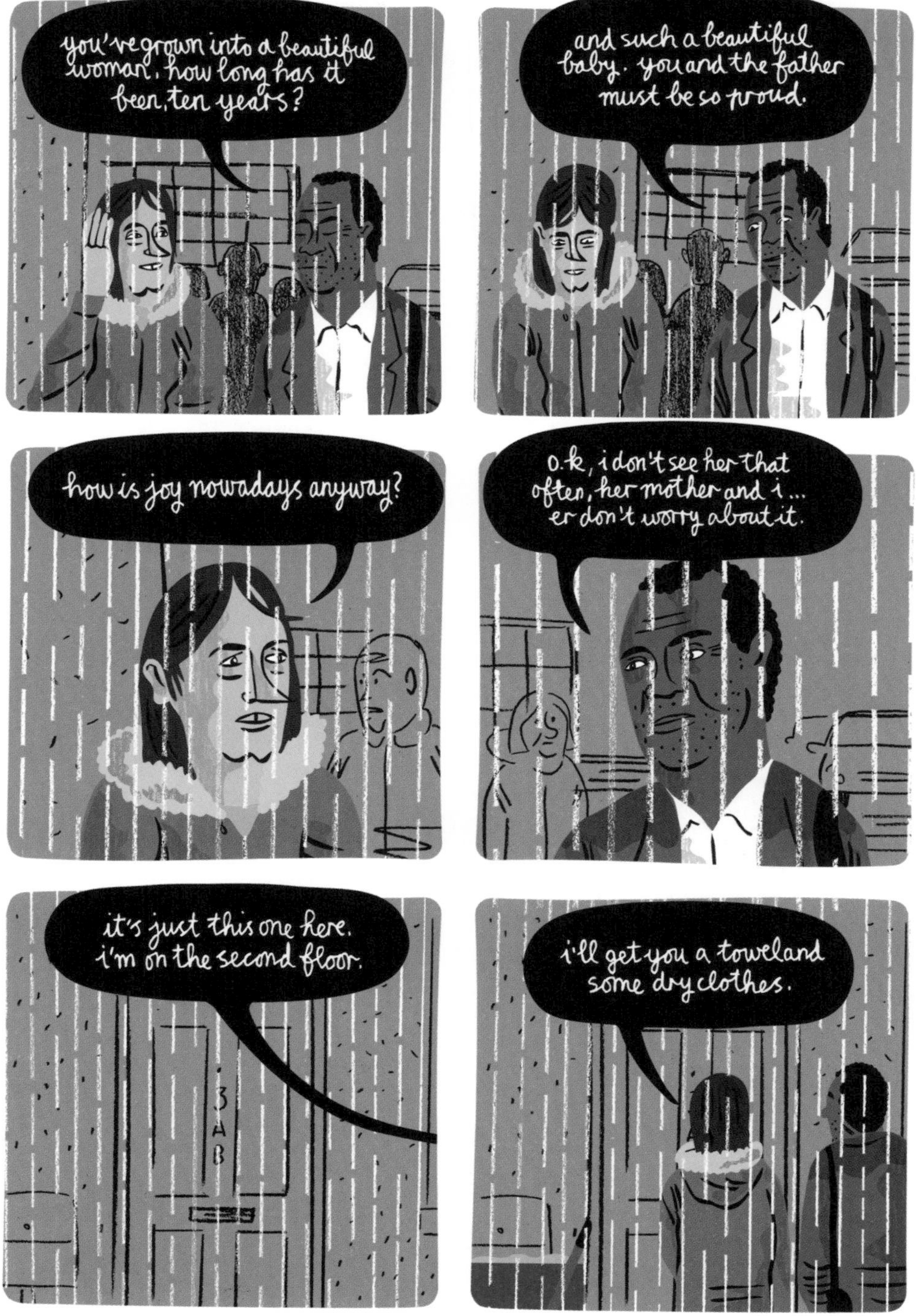
you've grown into a beautiful woman. how long has it been, ten years?
and such a beautiful baby. you and the father must be so proud.
how is joy nowadays anyway?
o.k, i don't see her that often, her mother and i... er don't worry about it.
it's just this one here. i'm on the second floor.
3AB
i'll get you a towel and some dry clothes.

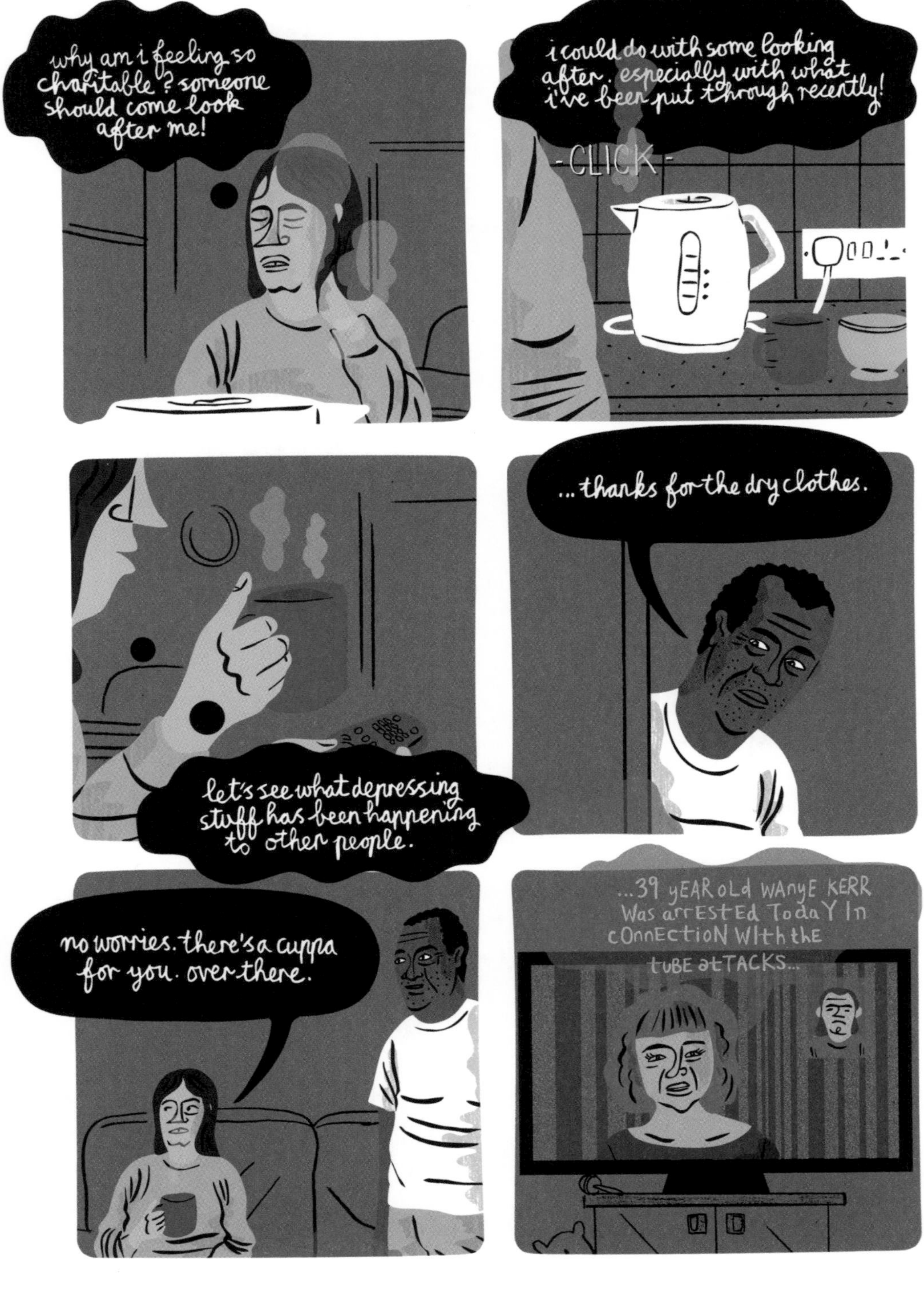
why am i feeling so charitable? someone should come look after me!
i could do with some looking after. especially with what i've been put through recently!
-CLICK-
let's see what depressing stuff has been happening to other people.
...thanks for the dry clothes.
no worries. there's a cuppa for you. over there.
...39 YEAR OLD WANYE KERR WAS ARRESTED TODAY IN CONNECTION WITH THE TUBE ATTACKS...

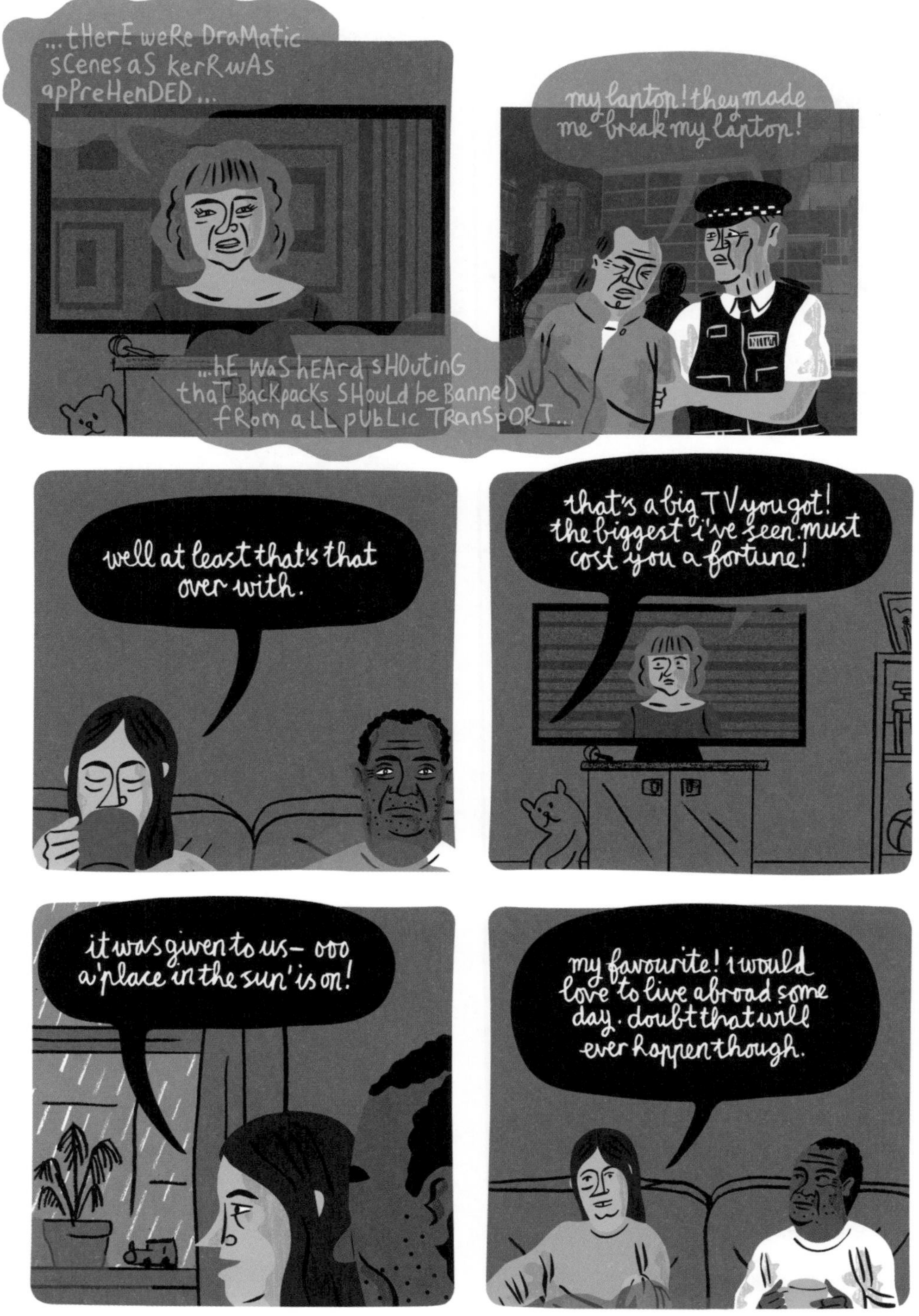
...tHerE weRe DraMatic sCenes aS kerR wAs appreHenDED...
my laptop! they made me break my laptop!
...hE WaS hEArd sHOutinG thaT BacKpacKs SHOULd be BanneD fRom aLL pUbLic TRansPORT...
well at least that's that over with.
that's a big TV you got! the biggest i've seen. must cost you a fortune!
it was given to us— ooo a 'place in the sun' is on!
my favourite! i would love to live abroad some day. doubt that will ever happen though.

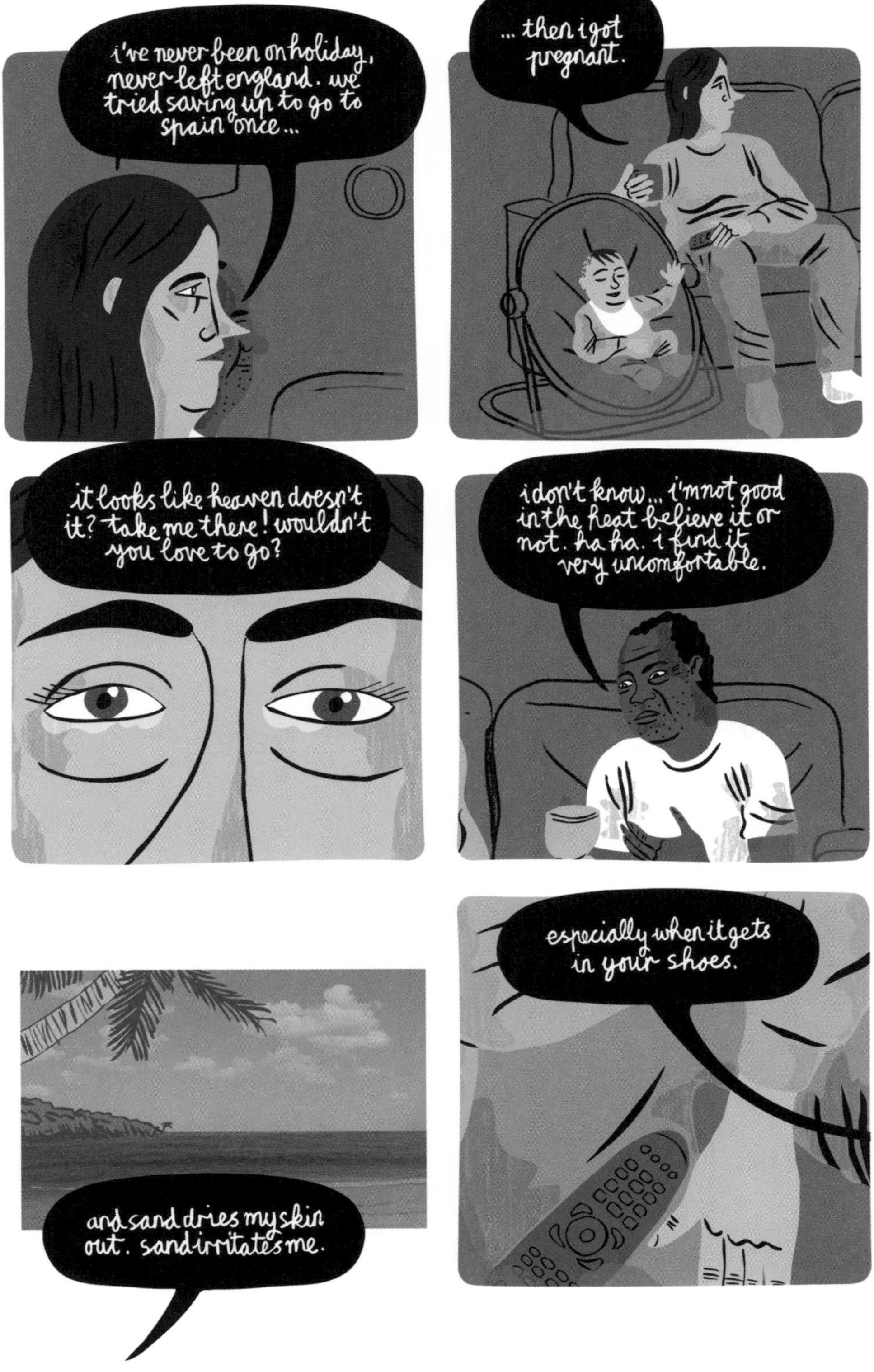
i've never been on holiday, never left england. we tried saving up to go to spain once...
... then i got pregnant.
it looks like heaven doesn't it? take me there! wouldn't you love to go?
i don't know... i'm not good in the heat believe it or not. ha ha. i find it very uncomfortable.
and sand dries my skin out. sand irritates me.
especially when it gets in your shoes.

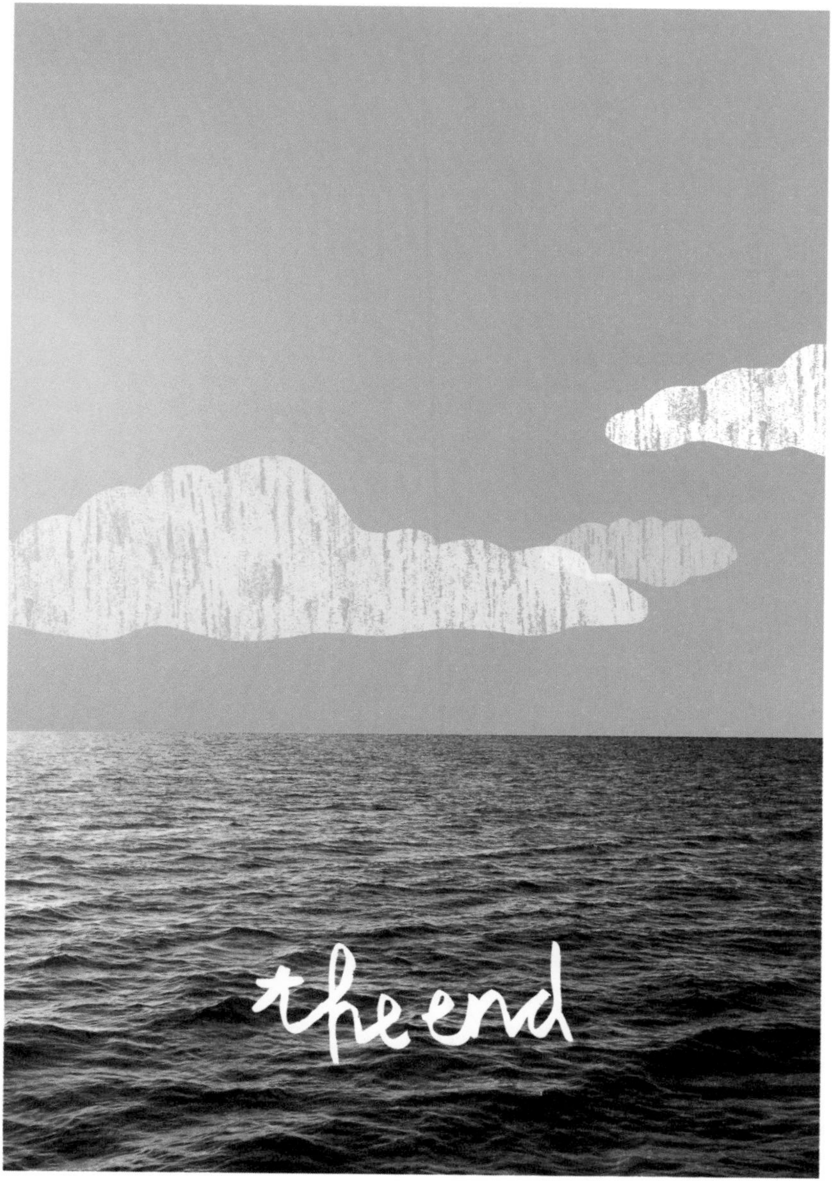
the end

scott jason smith was born in south london
in 1983, just before christmas. he attended
secondary school in chatham, kent and
picked up an art degree from the university
of east london. scott's comics have
appeared in various anthologies over the
last decade or so. marble cake is his first book.

thank you: rachel & crinkle and all at AHP

marble cake
by scott jason smith
published by avery hill publishing
first printing june 2019
copyright © scott jason smith, 2019

the creator has asserted his right under the copyright, designs and patents act 1988 to be identified as the author of this work. all rights reserved.

no portion of this book may be reproduced, stored in a retrieval system, or transmitted in any form or by any means, mechanical, electronic, photocopying, recording or otherwise (except for short excerpts for review purposes) without prior written permission from the publisher or the author.

ISBN: 978-1910395-47-9

averyhillpublishing.com

scottjasonsmith.com